Jimmy Carter as Peacemaker

JIMMY CARTER AS PEACEMAKER

A Post-Presidential Biography

Rod Troester

Praeger Series in Presidential Studies

 PRAEGER

Westport, Connecticut
London

Library of Congress Cataloging-in-Publication Data

Troester, Rod.
    Jimmy Carter as peacemaker : a post-presidential biography / Rod
Troester.
       p. cm.—(Praeger series in presidential studies, ISSN
1062–0931)
    Includes bibliographical references (p.) and index.
    ISBN 0–275–95444–7 (alk. paper)
    1. Carter, Jimmy, 1924– —Career in diplomacy. 2. Peace—
History—20th century. 3. World politics—1945– I. Title.
II. Series.
E873.2.T76   1996
973.927′092—dc20
   [B]   95–50469

British Library Cataloguing in Publication Data is available.

Library of Congress Catalog Card Number: 95–50469
ISBN: 0–275–95444–7
ISSN: 1062–0931

First published in 1996

Praeger Publishers, 88 Post Road West, Westport, CT 06881
An imprint of Greenwood Publishing Group, Inc.

Printed in the United States of America

The paper used in this book complies with the
Permanent Paper Standard issued by the National
Information Standards Organization (Z39.48–1984).

10 9 8 7 6 5 4 3 2 1

CONTENTS

PREFACE

This book project began several years ago when I presented a short paper entitled "Jimmy Carter: Ex-President and Peacemaker" to the Peace and Conflict Commission of the Speech Communication Association of America. As I prepared that paper, I came to admire and respect the work President Carter has done and the accomplishments he has achieved since leaving office. From that beginning, the more I read, and the more information I gathered, the more I became convinced that there was a unique quality to the role that President Carter had created for his post-presidency. As a country, we have never been quite sure what to expect from a former president. Post-presidencies have taken a number of different directions, usually based on the characters, personalities, and circumstances of the individuals, since there is no formally defined or established role prescribed for these individuals. In the case of the post-presidency of Jimmy Carter, I have found that his character, personality, and circumstances have combined to produce a significant force for peacemaking. There is truly no higher calling for a person, or a president, to pursue than to seek to further the cause of peace.

For the last fifteen years, President Carter has accepted the challenge of making peace and has demonstrated through his activities that a former president can make significant contributions to resolving armed conflicts and to building the foundations necessary for people to live in peace. This book tells the story of Jimmy Carter's post-presidency, chronicles his peacemaking activities, and highlights the accomplishments he has achieved.

While the writing of a book is in many ways a solitary endeavor, the process of taking an idea from inspiration to completion is a collaborative enterprise. When friends and colleagues would ask what I was working on over the last several years, I would explain that I was writing a book on the post-presidency of Jimmy Carter. While there were a number of different reactions to the project, most people encouraged me to pursue it and commented something to the effect that while Jimmy Carter may not have been the best president the country ever had, he is surely one of the best ex-presidents it has ever had. These comments suggested to me that there was a story that should be told and a career that deserved formal attention. It is for these people who have an interest in the work of President Carter, the study of peacemaking, and the contemporary American presidency that this book is intended.

I am grateful to Penn State Erie, The Behrend College, for providing the time and resources required to prepare this book. A grant from the Penn State Fund for Research provided the financial resources necessary to complete this project. I would also like to acknowledge the assistance of Wendy Gouldthorpe Eidenmuller, whose title of Staff Assistant VI fails miserably to describe the technical and editorial expertise she contributed to this project. I am also most grateful for the support and understanding I received from my family. I stole time and attention away from Erin and Patrick to work on this project. I depended on Judy to pick up my slack at home and to be an honest and supportive critic of this work. I am forever in their debt.

The assistance and encouragement provided by Dr. Robert Denton, Jr., who edits the Praeger Series in Presidential Studies, has also been most helpful. From my first inquiry to Dr. Denton through the acceptance of the proposal, he has provided useful suggestions and advice as the project developed. James Dunton and the staff at Praeger and the Greenwood Publishing Group have made taking my original proposal from its rough form to a completed volume a relatively painless and ultimately rewarding venture.

This book would not have been possible had it not been for the information and materials available through the Carter Center in Atlanta. While no one at the Carter Center was affiliated with or involved in the preparation of this volume, much of the information needed for it was available only through the Carter Center. On several occasions, more information was provided than requested. Documents and materials available through the Carter Center, supplemented by those available through traditional research sources, formed the basis for my work.

Finally, I would like to say that throughout my work on this book, I have on occasion felt it presumptuous for me to be writing a biography of someone of the stature of President Jimmy Carter. Throughout the preparation of this book, I was humbled by the magnitude of the accomplishments of my subject. As I contemplated the task, I would repeatedly remind myself that I was trying to tell a story. I was also continually aware of the fact that no single volume could capture every detail of the life of a man who, even fifteen years into his "retirement," shows no sign of retiring. I hope that the pages that follow begin to do justice to the continuing career of a man whom history will surely judge to be among its most significant "men of peace."

Jimmy Carter as Peacemaker

CHAPTER 1

AN INTRODUCTION TO THE POST-PRESIDENCY AND JIMMY CARTER

Moments after Ronald Reagan took the oath of office on January 20, 1981, final arrangements negotiated by President Jimmy Carter were executed for the release of fifty-two Americans who had been held hostage by the Iranian government. With the election and inauguration of Ronald Reagan, the presidency of Jimmy Carter passed into history, and he became former President Jimmy Carter—private citizen. In the wake of the Iranian hostage crisis, a stagnant economy, and a failed presidential campaign, what did the future hold for the man who, for the previous four years, had been one of the most powerful figures in the world?

Every four years, depending on the outcome of the presidential election, inauguration day marks a time of transition for the people of the United States and the leadership of the country. When a new president is elected, the nation prepares for the transition to a new administration with new programs and political directions. On inauguration day, the mantle of power in the United States and the leadership of the free world symbolically, and in reality, pass from one individual to another. The incumbent preparing to leave the White House also prepares for a transition, perhaps the most significant transition or adjustment he will ever have to make. The president-elect prepares to assume the role of president of the United States; the incumbent prepares to assume the role of ex-president and to return to life as a private citizen.

While the role of the president has been clearly established, the role of an ex-president is not clearly defined. The role of the president of the United States is established by the U.S. Constitution and the forty-two presidents who have occupied the office since the nation was founded. In the absence of any official status, the role of ex-president of the United States has been shaped and defined largely by the precedents and personalities of the individuals who have, willingly or otherwise, taken on the role. DeFrank observed, "It's never been easy to be an ex-president; a man with no power and no official role is somehow held to lofty standards of public and private conduct" (1990, p. 36). In the absence of constitutionally established guidelines or roles, and lacking any official power or status, a new ex-president has only the precedents of the men who have held and left the office to guide his behavior. In recent history, presidents have left office to write their memoirs, establish presidential libraries, act as senior statesmen, and travel the speaking/lecture/teaching circuit.

This book profiles and chronicles how the thirty-ninth president of the United States, James (Jimmy) Earl Carter III, has made the transition from president to ex-president and has established a new ex-presidential role, that of peacemaker, or what one writer has referred to as a diplomat without portfolio (Wines, 1992, p. A15). Upon leaving the office of the U.S. presidency, the White House, and the seats of power in Washington, D.C., Jimmy Carter joined the ranks of an elite group of men, former U.S. presidents. In contemporary times, there have been five members of this elite group.

Traditionally, the presidency of a particular individual, the period of time from inauguration to inauguration, has received considerable study and analysis by journalists, historians, political scientists, and others after the individual has left office. Young (1988) suggested that each presidency receives two different periods of study. The first period, the incumbency, is closely followed by Washington observers and journalists. The second, the post-incumbency, is the period when a presidency is reexamined in the light of historical hindsight by scholars using the documents of the president and his administration.

A third period, the post-presidency—what individuals choose to do after leaving the White House—is an equally important period of study in order to understand the historical and political significance of a president fully. However, the post-presidential period has generally not received much attention, analysis, or study. There are several notable exceptions to this lack of research. In *Beyond the Presidency: The Residues of Power* (1976), Marie Hecht examined post-presidential power and post-presidential citizens concluding with Richard Nixon. Two surveys on the topic of the post-presidency that appeared in the 1980s, James C. Clark's *Faded Glory: Presidents out of Power* (1985) and Homer Cunningham's *The Presidents' Last Years: George Washington to Lyndon Johnson* (1989), provided brief biographies of former presidents. A 1989 conference at the Hoover Presidential Library, which examined and discussed the role and responsibilities of America's former presidents, produced the book *Farewell to the Chief: Former Presidents in American Public Life* (1990), edited by Richard Smith and Timothy Walch. While these four books survey the subject, few detailed examinations or analyses of individual post-presidencies have been undertaken. Wilson (1990) provided a useful guide to the work that has been done.

In some cases, former presidents have retired to relative obscurity, and their activities have received little notice and limited comment. In more recent years, former presidents have attempted to rehabilitate their reputations, as in the case of Richard Nixon, joined the lucrative lecture-speaker circuit, as did Gerald Ford, or "cashed in" on their notoriety, as did Ronald Reagan.

This book is the story of a unique approach to the post-presidency of the United States—that of Jimmy Carter. It is the story of a man who left the White House defeated, who was blamed for a faltering economy and staggering interest rates, and who returned to his Plains, Georgia, home to find his family businesses in serious financial difficulty. More importantly, it is the story of a man who has succeeded in establishing his presidential library and founding a policy-study and advocacy center for domestic and world peace. It is the story of a man who has become a leading figure in world democratization, in peacemaking and international mediation, and in humanitarian development efforts at home and abroad.

This book tells the story of the post-presidency of Jimmy Carter and his activities under the auspices of the Carter Center of Emory University. His story and continuing accomplishments make him, as some have described, the best ex-president in the history of the United States.

In order to understand and appreciate the accomplishments of the post-presidency of Jimmy Carter, chapter 2 begins by contrasting the course Jimmy Carter has charted for his post-presidency with those of the other members of the elite group of contemporary former presidents. While he has also assumed all the traditional roles of his contemporaries—memoirs, libraries, lecturing—he has also redefined the role of the ex-president by demonstrating what a former president can contribute to humanitarian efforts and domestic and world peace, even in the absence of power or an official role. While in office, presidents invest their political capital and credibility to further their domestic and foreign policy agendas. Jimmy Carter's post-presidency demonstrates that after a president leaves office, considerable political capital and credibility remain, which can be invested both in the advancement of humanitarian efforts at home and abroad and in the development of peaceful relations within and among nations.

President Carter's perspectives on war and peace are important factors that must be considered in order to understand his post-presidency. Chapter 3 explores Jimmy Carter's transition from president to peacemaker. In many ways, the same ideals that shaped four years of U.S. foreign policy during the Carter administration (for example, his emphasis on human rights, humanitarian causes, and negotiation over confrontation) continue to shape and direct his post-presidency.

A deep concern for humanity, a respect for human rights, and a belief in democratic ideals and the importance of the creative management and resolution of conflict are some of the principles that guided the formation of the Carter Center of Emory University. With the establishment of the Carter Center, Carter embarked on his post-presidency. The various programs and organizations that comprise the Carter Center are briefly described in chapter 4. Following this overview of Carter Center programs, chapter 5 examines in more detail Carter's international peacemaking activities through negotiation and mediation. Three important peacemaking missions undertaken by former President Carter in 1994 are described in chapter 6. Democratization efforts in Latin American and African nations championed by Carter are described in chapter 7. The international humanitarian development activities and human rights programs of the Carter Center are discussed in chapter 8. While many Carter Center programs have had an international focus in the past, in more recent initiatives and programs former President Carter directed his energy and dedication to domestic humanitarian concerns. These are described in chapter 9. Finally, chapter 10 reflects on the last fifteen years of Carter's work, assesses what he has been able to accomplish through his peacemaking efforts and how he has accomplished these achievements, and speculates as to why his post-presidency has followed the course of peacemaking.

Jimmy Carter's transition from president of the United States to post-presidential peacemaker has been both difficult and extremely rewarding. Following his defeat by Ronald Reagan in 1980, Jimmy Carter could have retired quietly to his Plains, Georgia, home, content and satisfied with the accomplishments of his administration, and taken his place in history. However, at the age of fifty-six, Jimmy Carter instead embarked on a new and perhaps more rewarding career, unencumbered by partisan politics. In the fifteen years since he left office, Jimmy Carter has continued to make a positive difference in the world, internationally and domestically. His work is still far from complete. The pages that follow describe the differences made by the peacemaking post-presidency of Jimmy Carter.

REFERENCES

Clark, J. C. (1985). *Faded glory: Presidents out of power.* New York: Praeger Publishers.

Cunningham, H. F. (1989). *The presidents' last years: George Washington to Lyndon B. Johnson.* Jefferson, NC: McFarland & Co.

DeFrank, T. M. (1990, Apr. 2). A diminished Ron, a refurbished Jimmy: The perils of former presidents. *Newsweek,* p. 36.

Hecht, M. B. (1976). *Beyond the presidency: The residues of power.* New York: Macmillan Publishing Co.

Smith, R. N., and Walch, T. (Eds.). (1990). *Farewell to the chief: Former presidents in American public life.* Worland, WY: High Plains Publishing Co.

Wilson, D. W. (1990). Foreword. In R. N. Smith and T. Walch (Eds.), *Farewell to the chief: Former presidents in American public life.* Worland, WY: High Plains Publishing Co.

Wines, M. (1992, Nov. 9). Bush seems unsure about his plans. *New York Times,* p. A15.

Young, J. S. (1988). Foreword. In E. Hargrove, *Jimmy Carter as president: Leadership and the politics of the public good* (p. xii). Baton Rouge: Louisiana State University Press.

CHAPTER 2

CONTEMPORARY FORMER PRESIDENTS: NIXON, FORD, REAGAN, AND BUSH

STUDYING THE POST-PRESIDENCY

One day they are presidents; the next, they are once again private citizens. One day they are among the most powerful leaders in the world; the next, they formally and officially have no more power than any other citizen. Such has been the plight of the forty-one men who have occupied and left the White House. While they have no formal or official status or power because they are former presidents of the United States, they can exert and have exerted considerable influence on public opinion and policy.

How former presidents have elected to invest their time and to exercise their influence has been the subject of relatively little formal study. Historically, presidential administrations have received more attention and research than post-presidencies. However, several writers have examined the post-presidency and the activities of former presidents. Marie Hecht described her book, *Beyond the Presidency*, as follows: "This book does not attempt to be an exhaustive or encyclopedic account of the last years of the American presidents. Instead, it explores some aspects of their post–White House careers, seeking to determine the residues of power left to them" (1976, p. xv). In her analysis, Hecht (1976, p. xiv) pointed out that historically, ex-presidents have played many roles, including elder statesman, political outcast, discarded party leader, founder of colleges, eminent congressman, Confederate politician, chief justice, and presidential candidate. Hecht's exploration of the American post-presidency ends with that of Richard Nixon. A 1989 conference held at the Hoover Presidential Library invited historians, journalists, former staffers, and former President Gerald Ford to examine the post-presidency from Theodore Roosevelt to Jimmy Carter. The book *Farewell to the Chief* (1990), edited by Richard Smith and Timothy Walch, reported the results of this scholarly conference. In a more biographical and less analytical fashion, *Faded Glory: Presidents out of Power*, by James Clark (1985), provided short descriptive profiles of the post-presidential activities of each president from Washington to Carter. Homer Cunningham did much the same in *The Presidents' Last Years: George Washington to Lyndon B. Johnson* (1989) when he noted, "This book has been written to tell the stories rarely heard about the presidents in their last years" (p. xiii). These authors, and others, all note that the ex-presidency is a unique role and has become a unique institution. This unique institution has seen former presidents die in bitterness, try to regain the presidency (Van Buren, Fillmore, Theodore Roosevelt, and Cleveland—the only one to succeed), criticize their successors, chair government commissions (most notably Taft and Hoover), or leave office and retire quietly. Each former president has taken a somewhat different approach to his retirement, with contemporary former presidents being no exception.

Until the death of Richard Nixon in April 1994, there were five living former U.S. presidents: Richard Nixon (out of office since 1974), Gerald Ford (out of office since 1977), Jimmy Carter (out of office since 1981), Ronald Reagan (out of office since 1989), and George Bush (out of office since 1993). Not since Lincoln took office in the 1860s had there been five living former presidents (Scott, 1994, p. 2). With the exception of Nixon and Ford, all gained or left the White House through the electoral process. Upon leaving office, in recent times each former president has worked to establish his respective presidential library under the auspices of the National Archives and has penned his memoirs. However, they differ quite considerably in the other interests and activities they have chosen to pursue.

PRESIDENTIAL LIBRARIES

In recent times, the establishment of a repository or library for the written record of a presidency has become the norm for former White House residents. It was not until Franklin Roosevelt raised the question of what to do with presidential records that this modern norm of the presidential library developed. With the notable exception of Rutherford Hayes, who placed his papers in the custody of the state of Ohio, there was no systematic effort made to archive and record the papers of the first twenty-nine U.S. presidents ("Presidential libraries," 1989, p. 29). The 1978 Presidential Records Act allows presidents to restrict access to their papers for up to twelve years after they leave office (Scroggins, 1991, p. A10).

As the norm of establishing presidential libraries developed, raising the funds necessary to build these libraries became the responsibility of the individual president. Once established, these libraries are generally donated to the National Archives, which then staffs and manages the facilities. Recent changes made by the U.S. Congress will require former presidents, starting with George Bush, to provide an endowment to defray the cost of operating their libraries ("Presidential libraries," 1989, p. 29). As of 1991, the National Archives was administering eight such libraries at an annual cost to the taxpayers of some $24 million (Scroggins, 1991, p. A10). All told, from 1978 through 1988, Americans spent $112 million in support of ex-presidents' expenses, including pensions, travel, office expenses, and Secret Service protection ("President and accounted for," 1988, p. 9). Some would argue that this is a considerable amount of money. But it is interesting to compare these expenses to another "presidential tradition." When President Clinton followed the tradition established when Franklin Delano Roosevelt died of marking the death of a former president, in this case Richard Nixon, by declaring a national day of mourning and giving federal workers the day off, the cost of this tribute to the taxpayers was reportedly $308 million paid for workers not to work, in addition to the $23 million in overtime that was spent for those designated by the government as essential workers ("Honoring Nixon," 1994, p. 3A). The actual cost of the funeral for the federal government was estimated at $300,000 ("Nixon's Funeral," 1994, p. 6B). It is interesting that one day of tribute to Richard Nixon cost more than three times what ten years of support for former presidents had cost.

THE POST-PRESIDENCIES OF NIXON, FORD, REAGAN, AND BUSH

Each of the current former presidents has followed the traditions of establishing a library and writing memoirs, but each has varied somewhat in his other retirement activities. A brief biographical description of the post-presidency of each of the contemporary former presidents will provide a means of comparing and contrasting the traditional approaches to the post-presidency with the approach taken by Jimmy Carter. Despite his recent passing, these descriptions will begin with the post-presidency of Richard Nixon because his time out of office was considerable and his accomplishments significant.

Richard Nixon (1913–1994), President from 1969 to 1974

Richard Nixon, the thirty-seventh president of the United States, was elected to office in 1968, was reelected in 1972, and resigned from office in 1974 in the wake of Watergate. Nixon was the only president in the history of the United States to resign from office. At the time of his resignation, the possibility (some would say the probability) of impeachment loomed over his final days in office. Because of his resignation, questions regarding his involvement in Watergate, and his pardon by his successor Gerald Ford, much of Nixon's post-presidency was spent trying to rehabilitate his image and that of his presidency.

The Nixon Presidential Library in Yorba Linda, California, was built at a cost of $37 million and dedicated in July, 1990 (Fleeman, 1994, p. 2A). The library was built on the same land where, decades earlier, Nixon's father had tried and failed to establish citrus orchards ("Nation bids Nixon farewell," 1994, p. 14A). The Nixon Library was opened only after the legal status of some of his presidential papers and records was determined. Prior to Nixon, the government had assumed that presidents owned the papers of their administrations. With

Nixon's resignation and the controversy over his papers, Congress passed the Presidential Recordings and Materials Preservation Act and took control of Nixon's papers (Clark, 1985, p. 155). Unlike most presidential libraries, the Nixon Library is self-supporting and is not operated by the National Archives.

Nixon's post-presidency is perhaps best characterized as that of the elder statesman and author. In 1991, a spokesperson commented that Nixon spent most of his time "writing books and meeting with world leaders" (quoted in Scroggins, 1991, p. A10). These two activities consumed the bulk of the twenty-year post-presidency of Richard Nixon.

Throughout his political career, and certainly during his presidency, Nixon was an ardent anti-Communist. His early political fortunes were made during the national mood of anticommunism of the 1950s McCarthy era. In terms of foreign policy, his administration will be remembered for its conduct of the war in Vietnam, the establishment of relations with Communist China, and detente and early arms-control agreements with the Soviet Union.

With the breakup of the Soviet Union, the geopolitical landscape has changed significantly from the late Cold War era presided over by the Nixon presidency. In characterizing the elder statesman Richard Nixon in the 1990s, Schmemann noted, "In speeches, on Op-Ed pages and today in Russia (which was a frequent travel destination), the former President has become one of the most dedicated advocates of the notion that the United States must not ignore Russia now that Communism has collapsed" (1993, p. A4).

Nixon's travels after leaving office often took him to the former Soviet Union. In February 1993, Nixon made his ninth trip to Moscow, his fourth since leaving the White House. During this visit, Nixon positioned himself as an advocate for U.S. economic investment in the former Soviet Union. At the time, Nixon said, "I'm an anti-communist but a pro-Russian" (quoted by Schmemann, 1993, p. A4). As an elder statesman, when Nixon traveled to Russia, he received considerable attention from and access to the Soviet and Russian leadership. Nixon was especially impressed with the leadership of President Boris Yeltsin. However, because he did not travel as an official representative of the United States, he could also meet with the opposition leadership. During Nixon's tenth and final trip to Russia in the spring of 1994, Russian President Yeltsin first canceled and then later rescheduled meetings with Nixon. This occurred after Nixon met with leaders of the October 1993 uprising against Yeltsin, including former Vice President Rutskoi and ultranationalist Vladimir Zhirinovsky ("Peeved Yeltsin snubs Nixon," 1994, p. 2A; "Yeltsin reverses snub," 1994, p. 3A).

These recent meetings and years of similar meetings by Nixon suggest that Nixon, while not an official representative of the United States, was still able to act in the unofficial role of elder statesman. It has been customary following such meetings between world leaders and former presidents for the current occupant of the White House to request a briefing upon the former president's return. For example, President Clinton asked Nixon to brief him on his discussions with Russian leaders following his spring 1994 trip ("Peeved Yeltsin snubs Nixon," 1994, p. 2A). President Clinton commented, "I have appreciated the wise counsel he [Nixon] has given me on the question of Russia and many other issues since I have been president" (quoted in "Get-well messages," 1994, p. 6A). These meetings afford a valuable opportunity for the incumbent to profit from the experience and contacts of former presidents. The unique status and access that former presidents have with world leaders can provide benefits and insights that formal channels may not provide. In addition to his travels to the former Soviet Union, Nixon made five trips to China, a country his administration worked to open to the world and with which the United States established diplomatic relations in 1972 ("Nixon lapses," 1994, p. 1A).

After leaving the White House, Nixon was a prolific writer, penning nine major books. In fact, on April 19, 1994, the day before he was stricken by his fatal stroke, Nixon received the page proofs for *Beyond Peace*, which would be his final book (Sullivan, 1994, p. 3A). Warner Books' offer of $2.5 million for his memoirs entitled *RN: The Memoirs of Richard Nixon* (1978) helped Nixon to solve his financial problems after leaving office (Clark, 1985, p. 152). Other books by Nixon include *The Real War* (1980), *Leaders* (1982), *Real Peace* (1984), *1999: Victory without War* (1988), *In the Arena: A Memoir of Victory, Defeat, and Renewal* (1990), and *Seize the Moment: America's Challenge in a One-Superpower World* (1992). His writing career allowed Nixon to remain active in commenting on foreign policy issues, as well as securing his financial future. Syndicated columnist Richard Cohen summarized Richard Nixon's post-presidency well when he noted, "Nixon's afterlife has been beyond reproach—devoted to causes, not to chasing the dollar. His career is blemished only by his time in public office" (quoted in Hackett, 1989, p. 40). Nixon was remembered at his death for his foreign policy achievements, but he had not escaped the shadow of Watergate.

Gerald Ford (1913–   ), President from 1974 to 1977

Following Richard Nixon's resignation on August 9, 1974, Gerald Ford became the thirty-eighth president and the first nonelected president of the United States. Ford had become vice president following the resignation of Spiro Agnew in 1973.

Ford's presidency was shadowed by the cloud of Watergate and his pardon of Richard Nixon. In marking his eightieth birthday in 1993, Ford reportedly said that he wanted to be remembered for healing the wounds left by Vietnam and Watergate ("Gerald Ford hits 80," 1993, p. 12A). In fact, his memoirs are titled *A Time to Heal* (1979). The theme of healing the nation was one that began at his inauguration and continued throughout his presidency. In reflecting on his presidency, Ford stated, "I strongly believe that in the major areas of domestic and foreign policy, I did the right things for the country." He concluded, "I thought it [his presidency] was a good record then, and I do today" (quoted in "Gerald Ford hits 80," 1993, p. 12A). As in the case of Nixon, much of the legacy of the Ford administration and Ford's post-presidency has been in defending and justifying his actions while in office.

When he left the White House, Ford was in his mid-sixties and could anticipate a lengthy retirement. Unlike Nixon, the elder statesman, Ford has perhaps been harshly characterized by some for "cashing in" on the notoriety of being a former president. One reporter commented, "He has occasionally joined hands with Mr. Carter to promote various causes, but he is spotted more often on the golf links and in corporate boardrooms" (Scroggins, 1991, p. A10). Ford does serve on a number of corporate boards. He continues to sharpen his golf game, and he travels the sometimes lucrative speaking circuit. It has been suggested that we can "credit Gerald Ford with opening up new territory for retired Chief Execs by snagging a raft of well-paid corporate directorships and assiduously working the big-money corporate and trade association speaking circuit" ("Elder $tatesman," 1989, p. 552). With the help of wealthy friends, associates, and business opportunities, Ford's net worth was estimated to be $6 million by 1984 (Clark, 1985, p. 158). Ford's wealth resulted from consulting deals with corporations, owning two radio stations, being part owner in several real-estate deals, delivering lectures at $10,000 to $15,000 per date, and pitching great-moments-of-the-U.S.-presidency commemorative medals (Hackett, p. 40). It should also be noted, however, that both former President Ford and his wife Betty devote a considerable amount of their time to charity work for causes such as the fight against chemical dependence and for such organizations as the Boy Scouts of America—Ford himself is a former Eagle Scout.

Upon leaving the White House in 1977, Ford received a number of offers from the business community, colleges, and universities. In his autobiography, *A Time to Heal* (1979), Ford wrote that he accepted the most appealing offer, which came from the American Enterprise Institute for Public Policy Research. This position involved traveling to twenty college and university campuses a year to talk to students and faculty about foreign affairs, national defense, American politics, and the domestic economy. In the three years following his presidency, Ford visited 58 campuses, taught more than 500 classes, answered countless questions, and "learned an awful lot about American youth" (Ford, 1979, p. xiii). By 1990, Ford had visited 170 college campuses and had met with hundreds of classes (Smith and Walch, 1990, p. 173). In this regard, his early ex-presidency was similar to that of Carter, who accepted a teaching position at Emory University. His association with the American Enterprise Institute continues as Ford hosts an annual World Forum involving economists, political figures, and business and government leaders addressing topics such as the international debt crisis, arms control, and U.S.-Soviet relations (Smith and Walch, 1990, p. 173).

Following the traditional ex-presidential mold, Gerald Ford established and located his presidential library in Grand Rapids in his home state of Michigan. The $11.5-million building includes a replica of the Oval Office (Clark, 1985, p. 159). Under the auspices of the Gerald R. Ford Foundation and the Gerald

R. Ford Library and Museum, conferences, exhibits, and research and citizenship programs are organized and presented.

Following the assassination of Egyptian President Anwar Sadat in October 1981, former Presidents Nixon, Ford, and Carter were asked by President Reagan to represent the United States at the funeral. While the trip to Egypt was apparently tense, on the return trip Presidents Ford and Carter developed a friendship that has resulted in their collaboration on several programs and causes (Cloud, 1989, p. 62). Commenting on the trip, Ford noted that "I mark the beginning of my close association with Jimmy Carter with that trip" (quoted in Smith and Walch, 1990, p. 176).

One result of the collaboration between Ford and Carter was the book *American Agenda: Report to the Forty-First President of the United States of America* (1988). In this book, these former presidents drew upon their experience and offered President-elect George Bush their analyses of the most difficult problems his administration would face and their suggested possible solutions. The book was the result of a bipartisan committee of experts and the former presidents' in-depth study of national issues. Ford and Carter made a special trip to Washington to present the report to President-elect Bush, but Ford would later note, "As far as I know, very few of these proposals ended up in any of the recommendations of the newly elected president" (quoted in Smith and Walch, 1990, p. 149). Ford has also traveled with Carter to Panama to serve as an international election monitor (Hackett, 1989, p. 40), and Betty Ford has been involved with several mental health programs and lobbying efforts organized by Rosalynn Carter at the Carter Center in Atlanta.

In addition to his lecturing and charitable activities, as the country debated what to do with the nation's health-care system in 1994, Ford added his voice to the discussion. During an appearance with former President Bush at a business conference in California, Ford recognized that the system was in need of reform but was highly critical of Clinton administration proposals that would create a national health board to regulate insurance and health-care costs. Ford commented, "Whenever the government tries to solve a social problem, I become apprehensive" (quoted in "Ford blasts health care proposal," 1994, p. 11A). While it is unclear what effect comments by Ford might have on the formulation of policy, the comments do suggest that he continues to be interested and involved in national issues and public policy.

Ronald Reagan (1911–   ), President from 1981 to 1989

Ronald Reagan, the fortieth president of the United States, followed Jimmy Carter to the White House and left after serving the maximum two terms. Upon leaving office, Reagan was in his late seventies and was the oldest of the recent group of former presidents. Like his predecessors, Reagan raised private donations for his presidential library—a record $56.8 million, making it the most expensive presidential library to date. On November 4, 1991, the Ronald Reagan

Presidential Library was dedicated in Simi Valley, California. Then President Bush and all the living former presidents at the time attended the dedication.

The years of Reagan's post-presidency are similar to those of Ford in that "cashing in" seems to be the dominant characteristic. At the time of the dedication of Reagan's presidential library, one reporter noted that "he [Reagan] prowls the international lecture circuit, collecting upwards of $30,000 a speech" (Scroggins, 1991, p. A10). In addition, Reagan remained involved in Republican political circles but did not appear to have any grand plans for his retirement.

Reagan's largest "cashing in" occurred during a tour of Japan as the guest of the Fujusankei Communications Group in November 1989. Reportedly, the Reagans received a fee of $2 million plus $5 million in expenses for an eight-day visit marked by photo opportunities, appearances, and exclusive interviews with Fujusankei Communications Group interests ("Elder $tatesman," 1989, p. 552). In 1990, following the traditional precedent, Reagan published his memoirs under the title *An American Life*.

With the exceptions of his support for gun-control measures like the Brady bill (which he opposed while in office) and joining his ex-presidential contemporaries in supporting the North American Free Trade Agreement (NAFTA), Ronald Reagan has publicly remained fairly quiet on political issues during his retirement. Reagan, described as the "great communicator," appears content with the legacy of being the president whom some credit with the defeat of communism and the "Evil Soviet Empire."

Recently, along with former President Carter, Ronald Reagan was selected by the board of directors of the U.S. Institute of Peace to be among the first recipients of the Spark M. Matsunaga Medals of Peace. This award, created by Congress, honors Spark M. Matsunaga, the former U.S. senator from Hawaii ("Carter, Reagan are honored," 1993, p. 3A).

Tragically, in November 1994 Reagan announced that he had been diagnosed with Alzheimer's disease. Eventually, the disease will severely limit any future involvement he might have in public life. The revelation was made, in part, to promote greater awareness of this mind-crippling disease. In a handwritten letter to "my fellow Americans," Reagan wrote that he intends "to live the remainder of the years God gives me on this Earth doing the things I have always done. I will continue to share life's journey with my beloved Nancy and my family. I plan to enjoy the great outdoors and stay in touch with my friends and supporters" (quoted in Wilson, 1994, p. 13A). This disease will eventually end President Reagan's impressive political career.

George Bush (1924-   ), President from 1989-1993

George Bush, who served for eight years as Ronald Reagan's vice president, followed Reagan into the White House in 1989 as the nation's forty-first president. He was defeated at the polls by Bill Clinton in the fall of 1992. The presidency was the final crowning achievement of a long career in public service by George Bush, including terms as U.S. congressman from Texas, ambassador to China, director of the Central Intelligence Agency, and vice president of the United States. Because of his long government career, President Bush had no real home base of operations. Reportedly, one of the first acts of President Bush after conceding the election was to assign his wife Barbara the task of finding a new home in Houston (Wines, 1992, p. A15). The Bushes were legal residents of the state of Texas, but their legal residence was a hotel suite. The only property they owned was a small vacant lot. The summer home the Bush family owned in Kennebunkport, Maine, was not considered suitable as a year-round residence.

Immediately after his defeat in the fall of 1992, Bush had several options available to him. These included academia, possibly becoming the commissioner of professional baseball, writing his memoirs, and delivering speeches (Wines, 1992, p. A15). According to the student newspaper of his alma mater, alumni even recommended him for the position of president of Yale University. It is likely that Bush will follow his ex-presidential colleagues and write his memoirs, join the speaking circuit, and accept positions on corporate boards. Friends, aides, and reporters at the time of his election defeat suggested that George Bush's post-presidency would probably fall somewhere between the extremes demonstrated by those of Ford and Reagan and that of Carter.

During his first years out of office, George Bush was content to pass gracefully and quietly into retirement. Soon after leaving office, George and Barbara Bush could be found relaxing on a Caribbean cruise, enjoying the company of their fellow shipmates, with George Bush refusing to answer reporters' questions about the politics of his successor and noting that he had returned to private life (Beard, 1993, p. 5A). Two months after leaving office, in his speech to the National Security Industrial Association, where he accepted the Forrestal Memorial Award, Bush quipped that "there is a life outside D.C." ("George Bush, citizen," 1993, p. 3A).

In a most public trip only three months out of office, George Bush received a hero's welcome from the country of Kuwait. Many Kuwaitis viewed him as their liberator following the invasion of Kuwait by Iraqi leader Saddam Hussein and the successful completion of Operation Desert Storm in early 1991. During his three-day visit, Bush received Kuwait's highest civilian award, the Mubarak al-Kabeer Medal (the Mubarak the Great Medal). Kuwait's leader, Sheik Jaber, said that the medal was "in gratitude and appreciation for your enormous efforts in liberating Kuwait and your services toward world peace and understanding" ("Kuwait gives Bush hero's welcome," 1993, p. A4). Bush also addressed the Kuwaiti Parliament, received an honorary doctorate from Kuwait University, and visited with U.S. servicemen still stationed in the country.

Bush's trip to Kuwait was not without international intrigue when reports surfaced of an Iraqi-backed assassination plot (Lelyveld, 1993, p. 3A). In June 1994, five Iraqis and one Kuwaiti were sentenced to death by a Kuwaiti court for their involvement in the failed assassination attempt (Elias, 1994, p. 4A).

Later in 1993 during a trip to Great Britain, Bush received the Knight Grand Cross of the Order of the Bath, the highest honor Britain can bestow on a foreigner ("Bush made honorary knight," 1993, p. 6A) The award was in recognition of the close relationship between Bush and the British government during the Gulf War. The only other American to receive the award since World War II was George Bush's former boss, Ronald Reagan.

After leaving the White House, George Bush's involvement with domestic politics included lending his support to the passage of NAFTA in the fall of 1993. In a rare display of bipartisan support, Bush strongly advocated the passage of the agreement, which had been negotiated by his administration (Leicester, 1993, p. 4A). At the time of the debate over this agreement, all former U.S. presidents lent their support to President Clinton's efforts to secure the ratification of NAFTA. In addition to his support of NAFTA, Bush spoke out strongly against a National Rifle Association (NRA) fund-raising letter sent to the NRA's 3.5 million members that referred to some federal agents as "jack-booted thugs." The letter led Bush to condemn the NRA fund-raising effort and to resign his membership in the organization ("NRA apologizes for controversial statement," 1995, p. 4A).

In the fall of 1993, Bush turned his attention to the speaking circuit and to fund-raising for his presidential library to be built on the campus of Texas A&M University. Bush spoke to groups like the executives of Choice Hotel International and Amway Distributors. Reportedly, his Amway appearance fetched a fee of approximately $100,000 (Langford, 1993, p. 8A). During his public appearances, Bush has tried to keep an early promise not to comment on his successor's actions, but rather to reflect on his own administration's foreign policy accomplishments. In addressing the hotel executives, Bush said, "I'm proud of what we did and I have a funny, satisfied feeling . . . that history will judge this period [his administration] kindly" (quoted in Langford, 1993, p. 8A).

In recent years, George Bush has spent part of his retirement "stumping" for his children's political fortunes in Texas and Florida and for GOP candidates in general. In support of son Jeb's race for the governor's office in Florida, George and Barbara Bush reportedly raised $1.1 million for his campaign ("George Bush happy," 1994, p. 2B). Bush also supported the successful candidacy of Tom Ridge for governor of Pennsylvania by helping to raise $400,000 (Neri, 1994, p. 1A). As he campaigned for his sons and other GOP candidates during the fall of 1994, Bush said, "I'm relaxed, I'm unemployed and retired," none of which stopped him from raising millions and crisscrossing the country stumping for GOP candidates (Raum, 1994, p. 7A).

George Bush is a relatively new ex-president. Unlike his fellow ex-presidents, he has yet to establish a clear direction or character for his retirement years beyond what has been described. While we have yet to see President Bush's memoirs, Barbara Bush's autobiography *Barbara Bush: A Memoirs* has sold very well, with the proceeds benefiting her favorite cause as first lady, literacy programs (Sloan, 1994, p. 8N). On occasion, Barbara has upstaged

George Bush, as happened when he was honored by the Perkins School for the Blind in the fall of 1994. Bush received the Anne Sullivan Medal for his support of the 1990 Americans with Disabilities Act, but he commented that "I've been here five minutes, and everyone is saying, 'it's fine to see you, but where's Barbara?'" ("Barbara Bush upstages George," 1994, p. 14A). Other activities of the Bushes include a trip to Guatemala in the fall of 1994 where they visited housing and school projects and gave donations of medicine and clothing on behalf of the private charity Americares, which Barbara Bush serves as ambassador-at-large.

Commenting on his life in retirement, Bush said, "I am no longer in public life and my interest now is in the concept of volunteerism, one American helping someone else" ("Bush visits," 1994, p. 2A). Perhaps this is an indication that the post-presidency of George Bush will pursue the "thousand points of light" theme of volunteerism that he initiated during his administration.

POST-PRESIDENTIAL POSSIBILITIES, PAST RECORDS, AND FUTURE POTENTIALS

As a country, we have expectations for our presidents. As a country, we are less sure of our expectations of former presidents. The Constitution establishes and guides the behavior and our expectations of the president. Tradition and precedent guide the behavior and our expectations of former presidents. Several interesting proposals have been made regarding how ex-presidents could best serve the country. In her book *Beyond the Presidency*, Marie Hecht provided several interesting possibilities and past proposals (pp. 311–313). For example, on the humorous side, a *Louisville Courier-Journal* newspaper editor suggested that we "take them out and shoot them," which Grover Cleveland noted at the time was a proposal "worthy of attention." President Taft, after leaving office, proposed (tongue-in-cheek) "a dose of chloroform or . . . the fruit of the lotus tree" as a means to protect his countrymen "from the troublesome fear that the occupant [of the nation's highest office] could ever come back" (reported by Wilson, 1990, p. xi).

More serious proposals have been put forth to make former presidents either voting or nonvoting members of the U.S. Senate. During the Kennedy administration, a bill was introduced in Congress to make former presidents nonvoting senators-at-large as a way for the country to benefit from their experience and knowledge. A similar proposal was made by Mike Mansfield to President Kennedy to make retired presidents a consultative council to serve the sitting president. Former Librarian of Congress Daniel Boorstin has suggested the establishment of a "House of Experience" to institutionalize the ex-presidency and use the insights former presidents could provide (Smith and Walch, 1990, p. xiii).

While these proposals are all interesting, and some may be useful and valuable, none have, are likely to, or perhaps should become policy or practice.

Hecht (1976) concluded her book on the post-presidency by stating, "The proper use of ex-presidents is to let them determine the disposition of their twilight years according to their own preferences and abilities" (p. 313). Gerald Ford noted at the conclusion of a 1989 conference on the post-presidency that "historical circumstance, personal experience, and aptitude conspire against predetermined roles. Let former presidents decide what interests to pursue, what contributions to make, on their own" (quoted in Smith and Walch, 1990, p. 172).

While recent post-presidencies have taken different directions and seen former presidents pursue different activities in their retirement, they also share certain common characteristics. All U.S. presidents since Truman have left office to establish their libraries and write their memoirs, and most speak or lecture in a variety of situations, to a variety of audiences, and for a variety of purposes. Yet each of the four recent post-presidencies described in this chapter also has a somewhat unique character.

Much of Nixon's post-presidency was spent trying, indirectly, to rehabilitate the legacy of his presidency and attempting to overcome the negative perception left by his resignation from office. Nixon emphasized and capitalized on his foreign policy knowledge and expertise, and through his speeches, books, and writings, he attempted to have an impact on world affairs and geopolitics. At the time of his death in 1994, he was remembered most for his foreign policy achievements and contributions. However, even with his death, his legacy could not escape his involvement in Watergate that forced him from office.

The post-presidency of Gerald Ford is perhaps less noteworthy than that of Nixon and appears to have been motivated more by financial considerations than by ideological commitments. It is unfortunate that despite Ford's distinguished career in the U.S. House of Representatives prior to becoming vice president and later president, his political career will always be shadowed by the legacy of Watergate. His post-presidency is characterized, in part, by his serving on corporate boards, collecting large speaking fees, and commenting on domestic policy issues. While nothing prevents a former president from exploiting the status that surrounds former U.S. Presidents, both Ford and Reagan have been criticized for doing so. On a more positive note, Ford's charitable activities and collaboration with Jimmy Carter on several projects have made contributions to peace and democratization in developing countries.

During his administration, Reagan was characterized as the "great communicator." Early on, his post-presidency fully exploited his perceived skills as a communicator, most notably in his much-publicized trip to Japan. Like Nixon and Ford, Reagan also remained involved in GOP politics and domestic policy. This involvement will certainly decrease as his struggle with Alzheimer's disease continues.

While George Bush has not been out of office very long, his post-presidency has taken a fairly traditional course. He has been able to bask in the glow of the successes of the Persian Gulf War and celebrate the foreign policy accomplishments of his administration. Bush is still in the process of establishing his presidential library and has yet to follow his contemporaries and pen his memoirs. Perhaps Bush will opt instead to leave his legacy to the historians. He remains involved in GOP politics, most notably in support of his sons' campaign efforts in Texas and Florida.

Once out of office, contemporary former U.S. presidents have followed the traditional roles of their predecessors. Some have been motivated by particular ideological beliefs, while others have sought to make the most of their statuses. All, to varying degrees, have made contributions to what they consider to be important domestic and foreign policy concerns. None, with the possible exception of Nixon, has systematically set out to pursue a particular agenda during his retirement. None has made the kind of contribution to world peace and humanitarian causes that Jimmy Carter has made during his post-presidency.

REFERENCES

Barbara Bush upstages George. (1994, Oct. 7). *Erie Daily Times* (Associated Press), p. 14A.

Beard, D. (1993, Feb. 16). Citizen George Bush lives it up on sea cruise. *Erie Daily Times* (Associated Press), p. 5A.

Bush made honorary knight. (1993, Nov. 30). *Erie Daily Times* (Associated Press), p. 6A.

Bush visits Guatemala Garbage Dump. (1994, Oct. 3). *Erie Daily Times* (Associated Press), p. 2A.

Carter, Reagan are honored as peacemakers. (1993, Jan. 4). *Erie Daily Times* (Associated Press), p. 3A.

Clark, J. C. (1985). *Faded glory: Presidents out of power*. New York: Praeger Publishers.

Cloud, S. W. (1989, Sept. 11). Hail to the ex-chief. *Time*, pp. 60–63.

Cunningham, H. F. (1989). *The presidents' last years: George Washington to Lyndon B. Johnson*. Jefferson, NC: McFarland & Co.

Elder $tatesman. (1989, Nov. 13). *Nation*, *249*, pp. 552–553.

Elias, D. (1994, June 5). Kuwaiti court sentences 6 to death for Bush plot. *Time News Weekender* (Erie, PA) (Associated Press), p. 4A.

Fleeman, M. (1994, Apr. 25). Nixon's hometown braces for world's attention. *Erie Daily Times* (Associated Press), p. 2A.

Ford, G. R. (1979). *A time to heal: The autobiography of Gerald R. Ford*. New York: Berkley Books.

Ford, G. R., and Carter, J. E. (1988). *American agenda: Report to the forty-first president of the United States of America*. Camp Hill, PA: Book-of-the-Month Club.

Ford blasts health care proposal. (1994, May 8). *Erie Sunday Times News* (Associated Press), p. 11A.

George Bush, citizen, returns to Washington. (1993, Mar. 19). *Erie Daily Times* (Associated Press), p. 3A.

George Bush happy as "little point of light." (1994, Mar. 29). *Erie Daily Times* (Associated Press), p. 2B.

Gerald Ford hits 80. (1993, July 14). *Erie Daily Times* (Associated Press), p. 12A.

Get-well messages pour in for Nixon. (1994, Apr. 21). *Erie Daily Times* (Associated Press), p. 6A.

Hackett, G. (1989, May 22). How to be an ex-president. *Newsweek*, p. 40.

Hecht, M. B. (1976). *Beyond the presidency: The residues of power*. New York: Macmillan Publishing Co.

Honoring Nixon to cost government $23 million extra. (1994, Apr. 26). *Erie Daily Times* (Associated Press), p. 3A.

Kuwait gives Bush hero's welcome. (1993, June 15). *New York Times*, p. A4.

Langford, T. (1993, Nov. 28). Bush hits the speaking circuit. *Times News Weekender* (Erie, PA) (Associated Press), p. 8A.

Leicester, J. (1993, Nov. 17). Former president Bush says NAFTA is U.S. leadership test. *Erie Daily Times* (Associated Press), p. 4A.

Lelyveld, N. (1993, May 9). U.S. probers look into Iraqi link to Bush assassination attempt. *Erie Daily Times* (Associated Press), p. 3A.

Nation bids Nixon farewell. (1994, Apr. 27). *Erie Daily Times* (Associated Press), pp. 1A, 14A.

Neri, A. J. (1994, Oct. 26). Bush helps Ridge raise about $400,000 at Philly breakfast. *Erie Daily Times*, pp. 1A, 14A.

Nixon lapses into very deep coma. (1994, Apr. 22). *Erie Daily Times* (Associated Press), pp. 1A, 14A.

Nixon's funeral cost taxpayers $311,000. (1994, Oct. 4). *Erie Daily Times* (Associated Press), p. 6B.

NRA apologizes for controversial statement about "jack-booted thugs." (1995, May 18). *Erie Daily Times* (Associated Press), p. 4A.

Peeved Yeltsin snubs Nixon after Rutskoi meeting. (1994, Mar. 9). *Erie Daily Times* (Associated Press), p. 2A.

President and accounted for. (1988, Sept./Oct.). *Common Cause Magazine, 14*, p. 9.

Presidential libraries: His second term. (1989, Sept. 2). *Economist*, pp. 29–30.

Raum, T. (1994, Sept. 18). Ex-president here, there, everywhere raising cash. *Times News Weekender* (Erie, PA) (Associated Press), p. 7A.

Schmemann, S. (1993, Feb. 19). Who hails Russia? Nixon, no less. *New York Times*, p. A4.

Scott, W. (1994, July 3). Personality parade. *Parade Magazine* (supplement to) *Times News Sunday* (Erie, PA), p. 2.

Scroggins, D. (1991, Nov. 3). Library will dramatize Ronald Reagan the cold warrior. *The Atlanta Journal/The Atlanta Constitution*, p. A10.

Sloan, R. A. (1994, Dec. 25). Rallying around Reagans. *Erie Daily Times* (Associated Press), p. 8N.

Smith, R. N., and Walch, T. (Eds.). (1990). *Farewell to the chief: Former presidents in American public life*. Worland, WY: High Plains Publishing Co.

Sullivan, T. (1994, Apr. 20). Nixon takes a turn for the worse; listed in critical condition. *Erie Daily Times* (Associated Press), p. 3A.

Wilson, D. W. (1990). Foreward. In R. N. Smith and T. Walch (Eds.), *Farewell to the chief: Former presidents in American public life*. Worland, WY: High Plains Publishing Co.

Wilson, J. (1994, Nov. 6). Reagan says he has Alzheimer's. *Times News Sunday* (Erie, PA) (Associated Press), p. 13A.

Wines, M. (1992, Nov. 9). Bush seems unsure about his plans. *New York Times*, p. A15.

Yeltsin reverses snub of Nixon. (1994, Mar. 13). *Erie Daily Times* (Associated Press), p. 3A.

CHAPTER 3

JIMMY CARTER: FROM PRESIDENT
TO PEACEMAKER

FROM THE WHITE HOUSE TO PLAINS, GEORGIA

At noon on January 20, 1981, Ronald Reagan was sworn into office as the thirty-ninth president of the United States, and President Jimmy Carter became Jimmy Carter, private citizen. Carter spent his last several sleepless days and nights in office negotiating the final details for the release of the American hostages in Iran. Following their release on inauguration day—a final slap in the face to his presidency—Jimmy Carter had the bittersweet task of traveling to Wiesbaden, West Germany, to welcome and escort the hostages home to freedom. The release of the hostages was, in part, a vindication of his handling of the hostage crisis, but occurred too late to save his reelection campaign.

Following his defeat at the polls, the prolonged but successful negotiations to release fifty-two Americans who had been held hostage by the government of Iran, and lingering criticism over his handling of the economy, Jimmy and Rosalynn Carter returned home to Plains, Georgia. The Carters faced the same transition that had confronted all of their predecessors in the White House: What were they to do with the rest of their lives? Carter was fifty-six years old—certainly not old, and in fact he was the youngest ex-president in recent history. Jimmy Carter could anticipate a long retirement. As the Carters explained in their book *Everything to Gain* (1987), "We returned home to Plains almost three months after Election Day, and faced additional personal crises involving our home life, our health, our personal finances, and the need to carve out new careers that would best allow us to use our talents" (p. xv). This book tells of the transitions and changes the Carters, and others, experienced as they were confronted with major life changes and transitions.

The Carters returned to the house they had built in 1961, but had not lived in for ten years. Four years in Georgia's governor's mansion, two years on the presidential campaign trail, and four years in the White House resulted in their

Georgia home's falling into disrepair. The accumulation of four years of memories and memorabilia from the White House now filled the Carter family home beyond capacity.

In addition to the normal adjustments anyone would have to make, the Carters' peanut-warehouse business was in serious financial difficulty. Like all recent presidents, in order to avoid charges of potential conflicts of interest, Carter had placed his assets and those of his family business into a blind trust to be managed by a financial trustee during his presidency. Soon after the results of the election in November, the Carters were informed that three years of drought in Georgia, high interest rates on business loans, and management problems with the warehouse operations had left the business deeply in debt. While the Carters had not been wealthy when they entered the White House, they faced the prospect of leaving the White House in financial ruin. Their best chance to remain financially solvent was to sell the warehouse operations in order to retain their farms and family home. The warehouse operations were ultimately sold to the Archer-Daniel-Midland Company, and the resulting proceeds were used to pay off the debts and save the peanut-warehouse business from closing. It was important to the Carters to preserve the warehouse business because it had become an integral part of the financial health of the Plains area.

The personal transition to private life was also a painful one for the Carters. As Rosalynn Carter reflected on their election defeat, she wrote, "There was no way I could understand our defeat. It didn't seem fair that everything we had hoped for, all our plans and dreams for the country could have been gone when the votes were counted on Election Day" (Carter and Carter, 1987, p. 9). Immediately after the election, President Carter set about making the most of his remaining time in office. He reflected on that when he wrote, "It was not easy to scale down my wish list from great dreams—such as bringing peace to the Middle East, ridding the world of nuclear weapons, and ensuring the human rights of all people everywhere—to those things that were possible in the time left" (Carter and Carter, 1987, p. 7). At that time, the most significant challenge was to resolve the Iranian hostage situation successfully, which proved to be a daunting task that came to fruition only in the closing moments of the Carter presidency. The transition to private life was certainly shaped by the events, timing, and emotions of the last months in office. As the Carters recalled those days, weeks, and months following the election and the impending move to Plains in their book *Everything to Gain*, there was some bitterness, regret, and considerable reflection. President Carter's reflection led him to conclude that, given the circumstances, he had done the best job he could have done. Rather than dwell on what could not be changed, Jimmy Carter's reflections reminded him of what he, personally, and his administration had accomplished. As they anticipated their future, Carter wrote, "We had decided to postpone any serious decisions, because we understood the need to pause for a while, to come to terms with our circumstances" (Carter and Carter, 1987, p. 6). Choosing the course of the optimist, Carter wrote, "Privately, I commit myself to overcoming the obstacles or to figuring out a new course of action. This is what I had to do following the election in 1980" (Carter and Carter, 1987, p. 7).

FROM PRESIDENT TO WRITER

As was to be expected, the early days back in Plains were filled with unpacking and reorienting for a new life and contemplating new challenges. Among the challenges awaiting President Carter was the writing of his memoirs. Writing was not an unfamiliar endeavor for Carter. *Why Not the Best?* (1975) and *A Government as Good as Its People* (1977) preceded Carter's work on his presidential memoirs. *Why Not the Best?* was, in a way, a campaign book for the 1976 presidential campaign. The book addressed what Carter felt were two key questions Americans were asking in the wake of Watergate: Can our government be honest, decent, open, fair, and compassionate? and Can our government be competent? In outlining his answers, Carter laid out many of the positions and proposals that successfully led him to the White House in 1976. *A Government as Good as Its People* is a collection of the speeches of governor and then presidential candidate Jimmy Carter. The title reflected Carter's belief and campaign theme that the government of the United States could and should reflect the very best of the unique character of the American people.

In December 1980, before leaving the White House, President Carter and Rosalynn received numerous offers from various publishers to write their memoirs. As the Carters explained, "Not only would the contracts help us repair our financial status but they would also keep us immersed in hard and unfamiliar work for a number of months while we dealt with our political disappointments and made plans for the future" (Carter and Carter, 1987, p. 12). In the early months of their new life in Plains, both Jimmy and Rosalynn set about reflecting on and chronicling their years in public life. A friendly competition developed over whose book would be the most popular. Rosalynn Carter noted with some pride that her book, *First Lady from Plains*, was on the *New York Times* "best-seller" list for eighteen weeks, while Jimmy's *Keeping Faith* was on the list for thirteen, even though it did sell more copies (Carter and Carter, 1987, p. 29).

While in Washington, both the Carters had kept daily diaries. In President Carter's case, there were some 5,000–6,000 pages of unedited notes from his White House years, combined with official logs and records, so the raw material for the task was readily available. These materials formed the basis for *Keeping Faith: Memoirs of a President* by Jimmy Carter, published in 1982. Carter's memoirs provide a detailed description of the intricacies of the final negotiations for the release of the American hostages. They also trace the chronology of events and experiences during his term in office, from his unprecedented walk to the White House following his inauguration through the failed reelection campaign of 1980.

For Carter, writing his memoirs was an opportunity to recall and recount the successes, as well as the failures, of his four years in office. According to

Carter, reviewing his diaries and writing his memoirs "gave me a chance to come to terms with the more unpleasant events and put them in perspective along with the important things we had been able to achieve" (Carter and Carter, 1987, p. 16).

Like his contemporary Richard Nixon, Jimmy Carter has been a prolific writer since leaving the White House. In Carter's 1984 book *Negotiation: The Alternative to Hostility*, he discussed the need for "bright thinking, unanticipated approaches and unorthodox ideas to achieve the ancient goals of better justice and peace in the world" (p. 6). This book argues for the use of negotiation and alternative dispute-resolution strategies to settle differences between nations. Drawing upon his negotiation experiences with the Panama Canal and SALT II treaties, the Camp David Accords, and the Iranian hostage situation, Carter outlined a set of steps to follow in initiating negotiations and a list of ground rules that should be followed in the pursuit of conflict resolution (1984, pp. 13–24). These ideas on conflict resolution were distilled from what Erwin Hargrove (1988), a Carter administration biographer, argued were Carter's major foreign policy achievements: the Panama Canal Treaty, the Camp David Accords between Israel and Egypt, the SALT II Treaty, and the establishment of full diplomatic relations with China (p. 122).

Originally published in 1985 and updated and revised in 1993, *The Blood of Abraham* was written by Carter in collaboration with Dr. Kenneth Stein, who directed an early Carter Center program on the Middle East. The book provides a careful historical analysis of the problem of peace in the Middle East. While in the White House, Carter had dedicated himself to the pursuit of peace in the Middle East—an effort that resulted in the historic Camp David Accords. This volume is a continuation, or perhaps a culmination, of the first consultation held at the Carter Center in November 1983. That consultation, cochaired by former Presidents Jimmy Carter and Gerald Ford, sought a definitive analysis of the political, social, and military situation in the Middle East.

A book that has already been mentioned, *Everything to Gain: Making the Most of the Rest of Your Life*, was coauthored by Jimmy and Rosalynn Carter in 1987. The book examines life changes and how to cope with change. While the Carters recounted the major changes and transitions in their lives, they also related their experiences to those of ordinary citizens.

In *An Outdoor Journal*, an unusual book published in 1988, Jimmy Carter provided the reader with his insights into and love for nature and the outdoors. He recalled his early days of fishing and hunting with his father, teaching his children the art of fishing, escaping from the press and concerns of state on the cross-country ski trails at Camp David, and enjoying numerous hunting and fishing trips in the United States and throughout the world since leaving office. The pages of this book present a different side of President Carter from that of head of state or international diplomat.

Three recent books continue Carter's publishing career. In 1992 Carter wrote *Turning Point: A Candidate, a State, and a Nation Come of Age*, which recounts his 1962 race for senator of the Fourteenth District of Georgia, his first campaign for public office. The book tells the story of a naive Jimmy Carter's early political education concerning the corruption that characterized Georgia politics in the 1960s. It is also the story of his fight to change and reform Georgia electoral policies in the wake of the civil rights movement. According to Carter, this early electoral experience and education in politics "set the stage for my future career" (1992, p. xix).

Carter shared his peacemaking experiences with young readers—the first former president to undertake such an effort—in *Talking Peace: A Vision for the Next Generation* (1993). He recounted for young readers the lessons of the Camp David Accords, the nature of conflict—the waging of peace and the making of war—the importance of addressing basic human needs like food, shelter, health care, and protecting the environment, and the necessity of preserving human rights. He also described how his experiences with mediation and democratic elections since leaving the White House provide viable alternatives to conflict and hostility. In many ways, he challenged young people to work for a more peaceful world—locally, nationally, and internationally.

In his most recent book, *Always a Reckoning* (1995), Carter joined former Presidents John Quincy Adams and Abraham Lincoln in publishing a book of poetry. This work is a collection of forty-four poems written by Carter about his childhood, family, and political life and is illustrated by his granddaughter. It is the end product of a long-cultivated interest in poetry, which Carter first expressed as he courted Rosalynn and later studied seriously under the direction of poets Miller Williams and James Whitehead ("New books by the Carters," p. 10).

As was the case for Nixon, Carter's publishing career serves a dual purpose. It provides an outlet for his ideas regarding issues of concern. It also raises financial resources for the Carters and the work of the Carter Center.

FROM PRESIDENT TO TEACHER

The transition to private citizen also afforded Jimmy Carter the opportunity to realize a lifelong ambition—to teach. Most former presidents give speeches and lectures after they leave office. However, not since William Howard Taft left the White House in 1913 to teach law at Yale University had a former president seriously pursued the challenge of academia (Leviton, 1983, pp. 91–92). In the waning months of his presidency, Carter received offers from several major universities but ultimately accepted a distinguished professorship at Emory University in Atlanta, Georgia, in his home state. Later, a mutually beneficial partnership would develop between Carter and Emory University when he chose to locate the Carter Center at this relatively small but well-endowed Southern institution.

In 1983, Carter said, "I have always wanted to teach. I want to be in a forum where expressions of opinions on issues which are vital to the public are addressed" (quoted by Leviton, 1983, p. 92). At Emory, Carter lectured on topics ranging from the SALT II Treaty to morality to human rights in public life. His teaching activities have addressed the disciplines of history, political science, law, and business in classes ranging from thirty to several hundred students. As his work with the programs of the Carter Center has consumed more of his time, Carter has curtailed his teaching career.

FROM PRESIDENT TO PEACEMAKER

Following the tradition established by presidents since Franklin Roosevelt, Jimmy Carter set about establishing his presidential library upon leaving office. Carter recalled, "For at least the first few months [out of office] there was one disagreeable prospect ahead of me that I tried to ignore: the need to raise large sums of money to build a presidential library for the records of my administration" (Carter and Carter, 1987, p. 17). Unlike the libraries of his predecessors, the Jimmy Carter Presidential Library and Museum and the Carter Center of Emory University serve as more than a mere repository for presidential papers and records. While the challenge of raising the necessary money was significant, a more important challenge for Carter was to determine a purpose and direction for the project that would result in something more than a monument to his presidency, a prospect Carter adamantly opposed.

Against the background of having left the White House, trying to salvage their family finances, beginning work on their respective memoirs, and raising funds for his presidential library, the struggle to make the project meaningful, beyond its library-museum functions, became a significant challenge. Rosalynn Carter told of the origins of the Carter Center after the Carters had seen and listened to several architectural presentations deemed unacceptable because they were found to be too "monumental" in their approach. In one version of the story recounted by Rosalynn, Jimmy woke up abruptly one night and spoke the words "conflict resolution" (Driemen, 1992, p. 172). Rosalynn also recalled that Jimmy woke and said, "I know what we can do at the library. We can develop a place to help people who want to resolve disputes" (Carter and Carter, 1987, p. 31). "A center to settle disputes" provided the direction and vision that would guide the formation and establishment of the Carter Center. As Rosalynn remembered the event, "For the first time since our return to Plains, I saw Jimmy really excited about possible plans for the future" (Carter and Carter, 1987, p. 31). As Jimmy Carter recalled the newly found direction for the Carter Center, he speculated, "Who knows what we can do if we set our objectives high? We may even be able to do more than if we had won the election in 1980" (Carter and Carter, 1987, p. 32).

In many ways, the Carter Center would become an extension of the principles that guided the Carter administration and a means of building upon many of the successful mediation and negotiation efforts—most notably the Camp David Accords and the Iranian hostage negotiations—that characterized the Carter administration. The Carter Center would enable the Carters to continue to make a difference on the world scene.

The Carter Center is located on Copenhill, a thirty-acre tract of land between downtown Atlanta and Emory University, which was the site of a Civil War battlefield. This provided an ideal location for the complex. A partnership between a Hawaiian developer and an Atlanta architectural firm allowed detailed planning and preparation to begin. The Jimmy Carter Presidential Library and Museum and the Carter Center of Emory University were founded in 1982 in temporary quarters at Emory University. The Carter Center was constructed using $28 million in donations from individuals, foundations, and corporations and was dedicated in October 1986. In chapter 4, the Carter Center of Emory University will be explained in detail and its programs described.

Key to understanding the establishment of the Carter Center and the direction that Jimmy Carter's post-presidency has taken is to understand Carter's perspectives on peace and war. There is no doubt that the issues of war and peace are central concerns for the president of the United States. Why are they also concerns for Jimmy Carter as a former president? It would have been easier for Jimmy Carter to retire quietly to Plains to write his memoirs and await the final judgment of history.

As an officer in the U.S. Navy and later as commander in chief of the U.S. armed forces, Carter was never far removed from the possibility and potential of war. As an officer in the nuclear submarine program, Carter clearly understood the potential destructive consequences of nuclear war. As commander in chief, President Carter was intimately aware of conflicts around the world, as well as the power of the U.S. military forces under his command. Perhaps because of these experiences, Jimmy Carter understood and appreciated the devastating toll war can inflict on countries and the people of the world. In a speech opening the 1992 Carter Center consultation that was entitled "Resolving Intra-National Conflicts," Carter very clearly articulated his views on war: "War is bestial. It is inhuman. It violates basic human values and ignores laws designed over centuries, even millennia, that protect the rights of one person living adjacent to another" (Carter, "Human Rights," 1992, p. 10). Jimmy Carter realizes that in human terms, the costs of war are immense.

The economic consequences of war are also significant. Working with figures published in *World Military and Social Expenditures, 1991* (Sivard, 1991), Carter noted that in the 1980s, the average worldwide expenditure for defense was one trillion U.S. dollars. The United States is a major player in supplying arms worldwide. According to the U.S. Arms Control and Disarmament Agency, between 1981 and 1991 the United States doubled its share of arms exports, replacing the former Soviet Union as the world's number one arms supplier ("U.S. doubled arms export share," 1994, p. A24). The same report noted that 60 percent of U.S. arms exports between 1987 and 1991 went to developing countries.

To put these statistics in perspective, Carter stated that "two million dollars a minute is spent on war or the preparation for war" (Carter, "Human Rights," 1992, p. 10). Such expenditures by developed countries or a "superpower" like the United States are certainly a drain on a country's economy and draw valuable resources away from more productive, long-term development concerns. The same type of expenditure for arms by a developing country, in many cases, can literally result in a choice between a country's equipping an army or feeding its people. According to Carter, "In developing nations, there are eight soldiers for every medical doctor. It costs about $30,000 annually, on average, to support a soldier. This is 30 times more than is spent on the education of a child. Speaking of education, you can take one U.S. submarine and pay for twice the cost of educating more than 126 million children in the 18 poorest countries on earth" (Carter, "Human Rights," 1992, p. 10). What these comments demonstrate is that whether war is considered in abstract or in concrete terms, whether we consider its humanitarian or economic consequences, war devastates countries and people. Jimmy Carter clearly understands the nature of war and the necessity of addressing the elimination of war as a means of resolving differences between peoples or countries.

The intensity of Carter's feelings regarding war and its costs is illustrated in an event he related at the conclusion of his memoirs. Carter's first visitor to the Oval Office was Max Cleland, a Vietnam veteran and triple amputee, who served as Carter's administrator of veterans affairs. Cleland was also the last official visitor to the Oval Office. During that final visit, Cleland presented Carter with a plaque engraved with the following quote from Thomas Jefferson: "I have the consolation to reflect that during the period of my administration not a drop of the blood of a single citizen was shed by the sword of war." Carter noted in his diary on that day that the plaque "is something I shall always cherish" (Carter, 1982, p. 596). As a naval officer, Carter understood the consequences of war. As commander in chief, he worked for and achieved a measure of peace during his administration. Since leaving office, Jimmy Carter has continued to work for peace.

Peace is a term that can have different meanings for different people. Both as president and former president, the cause of peace has been central to the life and work of Jimmy Carter. When he wrote *Why Not the Best?* in 1975, Carter outlined what he believed to be the key responsibilities of the president of the United States: "The foremost responsibility of any president, above all else, is to guarantee the security of our nation—a guarantee of freedom from threat of successful attack or blackmail, and the ability with our allies to maintain the peace" (1975, p. 205). In *A Government as Good as Its People*, he wrote, "Peace is not the mere absence of war. Peace is action to stamp out international terrorism. Peace is the unceasing effort to preserve human rights. And peace is a combined demonstration of strength and goodwill. We will pray for peace and we will work for peace" (1977, p. 205). In these early thoughts, Carter expressed the perspective that peace is not simply a state or end condition to be sought, it is also an active process. For Carter, peace requires action, effort, demonstration, and work. In fact, peacemaking is perhaps the hardest work a person, a president, or a former president can do. Gary Cox, a philosopher and peace-studies scholar, provided a similar perspective on peace. Cox defined peace as more than the cessation of hostilities or the achievement of inner tranquility; fundamentally, "Peace is an activity of cultivating the process of agreeing" (1986, p. 12). What the peace perspectives of Carter, the president, and Cox, the philosopher, have in common is the notion that peace is both a state and a process. To achieve the state of peace (the cessation of hostilities or inner tranquility), peacemaking activities and processes are essential (cultivating the processes of agreeing).

A useful perspective for conceptualizing peace and also for examining President Carter's peacemaking activities is to explore the conditions that are necessary for peace and to suggest those that are sufficient for peace. The cessation of hostilities is a necessary or required condition for peace to exist. Cultivating agreement and learning to live peacefully among people is a sufficient condition or prerequisite for peace. To state it more simply, fighting and hostilities must end in order for the promise or possibility of peace to exist. In addition, the parties involved must find new ways of dealing with each other and new ways of living together for the probability of peace to exist. The remaining chapters of this book will examine President Carter's post-presidential activities as they relate to establishing both the necessary and sufficient conditions for peace.

The Carter Center of Emory University has served as the base of operations for Jimmy Carter's peacemaking activities since its establishment in 1982. The founding, mission, and programs of the Carter Center are described in chapter 4. The work of the Conflict Resolution Program and the International Negotiation Network are described in chapter 5, "International Peacemaking through Mediation and Negotiation." Particular attention is given to Carter's efforts at mediating Africa's longest-fought civil war between Ethiopia and Eritrea, as well as more recent negotiation and mediation efforts throughout the world. Three 1994 peacemaking missions undertaken by President Carter are described in chapter 6, "Carter Missions to Korea, Haiti, and Bosnia." The activities of the Conflict Resolution Program and the International Negotiation Network are significant in terms of establishing the necessary conditions for peace, the cessation of hostilities.

The efforts of President Carter at spreading democracy in developing countries are described in chapter 7, "Peacemaking through Democratization." Working with a group called the Council of Freely Elected Heads of Government and various other agencies and organizations, Carter has helped to arrange free and fair elections in countries including Nicaragua, Panama, Ghana, the Dominican Republic, Haiti, and Zambia. In some cases, free and fair democratic elections can be a means of conflict resolution. More often than not, such elections are a useful means of helping establish the sufficient conditions for peace by providing new ways of cultivating agreement among the citizens of a country and providing the preconditions that can lead to peaceful relations.

While he is perhaps best known for his mediation, negotiation, and election-monitoring activities, Carter and the programs sponsored by the Carter Center have made significant contributions to the health of Third World peoples, as well as the economic, social, and agricultural development of Third World countries. Chapter 8, "Peacemaking through Humanitarian Development Abroad," describes these humanitarian programs and explores their track record. As with his efforts at democratization, Jimmy Carter's humanitarian commitment to the developing world helps provide for the sufficient conditions that enable peace to flourish. The probability and potential for long-term peace are enhanced if people are healthy, educated, fed, and prosperous.

While it may appear that Jimmy Carter's post-presidency has taken on a global perspective, a domestic perspective to his activities can be found in his work with organizations like the Interfaith Health Program, Habitat for Humanity, and the Atlanta Project. These domestic development efforts are described in chapter 9, "Peacemaking through Humanitarian Development at Home." Fundamental to all of these efforts is understanding the establishment of the Carter Center of Emory University and the programs operated through this organization, which are described in chapter 4.

REFERENCES

Carter, J. (1975). *Why not the best?* Nashville, TN: Broadman Press.

_____. (1977). *A government as good as its people.* New York: Simon and Schuster.

_____. (1982). *Keeping faith: Memoirs of a president.* New York: Bantam Books.

_____. (1984). *Negotiation: The alternative to hostility.* Macon, GA: Mercer University Press.

_____. (1985). *The blood of Abraham.* Boston: Houghton Mifflin.

_____. (1988). *An outdoor journal.* New York: Bantam Books.

_____. (1992). *Turning point: A candidate, a state, and a nation come of age.* New York: Times Books.

_____. (1992, Jan.). Human rights: The real costs of war. Plenary speech printed in "Resolving intra-national conflicts: A strengthened role for non-governmental actors." Conference Report Series, vol. 3, no. 2. Available from the Carter Center, One Copenhill, Atlanta, GA 30307.

_____. (1992). *Talking peace: A vision for the next generation.* New York: Dutton Children's Books.

_____. (1993). *Always a reckoning.* New York: Times Books.

Carter, J., and Carter, R. (1987). *Everything to gain: Making the most of the rest of your life.* New York: Random House.

Carter, R. (1984). *First lady from Plains.* Boston: Houghton Mifflin.

Cox, G. (1986). *The ways of peace: A philosophy of peace as action.* New York: Paulist Press.

Driemen, J. (1992, Jan.). Jimmy and Rosalynn. *Good Housekeeping*, pp. 100–102, 170–173.

Hargrove, E. (1988). *Jimmy Carter as president: Leadership and the politics of the public good*. Baton Rouge: Louisiana State University Press.

Leviton, J. (1983, Jan. 10). Jimmy Carter finds a new job. *People Weekly*, pp. 91–92.

New books by the Carters. (1995, Winter). *Carter Center News*, p. 10.

Sivard, R. L. (1991). *World military and social expenditures, 1991*. Washington, DC: World Priorities.

U.S. doubled arms export share in '80s. (1994, Apr. 1). *Washington Post* (Associated Press), p. A24.

CHAPTER 4

ESTABLISHING THE JIMMY CARTER PRESIDENTIAL LIBRARY AND MUSEUM AND THE CARTER CENTER OF EMORY UNIVERSITY

Among the challenges facing former President Carter after he left the White House was raising the funds necessary to build his presidential library. Carter recalled that as he contemplated this task, as "a defeated Democrat with no desire to seek public office again, the thought of having to go hat in hand for cash contributions was disheartening, to say the least" (Carter and Carter, 1987, p. 18). Not only was the practical task of raising the funds a significant challenge, but a more important challenge for Carter personally was to make his presidential library a project that would have long-term meaning and significance for both the Carters and the people of the world.

The last thing Carter wanted was to raise funds for a library that would serve as a monument to his presidency or simply as a repository for his administration's documents. Carter reflected on this challenge when he wrote, "I was very concerned about building a library that would function not merely as a memorial to my administration but would be a workplace that would serve some greater purpose in the world. I would also have to make a living for my family. I was not ready for retirement!" (Carter, 1993, p. 27). After considerable soul-searching and contemplation, establishing a policy-study center for world affairs, and specifically for the study of alternative means of conflict resolution and peacemaking, provided the direction Carter sought to guide the planning for his library. According to Rosalynn Carter's recollection, the "spark" that guided the formulation of the Carter Center occurred late one night when Jimmy woke with the idea for a center for the study of conflict resolution. Such a dream and center required an appropriate physical location in order to grow.

In 1982, soon after leaving office and returning to his Georgia home, former President Carter received an invitation from Dr. James Laney, the president of Emory University, to accept a distinguished professorship. Carter's acceptance of this invitation marked the beginning of a long-term, mutually productive relationship between Laney and Carter and formed the basis for a long-term association between Emory University and the Carter Center ("Emory president," 1993, p. 9). The link between Carter's desire to establish a center for the study of conflict resolution and his desire to teach found a home in the partnership that developed between Emory University and the Carter Center.

The Carter Center of Emory University opened in temporary offices at Emory University's Woodruff Library in 1982. These temporary quarters served as the home for the Carter Center during the four-year period of fund-raising and construction needed in order for the Carter Center and the Jimmy Carter Presidential Library and Museum to become a reality. The Carter Center and the Jimmy Carter Presidential Library were constructed using $28 million in individual, foundation, and corporate donations.

The complex was dedicated in October 1986 in ceremonies attended by five thousand supporters, including then President Ronald Reagan. At the dedication, President Reagan said of President Carter, "You gave of yourself to your country, graced the White House with your passion and intellect and commitment" (quoted by Pasley and Weisman, 1987, p. 13). Emory University President Laney described the Carter Center as a "location where scholars and statesmen, in reflection and consultation, seek those things that make for peace. That surely is what the ultimate aim of all of our study and research should be—the well-being of peoples everywhere" (quoted in "Carter Center dedicated," 1987, p. 3).

In the early years of its operation, the Carter Center dispensed $16 million a year to support projects ranging from agricultural development programs in Ghana to seminars in conflict resolution (Hackett, 1989, p. 40). Roughly half of the money raised and dispensed by the Carter Center comes from domestic sources, while the rest comes from foreign contributions (Applebome, 1989, p. A9). By the early 1990s, the Carter Center operated with a budget of $25 million, employed a staff of some 250, and had open several overseas field offices ("Waging peace," 1993, p. 5). In order to ensure the Carter Center's future, on September 1, 1994, the Carter Center became a separately chartered, independently governed part of Emory University (Hardman, 1995, p. 2).

In 1986, the Carter Center complex consisted of four interconnected buildings laid out on thirty acres of land located between Emory University and downtown Atlanta. Three buildings in the complex housed the Carter Center's nonprofit international and domestic programs, while the fourth building housed the Jimmy Carter Presidential Library and Museum. In the fall of 1990, the Carter Center launched a $60-million capital campaign to secure the financial future of the Carter Center. Half of the funds raised would provide a permanent endowment for the future operation of the Carter Center, while the remaining money would be used to create an extraordinary-needs fund. The campaign was directed by six prominent corporate CEOs ("Center launches," 1990, p. 12).

Since its inception in 1982, the growth of programs at the Carter Center has made expansion of the physical plant necessary. In 1992, the Carter Center broke ground for the fifth building in the complex to provide much-needed meeting and conference space, including a 425-seat auditorium. This building, including the Ivan Allen III Pavilion and the Cecil B. Day Chapel, was dedicated in the fall of 1993. Andrew Young, former U.N. ambassador, Atlanta mayor, and long-time Carter supporter, told the audience at the dedication of the new building, "This place is about breaking down walls. This place is about making peace. This place is about human rights and justice. . . . we commit it to the continuation of breaking down barriers between races, clans, creeds, rich and poor, and to the waging of peace" (quoted in "Carter Center celebrates opening," 1993, p. 1).

Both the Jimmy Carter Presidential Library and the Carter Center have unique missions and programs that have characterized their development and operation. The Jimmy Carter Presidential Library and Museum is dedicated to serving as a research center for the Carter presidency by providing access to the documents and records of his administration. It is similar in this regard to presidential libraries dating back to the Truman administration. The Carter Center of Emory University is unique in its mission, its vision, and the programs it operates.

THE JIMMY CARTER PRESIDENTIAL LIBRARY AND MUSEUM

The Jimmy Carter Presidential Library and Museum houses twenty-seven million documents and thousands of pictures from Carter's term in the White House. Like other presidential libraries, it is deeded to and operated by the National Archives and Records Administration. When the Carter Library opened its research facilities in January 1987, it initially made available to researchers more than six million pages of documents ("Carter library," 1987, p. 12). Researchers who visit the library have access to the White House central subject and name files, some of the papers of White House staff members, and the federal records of presidential commissions and various White House conferences held during the Carter administration, as well as pre-presidential papers from Carter's years of campaigning ("Carter library," 1987, p. 12; "Library offers unique views," 1990, p. 16). Many of the papers available are written in President Carter's own hand or are documents annotated by President Carter ("Library offers unique views," 1990, p. 16). Much of the material now available to researchers concerns domestic policy and politics because many of the documents related to foreign policy remain classified and will not be available to the public for a number of years ("Library offers unique views," 1990, p. 16).

The museum facilities of the Jimmy Carter Presidential Library and Museum are open to the general public with exhibits that trace the history of the U.S. presidency during the twentieth century and highlight major events and issues of the Carter years ("Carter Center dedicated," 1987, p. 2). Modern interactive video technology provides visitors the opportunity to ask Jimmy Carter questions about his presidency and life in the White House. Visitors to the library are able to pose questions to President Carter's life-size video image ("Carter library," 1987, p. 12).

Since its dedication in 1986, the Jimmy Carter Presidential Library and Museum has regularly sponsored a variety of special programs and events related to American history and the presidency. One of the first special events was a symposium celebrating the bicentennial of the U.S. Constitution entitled "Women and the Constitution" ("Women and the Constitution," 1987, p. 5). The conference focused on women and the Constitution from political, economic, and sociological perspectives and featured speeches by Supreme Court Justice Sandra Day O'Connor, Barbara Jordan, Geraldine Ferraro, and Coretta Scott King. Programs in 1988 included a traveling Smithsonian exhibit focused on the Great Depression and highlighting eighty depression-era photographs and also an exhibit of the paintings by Israeli artists commissioned to celebrate the tenth anniversary of the Camp David Accords ("Jimmy Carter library," 1988, p. 16). A program called "Primed on the Presidency" was created at the library to help elementary-school students better understand how the U.S. government works. The work of Mexican artist Octavio Ocampo, whose portrait of Jimmy Carter is on permanent display in the library, and the political cartoons of Thomas Nast traveled to the library in 1989 ("Primed on the presidency," 1989, p. 16). The museum celebrated life in rural southern Georgia with an exhibit called "Folklife of the Georgia Wiregrass" created by folklorists and photographers who documented the architecture, agriculture, family and religious life, arts, and recreational activities of southern Georgia ("Wiregrass exhibit," 1990, p. 16). An exhibit of seventy-five photographs called "LBJ: The White House Years" also visited the library in 1990 to commemorate the twenty-fifth anniversary of Johnson's inauguration as president ("Wiregrass exhibit," 1990, p. 16). President Carter's love of the outdoors and fly fishing, in particular, was featured in a 1991 exhibit created in conjunction with the American Museum of Fly Fishing called "The Tie That Binds." The exhibit featured the historic and modern materials related to the sport of fly fishing ("Tie that binds," 1991, p. 16).

After more than two years of work by archivists at the library, the handwritten documents from President Carter's daily outbox while in the White House were made available to researchers. According to Donald Schewe, director of the library, because President Carter preferred memos to meetings, these handwritten documents are particularly important because they provide researchers insight into what President Carter knew, when he knew it, and what he thought about it—Carter was well known for making notes on documents ("Handwriting file," 1991, p. 16). Following the fall of the Berlin Wall in 1989, a two-and-one-half-ton segment of the wall was erected in front of the library and museum as part of a traveling exhibition called "The Symbol of an Age: Berlin and the Wall" ("Berlin Wall," 1992, p. 16). In 1992, the library and museum celebrated the two hundredth anniversary of the White House by mounting "The White House, 1792–1992: Image in Architecture" in cooperation with the American Architectural Foundation and the White House Historical Association. This exhibit was the first to explore the architectural history of the White House and included a special exhibit, "More Than Fabric and Frills—First

Lady Gown Reproductions," featuring gowns from Dolly Madison to Rosalynn Carter ("Celebration," 1992, p. 16). The work of combat artists in World War II was featured in a traveling exhibit sponsored by the National Archives called "World War II: The Artists View" designed to commemorate U.S. participation in World War II ("World War II," 1993, p. 16). The portrait work of Mathew Brady traveled to the museum and was featured in an exhibition sponsored by the National Portrait Gallery. Sixty of his photographs of nineteenth-century American politicians, personalities, and actors called "Lincoln and His Contemporaries" were on display ("Portraits of Mathew Brady," 1994, p. 15).

THE CARTER CENTER OF EMORY UNIVERSITY: MISSION, VISION, AND PROGRAMS

The Carter Center's mission statement is as follows:

The Carter Center brings people and resources together to promote peace and human rights, resolve conflict, foster democracy and development, and fight poverty, hunger, and disease throughout the world. The nonpartisan Center, which is affiliated with Emory University, builds partnerships to address complex and interrelated problems. By drawing on the experience and participation of former U.S. President Jimmy Carter and other world leaders, by fostering collaboration and avoiding duplication of existing efforts,and by combining effective action plans with research and analysis, the Center can achieve goals beyond the reach of single individuals or organizations. The Center is guided by the principle that people, with the necessary skills, knowledge, and access, can improve their own lives and the lives of others. ("Waging peace," 1993, p. 2)

The Carter Center has described itself as a consortium of nonprofit organizations that "seek to alleviate conflict, reduce suffering, and promote better understanding among peoples" ("The Carter Center" brochure). As described by President Carter in his 1993 book *Talking Peace*:

The Carter Center is founded on the principle that everyone on earth should be able to live in peace. In pursuit of this goal, the Center has earned an international reputation for bringing people and resources together to resolve conflict, foster democracy and development, and fight hunger, disease, and human rights abuses. By seeking ways to meet basic human needs, the Center draws on President Carter's access to world leaders and forms partnerships with other institutions and individuals to achieve larger goals. (1993, p. 29)

This statement clearly expresses the peacemaking mission of the Carter Center and articulates President Carter's vision for what the Carter Center seeks to accomplish through its activities and programs.

The Carter Center draws upon a unique combination of resources as it seeks to work toward peace in the world. First and foremost, there is the presence and daily involvement of former President Carter. While there is no shortage of public policy institutes and think tanks, the Carter Center is the only such institution that profits from the daily active involvement of a former U.S. president and the access to national and world leaders such involvement affords. Warren Christopher, former deputy secretary of state in the Carter administration and secretary of state in the Clinton administration, stated at its dedication that "the Carter Center draws upon the former President's ability to rally resources and command attention as only a former President can" (quoted in "Carter Center dedicated," 1987, p. 3). Christopher further noted that "this Center is devoted not to the past status but present works. Its purpose is not to aggrandize or justify, but to contribute. It has no object but the public good" (quoted in "Carter Center dedicated," 1987, p. 3).

Having designed the Carter Center and established its guiding mission, President Carter has been active in the day-to-day operations and programs of the center since its inception. The Carter Center is intended to be an active organization, one that can address difficult problems and formulate real solutions and programs to further its mission of peacemaking. As a former U.S. president, Jimmy Carter, through his presence at the Carter Center, provides access to world leaders and openings to organizations throughout the world that would not be possible if he were not actively involved. Dr. William Foege, former executive director of the Carter Center, described the uniqueness of the center when he said, "What makes us different is that we try to develop a policy or an approach to a problem and then actually intervene in order to solve that problem. Having President Carter makes it much easier" (quoted in "Thriving partnership," 1989, p. 2).

President Carter can and does call on world leaders, and when he calls, he is usually able to make contacts that might otherwise have been impossible. By the same token, the leaders of foreign countries can and have called upon the "good offices" of Jimmy Carter to mediate and address various conflict situations. Several of these conflict situations are described later in this book. In some cases, leaders in conflict situations contact Carter instead of the official representatives of the United States. For example, while monitoring elections in Nicaragua in 1989, Carter met with then Nicaraguan President Daniel Ortega, who shared with Carter a new proposal for resolving the war with the contras ("Quayle chides Carter," 1989, p. A3). Similar personal contacts were instrumental to Carter's involvement in the North Korean nuclear dispute, Haiti, and Bosnia-Herzegovina. While it may be problematic for a former U.S. president to meet with parties not officially recognized by the United States, Carter has said, "I would never do anything contrary to our nation's policy knowingly. We are not competitive; we are not trying to intrude" (quoted in Barrett, 1991, p. 5). Clearly such unofficial contacts have provided opportunities to mediate and defuse potentially devastating conflict situations that might not have been possible through traditional diplomatic channels.

As a resource for working toward world peace, Jimmy Carter's status as a former world leader is extremely valuable. Carter's status means that he has enjoyed unique access to the U.S. State Department in the form of a secure phone line (Bird, 1990, p. 562) and on numerous occasions has consulted with sitting presidents on international issues.

President Carter's personal commitment to peace led to the founding of the Carter Center, which, in turn, has provided a forum for him to further the cause of peace. The value of Carter's post-presidential credibility and the resulting stature of his good offices as a mediator have become significant tools in the peacemaking work of the Carter Center.

A second key resource available at the Carter Center is a group of knowledgeable and dedicated experts in a variety of areas essential to peacemaking. Because of its association with Emory University, the Carter Center is able to draw upon the expertise of the university's faculty. In many cases, the research fellows of the Carter Center hold faculty appointments in various departments at Emory University and other universities around the country. In 1990, the Carter Center established a Visiting Fellows Program to expand and enhance the research and outreach capabilities of the center. According to William Foege, "The pool of talent we have available to us through Emory University and the international academic community will considerably strengthen our ability not only to conduct first-rate research, but also to continue to apply what we have learned in the field" (quoted in "Visiting fellows," 1990, p. 11).

The research resources of Emory University, and the academic community at large, enhance the work of the center and provide an outlet for the implementation of practical solutions to real-world problems. The Carter Center provides a vehicle for scholarly research on contemporary global problems to become programs that, when implemented, actually address and solve problems. Numerous examples of this translation of academic research into practical solutions and programs can be found in the various organizations that operate under the auspices of the Carter Center. According to James Laney, "What the Carter Center adds up to academically is a new way of conceiving how to do foreign policy and is changing how we do political science" (quoted in "Thriving partnership," 1989, p. 2). The Carter Center programs also draw upon the research resources of Emory University to assist with special projects. For example, the International Negotiation Network has called upon the expertise of Emory University scholars and the academic community at large to conduct background research on particular conflict situations in preparation for major Carter Center consultations.

The relationship between the Carter Center and Emory University also benefits Emory University students through an active internship program ("Internship program," 1987, p. 2). The program allows students from Emory and other colleges and universities to work on various projects with Carter Center fellows. According to James Laney, "The work of the fellows with undergraduate students is a way of bringing the world to the doorstep at Emory" (quoted in "Thriving partnership," 1989, p. 2).

The various organizations and programs of the center combine the status and access a former U.S. president affords with the scholarly and academic research generated by center fellows and visiting scholars to produce outreach, demonstration, or public policy programs targeted at effecting positive change in conflict situations around the world as well as close to home. While the structure of the Carter Center has evolved and developed since its inception in 1982, a core collection of programs still comprises the work of the Carter Center. The Carter Center initiatives fall into three basic areas: International Democratization and Development, Global and Domestic Health, and Urban Revitalization ("Carter Center programs," 1995, p. 1). Carter Center programs are targeted at problems neglected or ignored by other international organizations and are guided by several principles, including being strictly nonpartisan, not duplicating the successful efforts of other agencies and institutions but rather collaborating and coordinating efforts with existing organizations, and seeking practical applications for scholarly research ("Challenges of faith and health," 1994, p. 72; "Waging peace," 1993, p. 5). Each of the major initiatives and programs will be introduced briefly and profiled, while subsequent chapters will detail the activities and accomplishments of some of these varied programs. (These overviews were abstracted from several sources, the most important being yearly summaries called "Carter Center Programs.")

OVERVIEW OF INTERNATIONAL DEMOCRATIZATION AND DEVELOPMENT

Conflict-resolution efforts, a focus on human rights, studies of governance in Africa and Latin America, and election-monitoring programs and postelection consolidation programs have helped to foster the transition to democracy in countries formerly controlled by military or dictatorial regimes in the Western Hemisphere and Africa. Currently, there are seven major programs pursuing initiatives under the International Democratization and Development area. These include the African Governance Program, the Commission on Radio and Television Policy, the Conflict Resolution Program, the Global Development Initiative, the Human Rights Program, the Carter-Menil Human Rights Foundation and Prize, and the Latin American and Caribbean Program.

The African Governance Program

The African Governance Program focuses on issues of governance in sub-Saharan Africa, including the monitoring of democratic elections and providing advice and counsel to newly elected democratic governments. The program is directed by Dr. Richard Joseph, an expert on African studies and a professor at Emory University, who joined the Carter Center in 1988. In 1990, the program instituted a research project to gather information on trends in political transition in Africa, to identify the major problems in political reform, and to suggest ways such transitions could be assisted by outside individuals and organizations.

To date, the African Governance Program has helped arrange and organize free multiparty elections in Zambia and Ghana and has conducted election-monitoring programs that have ushered in, for the first time, democratically elected governments for these countries. These efforts have been followed by ongoing postelection consolidation projects and consultation. The program has also worked in recent years to foster democracy in war-torn Liberia. The African Governance Program publishes *Africa Demos*, a bimonthly bulletin, which provides an outlet for the program's research and consultative efforts. The African Governance Program also facilitated the establishment of the Mickey Leland Community Development Fellowship Program, designed to strengthen democratic reforms and the transition to democracy in African nations.

The Commission on Radio and Television Policy

The Commission on Radio and Television Policy, as of January 1994 a joint initiative between the Carter Center and Duke University, examines U.S.-Soviet/Russian relations through the medium of television. The commission was formed in 1990 when President Carter met with former Soviet President Mikhail Gorbachev. Recognizing that in the era of glasnost, the television medium could have a significant influence on the restructuring of the former Soviet Union, the commission examines the role of television in the democratization of the former Soviet Union. The commission, under the leadership of Dr. Ellen Mickiewicz, has enjoyed unprecedented access to the most popular Russian television program, "First Program," and has conducted a poll of 2,500 Russians concerning their positions and attitudes on issues. Drawing upon the expertise of both the academic and professional communities, the commission is attempting to offer guidance for the establishment of independent broadcast media within the Commonwealth of Independent States (the former Soviet Union) and other countries enjoying such new freedoms.

Since its inception, the commission has developed models for the fair coverage of elections and ethnic minorities for television stations and governmental policymakers in countries being introduced to new press freedoms. The commission copublished the guidebook *Television and Elections* with the Aspen Institute, drafted a Charter of Media Independence for the states of the former Soviet Union, and has convened meetings between President Carter, the president of the Moscow Independent Broadcasting Corporation, and television executives to explore media ownership, technology, and regulation.

The Conflict Resolution Program

In 1992, Sweden's Uppsala University reported that there were 32 major armed conflicts among the 112 intranational conflicts ongoing around the world. The Conflict Resolution Program (CRP), through the International Negotiation Network (INN), tries to address these conflicts in new and effective ways in an effort to end the suffering caused by these conflicts. The INN monitors, analyzes, and, when requested by involved parties, becomes involved in the mediation of the conflicts.

The leadership body of the INN, the INN Council, is composed of eminent former world leaders who have the stature and ability to bring together parties in conflict, mediate conflicts, and monitor free elections to resolve disputes. Each year the CRP convenes a consultation, chaired by President Carter, to bring together world experts who try to find solutions to selected long-standing intranational civil conflicts. Consultations convened by the INN have addressed conflicts in Angola, Armenia, Azerbaijan, Burma, Cyprus, Haiti, the Korean Peninsula, Kosovo, Liberia, Macedonia, Sudan, and Zaire.

The INN's success in mediating these types of conflicts was demonstrated during the fall of 1989 with its involvement in mediating the Ethiopian-Eritrean civil war. In 1992 and 1993, the INN tried to increase international attention to the situation in Burma and the plight of Nobel laureate Daw Aung San Suu Kyi, who had been held under house arrest for several years until her release in 1995. In 1993, the CRP explored the possibilities for peace in the Sudan by hosting a meeting between the Sudan People's Liberation Army United and the Sudan People's Liberation Army (a southern Sudanese faction) and continues to monitor and communicate with the involved parties. More recently, the INN began a project on preventative diplomacy designed to reduce ethnic tensions between the Baltic States and Russia. The INN has also been involved since 1989 in peacemaking efforts to resolve the civil conflict in Liberia.

The Global Development Initiative

The Global Development Initiative (GDI) developed from a December 1992 conference, cochaired by President Carter and U.N. Secretary General Boutros Boutros-Ghali, that explored ways to improve the development aid process. The conference, held in collaboration with the Carnegie Commission of Science, Technology, and Government, involved donor agencies, recipient countries, and other interested groups. The conference sought to expand the measure of international aid success by focusing more on political, environmental, social, and cultural factors and concentrating less on economic growth. The GDI "seeks to marshal support among international donors and recipient countries to better coordinate and deploy development aid. The goal is to help developing nations address their needs in partnership with the donor community" ("Waging peace," 1993, p. 14). The overall objective of the GDI is to promote sustainable development in target countries. According to Boutros-Ghali, "A new vision of development is emerging. Development is becoming a people-centered process whose ultimate goal must be the improvement of the human condition" (quoted in "Waging peace," 1993, p. 14).

The first target country for the GDI was Guyana, where President Carter had helped monitor elections in 1992. While the elections were important in establishing democracy, Guyana requires significant assistance to ensure the promise of both democracy and sustainable development. GDI staff are working with the Guyanese government and all interested groups to create a strategy for such sustainable development.

As a result of his commitment to the GDI, Carter attended a meeting in Guyana of the Caribbean Group for Cooperation in Economic Development. This meeting resulted in pledges of $320 million in new aid for Guyana. In anticipating the future of his country, President Cheddi Jagan said, "We want Guyana placed proudly among those countries which have been able to carve out for themselves a nation ready to meet the trials and prospects the new millennium will so bring" (quoted in "Waging peace," 1993, p. 15). The ongoing commitment of the Carter Center in Guyana will continue, since the opening of a field office in Georgetown, Guyana, in 1995 will allow Carter Center staff to continue to work on a long-term development strategy, as well as to assist the Guyanese Elections Commission with electoral reform ("Carter Center opens office," 1995, p. 15).

The Human Rights Program

As was true during Jimmy Carter's presidency, the protection and promotion of human rights remains a key focus of his post-presidency through the Human Rights Program (HRP) at the Carter Center. Recognizing that respect for human rights is essential to peace and democracy, the HRP staff offers technical assistance to safeguard human rights, intervenes in cases of human rights abuse, and sponsors public education programs. In the same way that President Carter stressed human rights issues during his foreign visits, Jimmy Carter's post-presidential foreign travels continue to focus on human rights. When the Carters travel to countries with oppressive governments, they regularly meet with human rights activists and government leaders.

Carter's personal commitment to human rights and the Carter Center's HRP have resulted in tangible results. On many occasions, Carter's brand of quiet contact with the leadership of countries who abuse human rights has led to the release of political prisoners and prisoners of conscience. For example, in August 1991, President Carter personally intervened on behalf of Mohammed Srifi, a Moroccan prisoner of conscience, and appealed to King Hassan for the release of Srifi on legal and humanitarian grounds. Srifi was subsequently released after seventeen years of imprisonment.

The HRP is directed by Jamal Benomar, who fled Morocco in 1985 after eight years of torture and imprisonment for his political beliefs. He joined the Carter Center after having served as an African human rights specialist for Amnesty International. Under his direction, projects have been initiated to help countries establish institutional protection for human rights. Complementing the efforts of the CRP and the African Governance Program, the HRP works to help transitional governments ensure and protect human rights. These efforts are designed to ensure that constitutions and legislation are compatible with international human rights standards, and are ongoing in Ethiopia, Liberia, and Chad. Staff members from the HRP have, at the request of the Guyanese government, conducted police-training workshops on human dignity and community policing based on the program's earlier success with such efforts in Ethiopia. The HRP held a 1992 conference to discuss ways that countries in transition to democracy can address their repressive pasts and prevent human rights abuses in the future, and in 1993 the HRP supported the creation of the new post of U.N. high commissioner for human rights.

The Carter-Menil Human Rights Foundation and Prize

Established in 1986, the Carter-Menil Human Rights Foundation was formed by President Carter and Dominique de Menil, the founder of the nondenominational Rothko Chapel in Houston, to promote the protection of human rights. To celebrate and commemorate the anniversary of the Universal Declaration of Human Rights, the foundation annually presents a $100,000 prize to one or more individuals or organizations that have advanced human rights principles. The award enables human rights groups to continue their work, as well as focusing international attention on specific human rights issues. Past awards have gone to a variety of human rights advocates and organizations, all of whom have demonstrated their commitment to the prevention of human rights abuses and to the protection of human rights. The annual presentation of the award also serves as the occasion for President Carter to deliver his "State of Human Rights Address."

The Latin American and Caribbean Program

The Latin American and Caribbean Program addresses problems facing Latin American democracies, inter-American relations, and U.S. policy in Latin America and the Caribbean. The program is directed by long-time Carter associate and advisor Dr. Robert Pastor. A unique feature of the program is the Council of Freely Elected Heads of Government. This group of twenty-three current and former world leaders from the region works to promote democracy and the peaceful resolution of regional conflicts. One of the most important activities of this group has been the monitoring of free and fair democratic elections in countries throughout the region. The program has assisted with organizing and monitoring elections in Panama (1989), Nicaragua (1990), Haiti (1990), the Dominican Republic (1990), Guyana (1990–92), and Mexico (1992). The council has also assisted with elections in Africa in conjunction with the African Governance Program. Following successful elections, the council works to consolidate democracy in targeted countries. The election-monitoring activities of the council have been collaborative ventures with the United Nations, the Organization of American States, and the National Democratic

Institute for International Affairs.

The program has a long-term interest in strengthening democracy in Mexico. The council monitored Mexican elections in 1992, invited representatives from Mexico to witness U.S. presidential elections in 1992, and analyzed election reforms in Mexico in 1993. Recently, the Latin American and Caribbean Program studied the impact of the North American Free Trade Agreement and advocated its passage. Several consultations have been sponsored by the program at the Carter Center, including those on debt crisis (April 1986), reinforcing democracy (November 1986), and the New Hemisphere Agenda (March 1989).

OVERVIEW OF GLOBAL AND DOMESTIC HEALTH

The programs of the Global and Domestic Health initiative foster healthy living by promoting preventive medicine and developing and implementing strategies for reducing health risks common to all nations. In addition, programs have also increased food production in developing countries. The four globally focused programs include Global 2000, Inc., Agriculture, the Guinea Worm Eradication Program, and the Environmental Initiative. Three programs address domestic health issues and programs: the Interfaith Health Program, the Mental Health Program, and the Tobacco Control Program.

Headed by Dr. William Foege, former Carter Center executive director and former director of the U.S. Centers for Disease Control, Global and Domestic Health programs have sponsored several Carter Center conferences and consultations, beginning with "Closing the Gap" in 1984. This conference outlined the potential for preventing unnecessary illness and premature death and helped define major health issues in the United States. A 1986 conference, "Risks Old and New," provided health-intervention recommendations to health leaders in developing countries.

Global 2000, Inc.

Global 2000, Inc., was established in 1985 to help improve health and agricultural services in developing countries by focusing on disease-control and crop-demonstration projects. Global 2000 projects work with individual countries to promote self-sufficiency in food production and to improve health-care conditions. Global 2000 has also been involved with efforts to help the mentally and physically challenged in China. Global 2000 acts largely as a technology-transfer agent by facilitating the dissemination of existing technologies to those countries in need of such technologies.

Agricultural Programs. Global 2000 programs draw upon the expertise of top scientists, including 1970 Nobel laureate Dr. Norman Borlaug, an expert in increasing crop yields and credited with the "Green Revolution" in India. Global 2000 agricultural development programs are using improved seed, fertilizer, and farming technologies to increase food production significantly in target countries.

This program grew from 40 farmers in 1986 to about 19,000 farmers in 1988 and resulted in fourfold increases in crop yields. Global 2000 agricultural programs have worked with more than 150,000 farmers since their inception. With the help of Global 2000, Ghana has recently achieved near self-support in food production, while similar programs are currently under way in Zambia and the Sudan. In 1992, Global 2000 formed the fourteen-member Agricultural Council of Experts composed of agronomists, agricultural economists, and experts on women's issues to advise President Carter and Dr. Borlaug on economic and agricultural issues in Africa.

Guinea Worm Eradication Program. In 1988, the International Task Force for Disease Eradication was launched. In Pakistan, Ghana, and Nigeria, Global 2000, through the Guinea Worm Eradication Program, has worked to provide clean drinking water in an effort to eliminate the Guinea worm disease caused by a debilitating waterborne parasite that affects 2 million people annually and puts 100 million at risk of being crippled or maimed. In conjunction with the World Health Organization, the goal of this Global 2000 program is the eradication of this disease by 1995. As a result of this program, the incidence of Guinea worm disease in countries where it is endemic was reduced by 80 percent from 1989 to 1993.

The Environmental Initiative

The Environmental Initiative is designed to build awareness of the relationship between the environment and development. Goals of the initiative include the prevention and reversal of environmental degradation, the promotion of equitable and environmentally sound public policy, and the encouragement of sustainable population policies ("Waging peace," 1993, p. 26). The first major project of the initiative was the production of a series of public service "advertorials" designed to educate policymakers and to raise awareness about the 1992 U.N. Conference on Environmental Development (the Earth Summit) that was held in Rio de Janeiro. The sixteen ads aired on the Cable News Network, on U.S. television and radio stations, and in 140 nations worldwide. Carter Center development efforts, especially the test case in Guyana, are shaped by the emphasis on environmental protection stressed by the Environmental Initiative.

The Interfaith Health Program

The Interfaith Health Program was created in 1993 to help close the gap between the current level of public health knowledge and the potential for improving the length and quality of life for U.S. citizens by using U.S. religious groups to provide health education ("Waging peace," 1993, p. 27). The Interfaith Health Program followed up on one of the first conferences sponsored by the Carter Center in 1984, called "Closing the Gap." This conference measured the gap between health-care knowledge and health-care practice. The results of this conference formed the basis for a 1989 conference called "The Church's Challenge in health," which explored the opportunities for greater involvement by faith communities in closing the gap by providing health-related activities ("Challenges of faith and health," 1994, p. 71). In January 1994, the National Conference on Faith and Health, held at the Carter Center, brought together more than one hundred members of various faith groups to discuss what local congregations could do to promote the health of their members. This conference also launched the quarterly newsletter *Faith and Health* to provide faith groups with practical information on successful health programs.

The Mental Health Program

The Mental Health Program's objectives are to help make Americans more aware of mental illness and to change public opinion regarding the mentally ill. This program continues the work that Rosalynn Carter first began as first lady of Georgia and for which she was appointed honorary chair of the President's Commission on Mental Health from 1977 to 1978 during the Carter administration. In 1991, Rosalynn Carter formed the Mental Health Task Force to improve the mental health of Americans and to work to reduce the stigma associated with mental illnesses. Each fall, mental health professionals, advocates, and consumers gather at the Carter Center for the Rosalynn Carter Symposia on Mental Health Policy.

The Tobacco Control Program

The Tobacco Control Program works to prevent tobacco-related disease and death and to promote smoke-free societies by sponsoring education programs and advocating legislation that will discourage tobacco use. The program operates both domestically and internationally. The importance of this program is demonstrated by the fact that the U.S. Centers for Disease Control and Prevention estimates that tobacco kills more than 8,300 Americans each week. In addition to the program's efforts, President Carter in 1993 advocated a $2 per pack increase in tobacco taxes, which would raise $30 billion that could be used to improve health care significantly and to defray the toll tobacco takes on society. The Carter Center, in conjunction with the Centers for Disease Control and the World Health Organization, has worked to help African nations control tobacco use through similar educational and legislative initiatives.

OVERVIEW OF URBAN REVITALIZATION PROGRAMS

The Atlanta Project

After years of focusing primarily on humanitarian needs in developing countries, President Carter and the Carter Center turned their attention to the plight of cities in the United States, beginning with Atlanta. The Atlanta Project, created in 1991, is a communitywide effort to attack the social problems associated with poverty in urban communities. While the program is based in Atlanta, once established and operating, it is designed to be duplicated in urban centers throughout the country. The Atlanta Project was launched in October 1992 when tens of thousands of volunteers, working with the residents of twenty targeted neighborhoods in Atlanta, identified needs and problems and proposed feasible solutions. The resulting programs address the areas of education, housing, criminal justice, community and economic development, and health care. The Atlanta Project has succeeded in forming partnerships among local, state, and federal government agencies, nonprofit service organizations, the business community, and volunteers from the targeted communities.

The America Project

Building on the success of the Atlanta Project, the America Project was initiated in 1992 to spread the successes of the Atlanta Project experience to other communities and organizations around the country. Like the Atlanta Project, the America Project develops programs designed to improve the quality of life in cities.

PROGRAMS AFFILIATED WITH THE CARTER CENTER

Three programs are affiliated with and have formed partnerships with the Carter Center, but are not a formal part of the center's operations. These include the Task Force for Child Survival and Development, All Kids Count, and Every Child by Two.

The Task Force for Child Survival and Development

Formed in 1984, the Task Force for Child Survival and Development facilitates immunization and other child-survival efforts in developing countries. This effort was launched in recognition of the fact that each year approximately 3.5 million children die from vaccine-preventable diseases. The task force seeks to improve the health and well-being of the world's children through an ambitious agenda including global eradication of polio by the year 2000, a 95 percent reduction in measles deaths, the elimination of neonatal tetanus, a 70 percent reduction in diarrhea deaths, a 25 percent decrease in deaths from acute respiratory infection, and a 50 percent reduction in maternal mortality rates. This agenda and the programs of the task force are carried out in association with major sponsors like the World Health Organization, the United Nations Children's Education Fund, the World Bank, the United Nations Development Programme, and the Rockefeller Foundation. According to the Carter Center, the task force helped raise the immunization rate of the world's children from 20 to

80 percent between 1984 and 1990. A major initiative of the task force has been the control of river blindness. By facilitating the distribution of Mectizan, a drug donated by Merck and Co., the task force in 1992 helped treat 5.4 million people.

All Kids Count and Every Child by Two

Among the easiest and most cost-effective preventive health-care practices is childhood immunization. While such immunizations should be completed by age two, the U.S. Centers for Disease Control and Prevention reports that in the mid-1990s, only 44–63 percent of preschool children have been properly immunized. The All Kids Count Program, begun in 1992 by the Task Force for Child Survival and Development in conjunction with U.S. public health departments, is developing computer programs to track childhood immunizations. The intent of the program is to ensure that all at-risk children are vaccinated for measles, mumps, rubella, polio, and other diseases.

Spearheaded in 1991 by former First Lady Rosalynn Carter and Betty Bumpers, the wife of Arkansas Senator Dale Bumpers, Every Child by Two is designed to promote the importance of early childhood immunizations. The program seeks to educate parents to the importance of immunizing their children, encourages them to have their children immunized, encourages health departments to improve access to immunization services, and lobbies for vaccination policies throughout the United States to include all children by age two. As of 1994, campaigns were under way in twenty-six states through the help of the spouses of state governors.

REFERENCES

Applebome, P. (1989, May 11). Unofficially era of Carter is still here. *New York Times*, p. A9.

Barrett, M. E. (1991, Mar. 15–17). How Jimmy will save the world. *USA Today Weekender*, pp. 4–5.

Berlin Wall goes up in Atlanta. (1992, Spring). *Carter Center News*, p. 16.

Bird, K. (1990, Nov. 12). The very model of an ex-president. *Nation*, pp. 560–564.

The Carter Center. (un-dated). Brochure available from the Carter Center, One Copenhill, Atlanta, GA 30307.

Carter, J. (1993). *Talking peace: A vision for the next generation*. New York: Dutton Children's Books.

Carter, J., and Carter, R. (1987). *Everything to gain: Making the most of the rest of your life*. New York: Random House.

Carter Center celebrates opening of new pavilion and chapel. (1993, Fall). *Carter Center News*, pp. 1, 8.

Carter Center dedicated. (1987, Summer). *Carter Center News*, pp. 1–3.

Carter Center opens office in Guyana. (1995, Winter). *Carter Center News*, p. 15.

Carter Center programs. (1995). Available from the Carter Center, One Copenhill, Atlanta, GA 30307.

The Carter library. (1987, Summer). *Carter Center News*, p. 12.

Carter library, museum open. (1987, Summer). *Carter Center News*, p. 12.

A celebration: 200 years of the White House. (1992, Fall). *Carter Center News*, p. 16.

Center launches major new capital campaign. (1990, Fall). *Carter Center News*, p. 12.

The challenges of faith and health. (1994, Jan.). A report of the National Conference of the Interfaith Health Program of the Carter Center, and supported by the Robert Wood Johnson Foundation. Available from the Carter Center, One Copenhill, Atlanta, GA 30307.

Emory president named ambassador to South Korea. (1993, Fall). *Carter Center News*, p. 9.

Hackett, G. (1989, May 22). How to be an ex-president. *Newsweek*, p. 40.

Handwriting file provides insight into presidency. (1991, Fall). *Carter Center News*, p. 16.

Hardman, J. (1995, Winter). A message from the executive director. *Carter Center News*, pp. 2–3.

Internship program. (1987, Summer). *Carter Center News*, p. 9.

Jimmy Carter library hosts depression era and Israeli exhibits. (1988, Fall). *Carter Center News*, p. 16.

Library offers unique views of history. (1990, Spring). *Carter Center News*, p. 16.

Pasley, J., and Weisman, A. (1987, Jan. 19). He's back. *New Republic*, pp. 13–15.

The portraits of Mathew Brady. (1994, Summer). *Carter Center News*, p. 15.

Primed on the presidency. (1989, Fall). *Carter Center News*, p. 16.

Quayle chides Carter for talks with Ortega. (1989, Feb. 3). *New York Times*, p. A8.

A thriving partnership. (1989, Fall). *Carter Center News*, p. 2.

The tie that binds. (1991, Spring). *Carter Center News*, p. 16.

Visiting fellows expand CCEU resources. (1990, Fall). *Carter Center News*, p. 11.

Waging peace around the world. (1993). Available from the Carter Center, One Copenhill, Atlanta, GA 30307.

Wiregrass exhibit highlights Georgia folklife. (1990, Fall). *Carter Center News*, p. 16.

Women and the Constitution. (1987, Summer). *Carter Center News*, p. 5.

World War II through the eyes of combat artists. (1993, Spring). *Carter Center News*, p. 16.

CHAPTER 5

INTERNATIONAL PEACEMAKING THROUGH MEDIATION AND NEGOTIATION

The wars and conflicts that receive the most media attention also tend to be those that receive the most diplomatic attention aimed at mediation or resolution. However, while a small civil or regional conflict in a remote corner of the world may receive little or no media attention, such a conflict, if left to escalate, may eventually destroy the lives of thousands of combatants and noncombatants alike. The nonviolent resolution of conflicts, regardless of where they might occur, is necessary if peace is to become a reality. Conflicts and disputes between the sovereign nations of the world can and have been peacefully mediated and resolved by organizations like the United Nations (U.N.) or regional organizations like the Organization of American States (OAS). Civil conflicts within nations are a much more difficult problem for which the world community has not yet established the institutional means for mediation or resolution.

THE INTERNATIONAL NEGOTIATION NETWORK: BACKGROUND, DEVELOPMENT, AND APPROACH

Given the Carter Center's goal of resolving conflicts, the Conflict Resolution Program (CRP) is one of the most essential programs operating at the center. The following statement summarizes the broad-ranging work of the CRP:

For several years, The Carter Center of Emory University's Conflict Resolution Program has been engaged in developing an International Negotiation Network to alleviate the tremendous suffering resulting from intra-national conflicts. Our efforts have led to the convening of direct negotiation between warring parties engaged in prolonged conflicts. We have been involved in activities advancing free elections and election monitoring where such efforts have helped to facilitate the peaceful transfer of power in previously conflict-bound countries. We have been involved in quiet, back-channel linkages of disputing parties and resources available to them. Some of our efforts have received widespread media coverage. However, the vast majority of our work has not been widely known. ("International Negotiation Network," 1991, p. 5)

The CRP was one of the earliest programs established at the Carter Center. According to Dayle Spencer, who helped to found and who directed the program, the CRP and later the International Negotiation Network (INN) were designed to offer "a neutral, facilitative, international approach to solving intra-national conflicts" (quoted in "Profile: Dayle E. Powell," 1989, p. 3). The CRP began organizing the INN in 1987 for the dual purposes of "finding non-military means of reducing armed conflicts—closing the mediation gap, and helping to prevent the escalation of lesser-scale conflicts into armed ones; focusing in both cases on intra-national arenas" ("International Negotiation Network," 1991, p. 10). According to Uppsala University in Sweden, in 1991 there were more than 100 armed conflicts being waged in the world, 32 of which were intranational wars that could be classified as major conflicts—those resulting in one-thousand or more battle-related deaths per year. These intranational wars "are the most common and destructive armed conflicts on the planet, resulting in millions of deaths and incalculable suffering" ("Resolving intra-national conflicts," 1992, p. 7). At the time of the INN's formation, only 10 percent of these conflicts were international in nature and, therefore, able to be addressed by organizations like the United Nations or similar regional organizations. The remaining 90 percent were intranational in nature, most commonly civil wars, which fall outside the statutory jurisdiction of existing international organizations. These intranational conflicts are generally begun by rebel groups seeking to secede, gain greater autonomy, achieve greater participation by minority factions, or have greater access to the economic resources of a country ("International Negotiation Network," 1991, p. 9). While intranational in scope, these conflicts exact a staggering toll not only in terms of lives lost, but in impeded development, excessive child morbidity and mortality, the creation of refugee and displaced populations, and the spread of disease and famine.

The United Nations and regional organizations like the Organization for African Unity (OAU) and the Organization of American States (OAS) can negotiate and mediate between nations but are prohibited from involvement in what are usually described as the internal affairs of countries. Involvement in such conflicts by governments, including the United States, is often constrained by diplomatic and/or strategic considerations. For example, Article Two, Section Seven, of the U.N. Charter prohibits U.N. involvement in the internal affairs of member countries ("International Negotiation Network," 1991, p. 9). U.N. employees working in member nations are also forbidden from gathering political information about member nations.

During the early formative stages in the development of the INN, the secretaries general of the OAS, the Commonwealth of Nations, and the United Nations acknowledged to President Carter that they could not more aggressively address the problem of civil conflicts. In Carter's words, this was "because of political and institutional impediments" (quoted in "Resolving intra-national conflicts," 1992, p. 12). President Carter reported that then U.N. Secretary General Javier Perez de Cuellar recognized the need for an institution like the INN for parties in conflict who are seeking an alternative to U.N. mediation, but do not know where to turn.

The INN was developed to fill what can best be described as a "mediation gap," those conflicts within neither existing regional nor international jurisdictions. The INN proposed to address such conflicts by providing a neutral third-party agency that could work without the constraints imposed on U.N. and regional organizations.

A three-day working session on international mediation was held at the Carter Center in May 1987. This meeting brought together President Carter, the secretaries general of the United Nations and the OAS, and experts in the field of international mediation and negotiation to explore the potential for collaborative efforts among academics, international and nongovernmental organizations, and the media in resolving conflicts. This working group was cosponsored by the Carter Center and the Program on Negotiation at Harvard Law School and was supported by a grant from the Dana M. Greeley Foundation for Peace and Justice. Participants explored the limitations and constraints of current international conflict- and dispute-resolution systems and developed a consensus that "there was an emerging need for more 'venturesomeness' on the part of world leaders to solve conflicts through alternatives to the use of force" ("International Negotiation Network," 1991, p. 9). The overall conclusion that emerged from this working session was that a new approach to addressing intranational conflict and dispute resolution was necessary.

Subsequent meetings in September and October 1988 of an advisory group to the INN chaired by President Carter established the structures and functions of the INN. The structure of the INN includes a chair—former President Carter—to coordinate the efforts of the INN, a three-member Secretariat that commissions and convenes academic studies of targeted conflicts, and an eleven-member Council comprised of prominent current and former world leaders and recognized peacemakers. The INN Council "consists of a small group of eminent persons who offer their skills and services to parties embroiled in intra-national conflicts" ("Resolving intra-national conflicts," 1992, p. 7). The Council is further described as "a group of prominent world leaders that has banded together at The Carter Center [and] hopes its efforts to help peacefully resolve conflict will eventually make war obsolete" ("World leaders join," 1991, p. 10). The Council's intent is that by "working collaboratively, the Council members maximize INN access to world leaders and conflicts, but more importantly, use their collective influence to advance the proposition that war is no longer acceptable as a means of resolving disputes" ("International Negotiation Network," 1991, p. 10). The ultimate goal of the Council is to "work at a global level to affect the way society deals with conflict—creating the necessary political will to make war unacceptable" ("World leaders join," 1991, p. 10). The Council and its members have the potential to convene talks between parties in conflict, serve as third-party mediators in peace negotiations, and lead election-monitoring efforts when and where appropriate.

The INN was designed to function "as a network linking various resources available at many levels of operations internationally, avoiding duplication of efforts, and rather than competing with existing organizations, working collaboratively with them to more effectively address the most intractable kinds of conflicts" ("International Negotiation Network," 1991, p. 10). As described by the Carter Center, the INN is a flexible, informal network that coordinates third-party assistance, expert analysis and advice, media attention, and funding to help bring about the peaceful resolution of intranational conflicts. Such conflict resolution is facilitated as the INN links the parties in the conflict with resources like academic experts, nongovernmental organizations, and international organizations like the United Nations, the OAS, and the OAU. Specifically, the INN mediates civil conflicts; monitors existing and emerging conflicts; spotlights conflicts that require third-party assistance; convenes confidential consultations for disputants and mediators; matches disputants' needs with potential third-party mediators, funding sources, and other experts; performs premediation services, undertakes issue analysis, and teaches dispute-resolution techniques; and convenes conferences for academics and practitioners ("International Negotiation Network," 1989, p. 5).

Meetings in October 1988 gathered top experts and researchers in conflict resolution from around the world, in addition to representation from and participation by eleven nongovernmental, university, and American foundation organizations ("INN planning," 1988, p. 10). These discussions determined that the INN could be most effective in conflicts in Central America, China and Tibet, Ethiopia and Eritrea, Nicaragua, southern Africa, and the Sudan. Having identified these areas of concern as a potential INN mediation agenda, the advisory group directed its efforts at conducting background research on these conflicts and examining possible strategies for future mediation activities.

Mediation by the INN begins when members of the Secretariat examine existing conflicts and identify those appropriate for the type of third-party mediation the INN can provide. Upon consultation with President Carter, the Secretariat convenes academic studies of the targeted conflicts drawing upon the expertise of practitioners, academics, and scholars. Potential mediation teams are identified and strategies are suggested for the particular conflict situation ("International Negotiation Network," 1991, p. 10). As the INN monitors and identifies potential conflicts for mediation worldwide, it works closely with the Harvard University Program on Negotiation, the Department of Peace and Conflict Research at Uppsala University in Sweden, the Peace Research Institute of Oslo, and organizations like the United Nations, the OAS, and the OAU.

In March 1990, members of the INN set three goals for the year. These included expanded participation by international leaders, sponsoring an annual consultation of a core group of international conflict-resolution organizations, and exploring the ways in which resolving individual conflicts can benefit an entire region ("INN seeks to expand network," 1990, p. 10). In pursuit of this agenda, President Carter and Dayle Spencer attended the OAU meeting in July 1990 in Addis Ababa, Ethiopia, to try to encourage the renewed delivery of relief supplies and the resumption of peace talks between Ethiopia and Eritrea. As of the end of 1991, the Secretariat had actively monitored twenty-five armed conflicts, undertaken active mediation efforts in two, and pursued back-channel interventions in eight others. Numerous other parties have been linked to the resources available from organizations other than the INN. By the early 1990s, the INN as an idea and organization had grown from the twenty persons who attended the first working sessions in 1987 to more than four hundred individuals and organizations working in forty-seven countries in 1992 ("International Negotiation Network," 1991, p. 10).

Annual consultations sponsored by the INN are designed to be a vehicle for the INN Council to focus on specific conflicts and to address current situations. According to Dayle Spencer, these INN consultations will be held to "spotlight and set action agendas for resolving intra-national conflicts—an approach designed by conflict resolution expert William Spencer" ("World leaders commit," 1992, pp. 4–5).

The First INN Consultation: "Resolving Intra-national Conflicts: A Strengthened Role for Non-governmental Actors"

The INN Council met for the first time in January 1992 when President Carter and former Soviet Foreign Minister Eduard Schevardnadze (who participated via satellite link) convened the first of the INN's annual consultations, entitled "Resolving Intra-national Conflicts: A Strengthened Role for Non-governmental Actors." At this consultation, two hundred invited guests, experts on negotiation, conflict resolution, and peacemaking, and representatives from parties in armed conflict gathered at the Carter Center. Participants represented forty countries on six continents and included former heads of state, scholars, government officials, and leaders of religious, humanitarian, and international development organizations. More than 150 organizations and governments were represented at this inaugural consultation. Participants represented a mix of parties engaged in conflict, scholars, practitioners of "two-track" diplomacy, and representatives of intergovernmental, regional, and nongovernmental organizations. The consultation was supported by grants from the Carnegie Corporation of New York and the John D. and Catherine T. MacArthur Foundation.

The basic objectives for this inaugural consultation were to examine the role of nongovernmental organizations in resolving intra-national conflicts, to launch the INN Council officially (nine of its members participated in the consultation), and to identify themes that are not unique to particular conflicts but cut across political and cultural boundaries ("Resolving intra-national conflicts," 1992, p.

5). Overall, in expressing the broadest intent of the consultation in his opening address, President Carter stated, "Our dream is that this assembled body will use the discussion here to learn the generic principles on which we can move forward to a time when wars are not treated as little nuisances or worse, ignored, but are elevated to their proper place as matters of pressing international concern" (quoted in "Resolving intra-national conflicts," 1992, p. 13).

Consultation participants focused their collective attention and expertise on eight civil conflicts targeted by the INN Council, including those in Afghanistan, Angola, Burma, Cambodia, Cyprus, the Korean Peninsula, Liberia, and the Sudan. These conflicts were targeted because they represented conflicts in different phases of evolution and resolution and posed diverse challenges ("Resolving intra-national conflicts," 1992, p. 6). Consultation participants used their skills to develop specific strategies and plans for the resolution of these conflicts. In preparation for the consultation and to initiate discussion, the INN Secretariat commissioned experts to prepare action memoranda that addressed the issues underlying each of the eight targeted conflicts. Following the presentation of these action memoranda, discussion was facilitated by members of the INN Council and the Core Group. Discussions focused on barriers to resolving the specific conflicts, strategies for overcoming the barriers, and action steps for the INN and others to pursue ("Resolving intra-national conflicts," 1992, p. 5). The proceedings of each working session were documented, and a summary list of recommendations for each conflict was presented to consultation participants.

Collectively, the consultation participants addressed two broad thematic concerns: the psychological dimensions of conflict and sustaining the peace. According to consultation participants, "The surprise visit of Father Jean-Baptiste Aristide of Haiti added a poignant and immediate dimension to the Sustaining the Peace session" ("Resolving intra-national conflicts," 1992, p. 6). At the time, President Aristide was living in exile following a military coup that had forced him to flee Haiti after democratic elections in 1991.

The consultation produced several tangible results. A recommendation by consultation participants that a special U.N. representative be appointed to coordinate all U.N. peacemaking activities in Angola was implemented. Dayle Spencer emphasized that the appointment was important "because it focuses attention and resources on resolving the conflict in Angola" ("Strategies for resolving conflict," 1992, p. 5).

The consultation also dispatched Spencer to the Korean Peninsula to prepare for an INN Council trip to the region to follow up on consultation recommendations ("Strategies for resolving conflict," 1992, p. 5). Tensions on the Korean Peninsula had been one of eight conflicts addressed by the consultation. This type of involvement by the INN would be valuable two years later when tensions would once again flare on the Korean Peninsula, and President Carter would travel to the area to mediate an agreement (see chapter 6). Finally, the consultation recommended the convening of a regional meeting of the INN Council in Senegal during the fall of 1992 to target African disputes and to recommend strategies for peacemaking ("Strategies for resolving conflict," 1992, p. 5).

The Second INN Consultation, 1993

The second annual INN Council consultation took place in February 1993 when two hundred scholars, world leaders, representatives of relief agencies, and representatives of warring parties from twenty-five countries gathered to discuss ways non- and intergovernmental organizations could better coordinate their efforts to manage, stop, and prevent internal conflicts. The consultation was chaired by President Carter and former U.N. Secretary General Javier Perez de Cuellar to pursue the following goals: to gather a "critical mass" of conflict-resolution experts, to open discussions among non- and intergovernmental organizations regarding their roles in conflict resolution, to target specific conflicts and to suggest specific steps to end these conflicts, and to form task forces to implement the conflict-management strategies and recommendations resulting from the consultation ("INN seeks cooperation," 1993, p. 8).

Dayle Spencer of the INN Secretariat characterized the mission for this second consultation as "firefighting" when she stated, "What if we could develop a system of detection devices, of alarms, of means of containment that would stop these conflicts in their tracks before they destroy whole cities or nations or regions of the world? If they are already blazing, what if we could marshall every conceivable resource to put them out?" (quoted in "INN seeks cooperation," 1993, p. 8). By pooling and coordinating the collective resources and expertise of the assembled world leaders, conflict scholars and experts, relief agencies, and warring parties, this three-day consultation attempted to fulfill INN goals and to realize the challenges of peace.

Spotlighted conflicts for this consultation were those in Burma, the Caucasus, Haiti, Zaire, Macedonia, and Kosovo. Consistent with the purpose of the INN, these conflicts were targeted because they could not be addressed by existing organizations like the United Nations ("INN seeks cooperation," 1993, p. 8). Because the Carter Center is independent and not constrained in its peacemaking activities by charters like those of the United Nations, its potential to act in intranational conflicts is significant. President Carter stated: "Let other organizations be timid because of restraints on their charters. If all parties in a conflict invite us, we'll make every effort to prevent the conflict from growing and to resolve differences peacefully" ("INN seeks cooperation," 1993, p. 8).

The results and recommendations from this consultation were later shared by President Carter with Secretary of State Warren Christopher. Following the consultation, the INN conducted follow-up activities based on the recommendations of the participants and the task-force groups working on the five spotlighted conflicts ("INN seeks cooperation," 1993, p. 9). The INN's approach of trying to defuse conflicts before they escalate also resulted in workshops in Estonia to begin a dialogue among ethnic Estonians, Russians in

Estonia, and Russians from Moscow. According to Dr. Joyce Neu of the Carter Center, who directed the workshop, "These workshops often provide the first opportunity for parties in conflict to speak directly to each other in a nonthreatening, unofficial capacity" (quoted in "Conflict resolution programs," 1994, p. 13). This type of conflict prevention is particularly important given the diversity of groups comprising the states of the former Soviet Union. The third INN consultation in 1994 was similar to the first two but focused on conflicts in Burma, Haiti, Liberia, Nicaragua, and Zaire.

The INN was not designed or intended to be an organization that simply convenes consultations and produces recommendations. It was and is intended to be an organization that takes practical action directed at the mediation of conflict and the alleviation of suffering. Several of the INN's more ambitious projects are highlighted in the pages that follow—those in Ethiopia/Eritrea, Liberia, and the Sudan. These efforts are among those that have been publicly reported by the Carter Center and the popular press. Because of the delicate nature of the mediation work of the INN, not all of its peacemaking efforts have been publicly reported.

THE INN IN ACTION

Peacemaking in Ethiopia/Eritrea

The viability of the INN as an approach to conflict resolution and a mediator of intranational conflicts was first demonstrated by its involvement with the thirty-year-old civil war between Ethiopia and Eritrea. According to commentator Coleman McCarthy, Carter's work in Ethiopia and the Third World in general reflects his commitment to peace and "means that he will be working on the margins of American awareness" (1989, p. A25). Public awareness of Third World conflicts is certainly low, and what is reported is largely framed in ideological rather than human terms. Carter critics have charged that two of the three conflicting parties in the Ethiopian conflict were Marxist, to which he responded that the Marxist politics of a country "doesn't mean that the people of Ethiopia won't be immediately better off if we stop the war. They will be immediately better off if we immunize their children against polio, or measles, or whooping cough, or increase their food production so people won't starve" (quoted in McCarthy, 1989, p. A25). Carter's mediation efforts and those of the INN are designed to alleviate the sorts of conditions he cited, regardless of the ideology of a country's leadership. It appears that for Carter, peace cannot be political, and peacemaking must be nonpartisan.

Background to the Conflict. Estimates suggested that since 1974, half a million civilians and 39,000 soldiers had been killed in the civil war that raged in Ethiopia (McCarthy, 1989, p. A25). The combatants included the People's Democratic Republic of Ethiopia (PDRE), the Ethiopian government of President Mengistu Haile Mariam, who sought to remain in power and who justified the war based on the principles of national unity and sovereignty; the Eritrean People's Liberation Front (EPLF), which sought self-determination and independence from Ethiopia; and a third group, the Tigray (Tigre) People's Liberation Front (TPLF), which desired a broader-based government ("Second rebel group," 1989, p. A6).

The roots of the conflict between Ethiopia and the Eritreans can be traced to events far predating the more recent thirty years of civil war. (This brief history and analysis is drawn from "International Negotiation Network," 1991). In modern times, Eritrea was made a part of the confederation that makes up Ethiopia. The 1889 Treaty of Wuchale between Italy and Ethiopia established the borders of Eritrea as they exist today. Following Italian colonial rule, Eritrea was administered by Great Britain until U.N. Resolution 390-A(V) declared that Eritrea be federated to Ethiopia. However, regardless of U.N. mandates, Eritreans saw themselves as Eritrean, not Ethiopian. The Eritreans petitioned the United Nations for the right to self-determination through referendum, but failed in their attempt when a U.S.-sponsored U.N. resolution in 1952 successfully federated Eritrea to Ethiopia.

When Ethiopian Emperor Haile Selassie ignored the terms of the U.N. federation resolution, which would have left Eritrea largely autonomous, an Eritrean resistance movement developed. This movement would become the EPLF and the major rebel opposition group in the civil war. The EPLF struggled for almost three decades against the Ethiopian government, and the civil war resulted in significant battle and civilian casualties. With 70 percent of the Ethiopian government's budget going to support the military, living conditions for the Ethiopian people were made even more difficult. Devastating droughts, crop failures, and famines struck in 1984–1985 and threatened again in 1991, brought about—at least in part—as a result of the sustained civil war.

True to the intent of the INN to "address the most intractable kinds of conflict" and "not look for easy victories that might be tracked on a score card, but to focus on the most horrendous conflicts in terms of human suffering or lives lost," the Ethiopian-Eritrean civil war became a first test of the viability of the INN ("International Negotiation Network," 1991, p. 10). The involvement of President Carter and the INN in the civil war in Ethiopia can be divided into three stages: preliminary negotiations, a second round of procedural talks in Atlanta, and additional procedural and substantive negotiations held in Nairobi, Kenya.

The Preliminary Talks. In the fall of 1988, during one of the early working sessions of the INN, participants were asked to identify a short list of "hot spots" or conflicts that were at or near the boiling point and were not being mediated by either international organizations or governments. Ethiopia/Eritrea topped the list ("International Negotiation Network," 1991, p. 12). The Secretariat of the INN began an initial analysis of the historical, political, sociological, and economic aspects of the conflict, as well as conducting a number of preliminary interviews with scholars, government and policy analysts, and relief organizations regarding the conflict. Several briefing sessions were conducted by the INN mediation team in Atlanta, New York, and Washington, D.C., with experts on the conflict, seeking advice on how best to approach the conflict.

As part of a trip to the Horn of Africa region concerning famine relief, human rights, and agricultural reform, members of the INN mediation team met directly with the leadership of both sides to explore their interest in a new mediation effort. In the spring of 1989, President Carter and the INN mediation team met in Khartoum, Sudan, with Isaias Afwerki, the general secretary of the EPLF, and with senior members of the EPLF leadership. President Carter explained his desire to mediate the conflict and explained the approach of the INN. Following talks with President Mengistu and the PDRE, the team held a second round of talks with the EPLF. At this point, both sides had expressed an interest in, and commitment to, a new mediation initiative. Because both parties were reluctant to take the first step, the international community was informed of the new negotiations in a public announcement by President Carter.

These preliminary talks led the INN team to two conclusions. First, more than thirty years of armed conflict and generations of animosity between the two sides would not be easily settled at the negotiating table. Second, the INN team determined that "our strategy was to devise and implement steps to transform the members of the negotiation teams from warriors into problem solvers" ("International Negotiation Network," 1991, p. 13). Short of complete success in mediating the conflict, "our [the INN team's] best role might be to create a process that would be used by the parties for their own purposes but which would result in a temporary cessation of the fighting, saving lives in the short term, and hope that changing circumstances would lead to long-term options for peace" ("International Negotiation Network," 1991, pp. 13–14).

The Atlanta Talks. The preliminary talks initiated by Carter and the INN's mediation team had secured agreement, without preconditions, from President Mengistu and the Eritreans to pursue a negotiated peace ("Ethiopian minister," 1989, p. A2; "Second Rebel Group," 1989, p. A6). In opening the Atlanta talks, which were held on September 7–19, 1989, Carter noted that the lack of preconditions and the agreement to hold talks in the presence of a third party marked a substantial break from previous attempts to resolve the conflict and that the lack of preconditions meant that either party could bring any topic to the negotiating table for discussion. President Carter defined his role and that of the INN as a neutral observer and facilitator in the initial round of procedural talks, which were designed to establish a general framework for a second round of substantive talks to be held in Nairobi, Kenya, in November 1989. Regarding the development of a framework or strategy, the INN team tried to devise "a multitrack, multiphased approach which called for simultaneously conducting a bargaining strategy, a single-text negotiating approach, and a joint problem-solving strategy" ("International Negotiation Network," 1991, p. 14).

The INN team paid careful attention to the physical environment for the talks. Recognizing that previous failed negotiation efforts had taken place in formal hotel environments, it prepared an empty conference room at the Carter Center with sofas and comfortable chairs replacing normal conference seating. In what was described as "a less than subtle touch," a sculpture of white doves was placed on a pedestal in one corner of the room near a painting of the signing of the Camp David Accords ("International Negotiation Network," 1991, p. 14). The traditional "bargaining table" was abandoned in favor of a room laid out in the shape of a horseshoe with the two parties facing each other and President Carter and the INN representatives serving as a buffer at the top of the horseshoe.

Since previous negotiations had been characterized by allegations that one side or the other had misrepresented the negotiations, the discussions in Atlanta were tape recorded. The recordings were transcribed at the end of each day, and copies were provided to the parties to ensure an accurate record of the talks. Language differences between the parties were also a problem. For both the PDRE and the EPLF, there were political and cultural reasons for their insistence on a certain language. While simultaneous translations were provided, English was the official language of the negotiating sessions. The INN team considered it a breakthrough when "they [the PDRE and the EPLF] became so engaged in their discussions that they dropped their insistence on Amharic and Arabic and began speaking directly to each other in English" ("International Negotiation Network," 1991, p. 15).

A basic objective of the Atlanta talks was to establish agreement on an agenda of what would, and what would not, be open for discussion during the talks, and to shape continued talks between the parties. Establishing an agenda for the talks began by the parties generating a comprehensive list of fourteen topics. Determining the order in which the topics would be discussed was difficult. To determine an order, the agenda items were listed on fourteen pieces of Post-It paper and placed on a larger sheet of paper. The representatives were asked to try to come to agreement by placing the notes in their preferred order and to determine if there was overlap in the placements. Reportedly, in a matter of twenty minutes the representatives had combined two points into one and had come to an acceptable ranking for the remaining items. The final agenda was signified by placing tape over the Post-It papers. While this was seemingly a minor task, the INN team suggested that "this visual symbol of their first step toward resolution of their three-decade conflict, the white chart with 14 yellow post-its taped in place, was left in the Zaban room throughout the next two weeks" ("International Negotiation Network," 1991, p. 16).

During the thirteen days of negotiating sessions from September 7 to September 19, 1989, the parties met almost daily from 9 A.M. to 5 P.M. in formal negotiating sessions or private meetings with President and Rosalynn Carter or members of the INN team. While there were many tensions, there reportedly was never a time when any side walked out of the talks.

Three key issues were particularly problematic during the Atlanta talks: who would chair the negotiations, who would observe the negotiations, and who would serve as the secretariat or staff for the peace process. The nature and function of each of these roles became problematic ("International Negotiation Network," 1991, pp. 19–20). While President Carter initiated the process and convened and chaired the negotiations in Atlanta, his continued chairmanship of the peace talks became a politically sensitive issue. President Mengistu had serious political concerns about the perception created by a white American trying to resolve what Mengistu perceived as an internal Ethiopian problem. The PDRE strongly favored an equal and permanent cochairman to work with President Carter, proposing initially President Mugabe of Zimbabwe and later former President Nyerere of Tanzania. For Mengistu, one of these African leaders as cochairman for future talks was politically more acceptable than a single former U.S. president. However, because Nyerere was a former African president and, therefore, might be perceived as an ally or peer of Mengistu, in addition to being a founding member of the Organization of African Unity (OAU), which adopted colonial boundaries as permanent national boundaries, he was unacceptable to the EPLF. The EPLF proposed that the negotiations be conducted under the aegis of the INN, with President Carter acting as chairman. In the end, former President Nyerere did serve as cochair of the second round of talks in Nairobi.

The question of who would observe the talks was complicated. The PDRE wanted few observers because it perceived the war as an internal affair. On the other hand, because the EPLF historically had sought to internationalize the Eritrean question, it desired a large number of observers including the OAU and the Arab League ("International Negotiation Network," 1991, pp. 19–20). President Carter proposed a compromise position where seven observers would be involved, two to be chosen by each side and the remaining three to be mutually agreed upon. At the conclusion of the Atlanta talks, the EPLF accepted this formulation provided that the observers could also act as mediators, and the PDRE accepted provided that it could express reservations about the choices of the other side and that the role of the observers be limited to that of witnesses.

The final question, the secretariat, was the least troublesome of the three major points of contention. The Eritreans wanted the secretariat to come from the Carter Center staff, the OAU, and the Sudan and proposed that members of the secretariat serve in official capacities as representatives of their government or organization. The Ethiopians insisted that the chairs select the secretariat and that members not represent their respective government or organization. The compromise position offered by President Carter recognized that others, in addition to the chair, would need to act as mediators, and the mutually approved observers and members of the secretariat could fill these roles.

The actual negotiating sessions not only employed traditional mediation techniques, but utilized computers in the form of single-text negotiation. As the negotiations progressed, the INN team would listen to the discussions between the parties and try to identify areas of agreement. When agreement was found, these items were immediately reduced to text, put on computer, and distributed to the parties for further editing. This mediation process was used to arrive at a single text acceptable to both parties. Once an item was finalized, it was initialed by the chairmen of each delegation and became a part of the final communiqué ("International Negotiation Network," 1991, p. 17). The INN team reported that the personal computer became an important tool as the parties neared a final agreement ("International Negotiation Network," 1991, p. 17). During the final negotiations, President Carter often gathered one side in his private office around his personal computer. Working with each party, he would produce, edit, and revise drafts of the agreements with delegates literally looking over his shoulder until final agreements were reached and formalized. According to the INN team, "The coupling of the computer with a skilled mediator alleviated the need for clerical support and the usual delay occasioned by writing the agreements after the discussion" ("International Negotiation Network" 1991, p. 17).

On September 19, 1989, the final communiqué from the Atlanta talks was issued and summarized the thirteen points of agreement and also the remaining points of contention. The delegations had agreed on the main agenda for the next round of talks, working languages, record-keeping, procedural rules, publicity, and the composition of the negotiating teams ("Carter convenes," 1989, p. 4). Between the end of the Atlanta talks and the beginning of the Nairobi round to be held on November 18, the two sides were asked to seek agreement on the remaining issues. In addition to the formal communiqué, the Atlanta talks resulted in a de facto cease-fire during the nearly two weeks of negotiations at the Carter Center.

The Nairobi Talks. Considerable work on the part of President Carter and the INN team was necessary following the completion of the Atlanta talks and prior to the opening of the Nairobi talks. Logistical concerns about the Kenyan government's ability to accommodate the talks, invitations to and acceptance from potential observers, confirmation of President Nyerere's willingness to serve as cochair, and additional procedural matters consumed the sixty days between the two rounds of peace talks. The INN team worked to "remove all possible barriers that would impede the parties from making the transition from preliminary negotiations to substantive negotiations as quickly as possible" ("International Negotiation Network," 1991, p. 21). In addition, the World Bank was contacted to arrange a package of incentives that might be used during the serious bargaining ahead.

Kenyan President Daniel arap Moi agreed to host the Nairobi peace talks and went to great lengths to contribute to the success of the peace process by remodeling what became known as the "peace house." The U.S. State Department was supportive of the peace talks by helping with travel arrangements, visas, and ground contacts. Soviet President Mikhail Gorbachev used his country's influence with the Ethiopian government, its former ally, to persuade it of the need to reach a mediated settlement. The INN team noted that "throughout the peace process we called on President Gorbachev to assist us, and in each instance he was cooperative" ("International Negotiation Network," 1991, p. 22).

The Nairobi talks were cochaired by President Carter and former Tanzanian President Nyerere. Both the Eritreans and the Ethiopians used the opportunity of the opening press conference to make disparaging remarks about the other and to engage in public political posturing. The opening sessions of the six days of talks in Nairobi soon bogged down over the ongoing issue of the selection of international observers ("International Negotiation Network," 1991, p. 22; "Ethiopian Talks Stall," 1989, p. A19). This issue had been contentious and unresolved in Atlanta and continued to be so in Nairobi. Talks with most potential observers had revealed a willingness to serve, but both the United Nations and the United Kingdom indicated that they would be unable to accept an invitation. U.N. involvement was only possible if both parties agreed to its participation, which the PDRE was unwilling to do. The Eritreans favored U.N. involvement given that U.N. mandates were perceived to be, in part, the cause of Eritrea's being federated to Ethiopia ("International Negotiation Network," 1991, p. 22).

The issues of chairmanship, observers, and the secretariat that had been left unresolved in Atlanta reemerged as early points of contention in Nairobi. Final agreements were ultimately reached between the parties and signed on November 28, 1989, following a Thanksgiving feast hosted by Presidents Carter and Nyerere. Seven observers would attend the main talks, of whom two would be selected by each side without restriction and without expression of reservation by the other side. The remaining three observers would represent the three venue countries and be invited by mutual consent. The secretariat would be chosen by the cochairmen to provide professional, administrative, and technical support. President Carter dispatched cables to the embassies of all invited observers and sought their earliest response. Carter also contacted the secretaries general of the United Nations and the OAU, problematic EPLF choices for observers.

On November 29, 1989, the final communiqué of the Nairobi talks was issued. By that time, six invited observers had responded, including Kenya, Tanzania, the Sudan, the Organization of African Unity, Zimbabwe, and Senegal. Two days prior to the issuance of this communiqué, the EPLF accused the PDRE of interfering with its freedom of choice in selecting observers and attempting to orchestrate a negative response from the United Nations. Further, the EPLF accused President Carter of acting in bad faith in not wanting to involve the United Nations, and announced its withdrawal from the negotiations. In an effort to save the talks, President Carter again reminded the EPLF that it had been informed, in advance, that the United Nations would decline an observer invitation. He went so far as to offer the EPLF the use of his private plane to fly to New York to consult with the secretary general of the United Nations to verify its refusal to serve.

Following the agreements and the final communiqué, the Nairobi talks ended with a press conference at which the EPLF expressed animosity toward the

PDRE and criticized Carter for his handling of the observer question. However, "Both sides reiterated their commitment to the peace process in spite of the obvious hard feelings" ("International Negotiation Network," 1991, p. 25). President Carter characterized the Nairobi talks as "sincere and dedicated" (quoted in "Ethiopian civil war talks continue," 1989, p. A9). A full-scale peace conference scheduled for January 1990 was to be based on the agreements reached in Nairobi ("Ethiopian talks stall," 1989, p. A19). Unfortunately, at the same time the EPLF was preparing to mount a full-scale offensive against the Ethiopian capital of Addis Ababa (Perlez, 1989, p. A6). While the potential for further talks existed, the Eritreans had succeeded effectively in ending, or at the very least suspending, the peace process. Upon leaving the Nairobi talks, the EPLF informed the INN team that it was ready to continue the peace process as soon as all seven observers had accepted the invitations—knowing that the United Nations would not accept the invitation.

The proposed January talks never took place. Rather, the military forces of the EPLF and the TPLF accomplished on the battlefield what they were unwilling or unable to accomplish at the peace table. Following the Nairobi talks, the EPLF renewed its assault on the Ethiopian cities of Asmara and Massawa in February 1990, and the TPLF mounted a large-scale offensive against the capital of Addis Ababa.

Attempts were made by Carter and the INN during April 1990 to renew the peace process. However, because of the EPLF's insistence on the presence of a U.N. observer in the peace process, these efforts were not successful. At the same time, famine and drought conditions worsened throughout the region (Perlez, 1989, p. A6). As the battlefield situation worsened for the Ethiopian army, the INN reported that on June 4, 1990, President Mengistu authorized the INN to extend an invitation to the United Nations to serve as an observer to the peace process. In effect, the PDRE acceded to the position of the EPLF, and, given that the invitation was now extended from the Ethiopian government, the United Nations reversed its earlier decision and announced that it would serve as an observer.

President Carter notified the parties that since all barriers to the peace process had been removed, the first round of substantive talks could begin in Nairobi on July 6, 1990. Unfortunately, given its success on the battlefield, the EPLF informed Presidents Carter and Nyerere on June 11, 1990, that it was withdrawing from the peace process and was appealing to the United Nations to conduct a referendum to determine Eritrea's future. In announcing this development, Presidents Carter and Nyerere called the decision a tragedy. According to Carter, "Both sides have been given the opportunity to participate in a forum to resolve this conflict peacefully," and he called on the armed forces to declare a unilateral cease-fire in order to facilitate relief aid to famine and drought areas (quoted in "International Negotiation Network," 1991, p. 26). President Carter noted, "Perhaps the most tragic aspect of the turn of events is that some three million people may simply starve to death if relief supplies cannot be delivered" (quoted in "International Negotiation Network," 1991, p. 26).

The withdrawal of the EPLF from the peace process and its military successes ended President Carter's and the INN's efforts to negotiate an end to the conflict peacefully. Lines of communication with both sides were maintained by Carter and the INN team, and they stood ready at any time to renew their efforts. One future role the INN could play would be in the arrangement and monitoring of elections as a way of settling the conflict. The Carter Center could bring to bear its considerable experience and expertise in this area to "assist the myriad Ethiopian/Eritrean parties in ending their differences with the ballot box rather than the military" ("International Negotiation Network," 1991, p. 27).

Following Carter's initial efforts, U.S.-brokered peace talks continued in London. In late May 1991, the EPLF took the Eritrean provincial capital of Asmara from the Ethiopian government, and the Ethiopian People's Democratic Front (an umbrella organization of several of the many revolutionary groups) and the TPLF took the capital of Addis Ababa and forced the resignation of Ethiopian President Mengistu (Miller, 1991, p. A1). U.S. officials mediating the talks urged that hostilities cease and elections be called.

In April 1993, a referendum was held in Eritrea to formalize the de facto independence Eritreans had won since taking the Eritrean provincial capital of Asmara ("Eritreans vote on independence," 1993, p. 2A). The referendum was reportedly the first free election in twenty centuries of recorded Eritrean history and granted sovereignty to a people ruled for the past four hundred years by Turks, Egyptians, Italians, the British, and Ethiopians. The Eritreans planned to apply immediately for membership in the United Nations. The leader of the provisional Eritrean government, Isaias Afwerki, renewed his government's pledge to move the new nation toward multiparty democracy ("Eritreans vote on independence," 1993, p. 2A). On May 24, 1993, the Eritreans formally pronounced their independence on the second anniversary of the taking of the provincial capital and the collapse of the Ethiopian government. Eritrean President Isaias Afwerki described independence as a "moment of joy and resurrection for Eritrea" ("World's newest nation," 1993, p. 2A).

The experience of President Carter and the INN in the Ethiopian-Eritrean peace process resulted in several lessons for future mediation efforts. These included the importance of private forums, the value of a joint problem-solving approach, the need for involving external players, the value of exploiting internally created solutions, the usefulness of employing neutral meeting sites and processes, the need to provide gains for both parties, and the need for active involvement by third-party mediators. Despite criticism from some who argue that private talks are best in the initial phases of a mediation effort, the INN found that both parties were unwilling to engage in negotiations without the presence of the media. While the parties publicly postured with the media, in private the parties assumed a more problem-solving orientation. Given that both sides were affected by the famine, disease, drought, and environmental devastation resulting from the war, the INN, by putting them in the position of being joint problem solvers, provided them with a way out of the situation. According to the INN team, "When their attention can be directed toward solving joint problems, rather than continuing to deal with each other adversarially, they can begin to work their way out of the trap" ("International Negotiation Network," 1991, pp. 34–35).

External players, such as regional and international agencies and other governments, play an important role in negotiations between parties in long-standing conflicts. Members of the INN team noted, "It is easier for a party to make a concession to a trusted friend, as a means of ending the conflict, than to the long-hated adversary" ("International Negotiation Network," 1991, p. 35).

When the parties in a conflict design their own solutions to the conflict, "they are empowered to resolve their own problems" ("International Negotiation Network," 1991, p. 35). Owning the problem and owning the solution tend to create more equality between the parties. In addition, solutions arising from the parties tend to be more acceptable to the parties than solutions suggested or imposed from someone outside the situation.

The careful attention to the physical surroundings demonstrated by the INN team at both the Atlanta and the Nairobi talks contributed to the successes achieved. Care was taken to provide equal accommodations for both sides, the negotiating rooms were designed to be conducive to a collaborative working environment, and the venues were selected so as not to favor either side.

While the EPLF/PDRE negotiations never reached the substantive level, the INN negotiating team tried throughout the preliminary talks to ensure gains for both sides. Had the talks proceeded to the substantive level, efforts by the INN were in the works for the World Bank and the International Monetary Fund to provide incentives to both parties ("International Negotiation Network," 1991, p. 35).

The involvement of third parties can facilitate and organize the peace process as well as assist with the implementation of any agreements that might be reached. The stature of President Carter as a neutral third party afforded both parties an eminent world leader with the credibility to satisfy both sides, in addition to the access to resources, governments, organizations, and the media he could provide.

A very basic lesson to be learned is simply that parties in conflict must communicate with each other. Because organizations like the United Nations are prohibited from even talking to rebel organizations like the EPLF, their ability as a peacemaker is severely limited. In the same way, many governments refuse to acknowledge revolutionary groups for fear of becoming alienated from the recognized government. Formal diplomatic relations are generally required in order for traditional diplomatic efforts to succeed. In the absence of formal diplomatic relations, President Carter and the INN provided the communication link that was necessary for parties in conflict, regardless of their diplomatic standing, to begin the difficult process of making peace.

The INN team concluded from the goals accomplished during the Ethiopian-Eritrean peace process that "if we can succeed in developing an international network that draws a larger number of eminent persons into close association for the purpose of making war the least acceptable means of resolving conflicts, rather than the method of first resort, we can have an impact at a systemic level" ("International Negotiation Network," 1991, p. 38). The INN team noted an encouraging development following the conclusion of its involvement with the Ethiopians and Eritreans in that "if we judge from the numbers of requests for INN assistance, there is one clearly evolving trend: the parties caught in the mediation gap are increasingly looking for more peaceful ways to resolve their differences" ("International Negotiation Network," 1991, p. 38).

Commenting on Carter's efforts, Copson concluded that while "the initiative has not borne fruit, Carter surprised many observers with his ability to bring the EPLF and the Ethiopian regime together in two meetings where substantive progress was made on procedural arrangements for substantive talks" (1991, p. 38). Carter's accomplishment of getting the parties to talk after more than thirty years of conflict is significant and illustrates "Carter's deliberate pursuit of hard problems to solve . . . reflecting his will and skill in facing and overcoming difficult obstacles" (Hargrove, 1988, p. 122).

Recent work by representatives of the Carter Center continues the work of peacemaking and conflict resolution in Ethiopia. Dan Phillips, former U.S. ambassador to the Republic of the Congo, joined the Carter Center in the fall of 1993, worked on mediation efforts between Ethiopia and the Sudan, and helped to develop human rights and democratization programs for the new government in Ethiopia. According to Phillips, "In Ethiopia, The Carter Center is attempting to build on President Carter's 1989 efforts to end Africa's longest-running civil war with programs designed to ensure that the country's post-war institutions reflect democratic and human values" ("Former ambassadors tackle human rights," 1993, p. 10). These ongoing efforts toward establishing democracy in Ethiopia have involved representatives of various Carter Center programs traveling to Ethiopia to discuss a new constitution, revising the judiciary, and ensuring the future protection of human rights ("Moving toward democracy in Ethiopia," 1993, pp. 11–12). While the Carter Center was not able to reach the ideal resolution of the Ethiopian-Eritrean civil war that would have been an acceptable agreement negotiated at the peace table, it directs its ongoing efforts in Ethiopia at building democracy.

Peacemaking in Liberia

Estimates are that since civil war erupted in the African country of Liberia in December 1989, 150,000 people have been killed in the violence and destruction. The Carter Center and the INN have played an ongoing role in trying to bring peace to this war-torn country. Early on in the peace process, a representative from the INN attended summit meetings in Yamoussoukro, Côte d'Ivoire ("Waging peace," 1993, p. 13). Liberia was one of the conflicts targeted during the annual 1992 INN consultation, "Resolving Intra-national Conflicts." At that time there were, in fact, two de facto governments in Liberia ("Strategies for resolving conflict," 1992, p. 5). The Interim Government of National Unity controlled the capital of Monrovia, while the National Patriotic Reconstruction Assembly Government controlled most of the rest of the country. Both factions were represented at the consultation along with experts on the situation in Liberia. The Liberian working session produced a list of ten specific short- and long-term steps to be taken in an effort to resolve the conflict. These included disarmament, appeals to international and regional aid organizations for financial and material assistance, and developing plans for elections, as well as the long-term rebuilding of infrastructure and repatriation of refugees ("Resolving intra-national conflicts," 1992, p. 33). Since the outbreak of fighting, several peace plans and cease-fires have been put into place. An eight-nation African peacekeeping force backed by the United Nations has had some success in bringing peace to the country by beginning to disarm the fighters, by inaugurating a transitional council and legislature, and by scheduling elections in 1994 (Shiner, 1994, p. A26). These efforts have been carried out under the auspices of the Economic Community of West African States and the July 1993 Cotonou Peace Accords. Despite these and other efforts, peace has eluded Liberia.

During the course of the civil war, President Carter, Rosalynn Carter, and members of the Carter Center's Conflict Resolution and African Governance programs have met with Liberian leaders. Commenting on these ongoing efforts, President Carter said, "The Carter Center has been closely involved in assisting the peace process in Liberia. We expect to play a major role, together with other U.S. and international organizations, to promote reconciliation, civic education, and free and fair elections under the terms of the Cotonou agreement" (quoted in "Carter Center supports peace," 1993, pp. 13–14). Among the efforts undertaken by the Carter Center was to agree to assist with arranging and monitoring elections. In the spring of 1992, Richard Joseph, director of the African Governance Program, observed that after three years of civil war, "what Liberia now needs is one government that is freely elected by the people" ("Liberia targeted," 1992, p. 10). To further this goal, the Carter Center established an election-monitoring office in Monrovia and was prepared to work with other international organizations on the elections. In April 1992, representatives of the INN traveled to Liberia and met with representatives of both major factions in the conflict and the Liberian Elections Commission ("Liberia targeted," 1992, p. 10). The Carter Center also established a consortium of nongovernmental organizations called Project Liberia: Peace, Elections, and Democracy designed to help bring peace and democracy to Liberia ("Carter Center supports peace," 1993, p. 14).

On a more humanitarian level, Paul McDermott, who directed the center's Monrovia office, in 1993 negotiated for the release of ten U.N. and World Food

Program workers who had been detained by one of the warring factions ("Prisoners are released," 1993, p. 14). Carter Center programs have also had a long-term focus in Liberia. In April 1991, the Mickey Leland Community Development Fellowship Program was launched at the Carter Center ("Leland Fellowships," 1991, p. 7). These fellowships, named in honor of the Texas congressman who lost his life while on a 1989 famine-relief mission to Ethiopia, will allow officials from African nongovernmental organizations to participate in a course of study designed to enhance their organizational, leadership, and consensus-building skills ("Leland fellows eager," 1993, p. 13). Six Liberians were among those chosen as Leland fellows for 1993.

Finally, while the conflict continued, the Carter Center took positive steps to aid in the continued development of Liberia. As peace efforts faltered in 1994, South African Bishop Desmond Tutu made a four-day trip to Liberia at the invitation of the Carter Center and the Liberian Council of Churches to help energize the peace process (Joseph, 1994, p. 10). During talks with the various leaders and factions, Tutu challenged Liberians to seek peace, suggesting, "If South Africa could achieve accommodation among its diverse ethnic, racial, and cultural groups, what prevents Liberia from doing likewise?" (quoted by Joseph, 1994, p. 10).

Since the civil war began in Liberia, the Carter Center has worked and will continue to work to resolve the conflict, to help establish democracy, and to facilitate humanitarian development efforts in the country. All of these efforts are directed at ongoing and long-term peacemaking for Liberians.

Peacemaking in the Sudan

The African country of the Sudan has experienced civil war almost since its independence from Britain in 1956. Fighting and hostilities resumed in earnest in 1983 between the Muslim-dominated north and Christian and animist factions in the south (Walgren, 1993, p. 1A). The fighting has been dominated by regional, religious, and ethnic differences between the various factions, with most of the fighting having taken place in the southern parts of the country. In the most recent flare-up of violence dating from 1983, the Sudanese People's Liberation Army and southern Sudanese have been fighting the government for a nonsectarian national government, the repeal of strict Islamic laws, and greater autonomy for the southern region of the country ("SPLA leader," 1989, p. 10).

President Carter and the INN have also been involved with conflict-resolution efforts in the civil war in the Sudan for a number of years. Carter's efforts and those of various Carter Center programs in the Sudan truly characterize the need to address both the necessary and sufficient conditions required for peace. Not only has President Carter sought to resolve the armed conflict, but at the same time, Carter Center agencies have worked to further humanitarian aid to the country.

In June 1989, Dr. John Garang, the founder and leader of the Sudanese

People's Liberation Army, led a delegation to Atlanta seeking the Carter Center's assistance in resolving this civil conflict. Garang later met with President Carter in Plains, Georgia, to discuss ways that the center might assist and facilitate negotiations designed to end this civil war. In October 1990, President Carter called on General Omar al-Bashir, the leader of the Sudan, to open relief routes to the south to prevent a repeat of a 1984 famine that claimed 150,000 Sudanese lives ("Carter calls for famine relief," 1990, p. 10).

The civil war in the Sudan was also among the eight conflicts spotlighted and targeted for analysis at the inaugural INN consultation in 1992. The major factions in the conflict were all represented at that consultation. Among the major barriers to resolution identified by participants were the official Islamic government, which was opposed by the rebel groups who were seeking a more secular state, the government's ties to Iran and accusations of state-sponsored terrorism, the rebel groups' call for pluralistic democracy, and the issue of who should represent the rebels in any negotiations with the government ("Resolving intra-national conflicts," 1992, p. 34). The consultation proposed three basic steps for resolving the conflict in the Sudan, including grass-roots efforts aimed at humanitarian relief aid as formal peace negotiations took place, involving outside parties like the INN, the OAU, the Arab League, or the country of Nigeria (all of whom were represented at the consultation) in peace talks and negotiations, and a three-step peace process involving meetings between the major parties, the continuation of humanitarian aid, and a cease-fire and release of prisoners ("Resolving intra-national conflicts," 1992, p. 35). There was agreement to draft an invitation to the parties and eventually to convene a roundtable conference. It was hoped that a cease-fire and the opening of peace talks could, in the interim, facilitate international relief support for the Sudan.

Following these talks, the Sudan was increasingly isolated by the world community during 1993 after a U.N. vote in December 1992 condemned the Sudan's human rights behavior. The Sudanese government did announce a cease-fire with the rebels in March 1993 in a move seen by Western diplomats as an attempt to improve relations with the West (Ford, 1993, p. 3). However, in the fall of 1993 the Sudanese government once again launched major offensives against the rebels (Walgren, 1993, p. 1A). At the same time, Carter continued his efforts at a mediated settlement. In mid-September, Carter met with President Clinton at the White House and discussed what could be done to facilitate an end to the war in the Sudan (McQuillan, 1993). Carter's mediation efforts had been complicated when the U.S. State Department added the Sudan to its list of terrorist states on August 18, 1993. Carter criticized this move because he felt that it was premature, was without proof, and "in effect aborted several weeks of [mediation] work on our part" to reach a cease-fire (quoted in McQuillan, 1993).

In late October 1993, the United States attempted unsuccessfully to bring together two of the rival rebel factions in the Sudanese civil war (Press, 1993, p. 2). These talks were followed by meetings between Carter and a Sudanese guerrilla leader. After these talks, Carter reported "guarded optimism about the prospects for a peace settlement in Sudan" ("In the news," 1993, p. 10). Still other talks were taking place under the leadership of governments in the region and chaired by Kenyan President Daniel arap Moi (Press, 1993, p. 2). These meetings came at a time when a Washington-based refugee group released a report that characterized the civil war in the Sudan as one of the worst on earth, having claimed more than 1.3 million lives. Not only had the fighting claimed thousands of lives, but famine and disease were claiming even more lives. Carter's mediation efforts failed in October when the Khartoum government accused Carter of working to repair relations between the rebel factions (Walgren, 1993, p. 1A). In the absence of a peaceful mediated settlement, the fighting and the dying in the Sudan would continue throughout much of 1994.

Renewed hope for stopping the fighting in the Sudan and reducing the human death toll came in the spring of 1995. On March 28, 1995, President Bashir, who was joined by President Carter, declared a unilateral two-month cease-fire ("Truce in the Sudan," 1995, p. A12). This cease-fire would permit the continuation of efforts to eradicate Guinea worm disease, to prevent river blindness, and to immunize children. Like other African countries, the Sudan had been fighting the spread of the waterborne parasite responsible for the crippling Guinea worm disease. While similar efforts in other African countries have controlled and almost eliminated the disease, the civil war had complicated eradication efforts in the Sudan (Schwartz, 1995). The cease-fire provided time for relief efforts, sponsored by the Carter Center and other relief organizations, to continue their life-saving humanitarian work. President and Rosalynn Carter visited relief sites and toured rural regions of the Sudan in July 1995. As they surveyed the relief efforts, President Carter met with government and rebel leaders to ensure that the efforts would continue and urged that the cease-fire be extended and that peace talks begin (Powell, 1995, p. 4A). It was the cease-fire that Carter helped arrange that made these relief efforts possible. Working on both mediation and humanitarian fronts, President Carter was seeking a long-term solution to the civil conflict and addressing the immediate and long-term humanitarian needs of the Sudanese people.

The work of the Carter Center and the INN to date has met with some success and considerable frustration as they have attempted to address some of the most intractable civil wars around the world. However, the mission of the INN in seeking to fill the mediation gap means that it tends to become involved where others either have failed or are not permitted to intervene. While large victories are difficult and rare, the small victories President Carter and the INN have achieved are nonetheless significant. Lives were saved as talks took place between the Ethiopians and the Eritreans. Following the end of the conflict and the establishment of a democratically elected government, the long-term prospects for the people of Ethiopia have been improved. Ongoing programs by the Carter Center designed to strengthen this emerging democracy do not draw significant media attention but, nevertheless, further peacemaking. Even while the fighting continued in Liberia and the Sudan, efforts sponsored by the Carter Center improved and saved the lives of thousands. These small successes characterize the work of the INN and will continue as it pursues the difficult work of making peace.

REFERENCES

Carter calls for famine relief in Sudan. (1990, Fall). *Carter Center News*, p. 10.

Carter Center supports peace in Liberia. (1993, Fall). *Carter Center News*, pp. 13–14.

Carter convenes historic Ethiopian/Eritrean peace talks. (1989, Fall). *Carter Center News*, pp. 1, 4.

Conflict resolution program begins project to ease tensions in Baltics. (1994, Summer). *Carter Center News*, p. 13.

Copson, R. W. (1991). Peace in Africa? The influence of regional and international change. In F. M. Deng and I. W. Zartman (Eds.), *Conflict resolution in Africa* (pp. 19–41). Washington, DC: Brookings Institution.

Eritreans vote on independence. (1993, Apr. 23). *Erie Daily Times* (Associated Press), p. 2A.

Ethiopian civil war talks continue. (1989, Nov. 21). *Denver Post*, p. 9A.

Ethiopian minister says civil war cost is high. (1989, Aug. 19). *New York Times*, p. 2A.

Ethiopian talks stall. (1989, Nov. 25). *Washington Post*, p. A19.

Ford, P. (1993, Mar. 24). Isolated and broke, Islamic Sudan tries to smooth ties with West. *Christian Science Monitor*, p. 3.

Former ambassadors tackle human rights, conflict resolution. (1993, Fall). *Carter Center News*, p. 10.

Hargrove, E. (1988). *Jimmy Carter as president: Leadership and the politics of the public good*. Baton Rouge: Louisiana State University Press.

In the news. (1993, Fall). *Carter Center News*, p. 10.

INN planning continues worldwide. (1988, Fall). *Carter Center News*, p. 10.

INN seeks cooperation to end internal conflicts. (1993, Spring). *Carter Center News*, pp. 8–9.

INN seeks to expand network, encourage regional conflict resolution. (1990, Spring). *Carter Center News*, p. 10.

International negotiation network fills "mediation gap." (1989, Fall). *Carter Center News*, p. 5.

The international negotiation network: A new method of approaching some very old problems. (1991). Occasional Paper Series, vol. 2, no. 2. Available from the Carter Center, One Copenhill, Atlanta, GA 30307.

Joseph, R. (1994, July 27). Many lessons for Liberia in South Africa's model. *Christian Science Monitor*, p. 10.

Leland fellows eager to help rebuild their native Liberia. (1993, Fall). *Carter Center News*, p. 13.

Leland fellowships to promote African development. (1991, Spring). *Carter Center News*, p. 7.

Liberia targeted for election observation. (1992, Spring). *Carter Center News*, p. 10.

McCarthy, C. (1989, Nov. 18). The best ex-president we have. *Washington Post*, p. A25.

McQuillan, L. (1993, Sept. 14). Clinton, Carter discuss ending Sudan civil war. Reuters News Service (available through CD NewsBank 1995 Comprehensive).

Miller, R. (1991, May 28). Ethiopian capital falls to rebels. *Erie Daily Times* (Associated Press), p. A1.

Moving toward democracy in Ethiopia. (1993, Spring). *Carter Center News*, pp. 11–12.

Perlez, J. (1989, Nov. 30). Amid new famine worries, talks with Ethiopia advance. *New York Times*, p. A6.

Powell, E. A. (1995, July 23). Carter brings safe water crusade to south Sudan. *Erie Daily Times* (Associated Press), p. 4A.

Press, R. M. (1993, Oct. 25). Seeking an end to Sudan's agony. *Christian Science Monitor*, p. 2.

Prisoners are released. (1993, Fall). *Carter Center News*, p. 14.

Profile: Dayle E. Powell. (1989, Fall). *Carter Center News*, p. 3.

Resolving intra-national conflicts: A strengthened role for non-governmental actors. (1992). Conference Report Series, vol. 3, no. 2. Available from the Carter Center, One Copenhill, Atlanta, GA 30307.

Schwartz, J. (1995, Apr. 12). Carter urges resumption of cease-fire in Sudan. Reuters News Service (available on CD NewsBank 1995 Comprehensive).

Second rebel group joins Carter's Ethiopia talks. (1989, Aug. 25). *New York Times*, p. A6.

Shiner, C. (1994, Apr. 1). 8-nation African force is peacekeeping model in war-torn Liberia. *Washington Post*, p. A26.

SPLA leader seeks negotiation avenues at Center. (1989, Fall). *Carter Center News*, p. 10.

Strategies for resolving conflict. (1992, Spring). *Carter Center News*, p. 5.

Truce in the Sudan. (1995, Mar. 28). *New York Times* (Reuters), p. A12.

Waging peace around the world. (1993). Available from the Carter Center, One Copenhill, Atlanta, GA 30307.

Walgren, J. (1993, Nov. 7). The lost boys: Refugee camp kids viewed as southern Sudan's future. *Dallas Morning News* (available from CD NewsBank 1995 Comprehensive), p. 1A.

World leaders commit to act for peace. (1992, Spring). *Carter Center News*, pp. 1, 4–5.

World leaders join INN peace efforts. (1991, Fall). *Carter Center News*, p. 10.

World's newest nation emerges today. (1993, May 24). *Erie Daily Times* (Associated Press), p. 2A.

The Carter Presidential Center and the Jimmy Carter Presidential Library and Museum in Atlanta, Georgia. Photo courtesy of The Public Information Office of The Carter Center.

Former President Jimmy Carter, the 39th President of the United States. Photo courtesy of Charles W. Plant of Americus, Georgia, and The Public Information Office of The Carter Center.

(from right to left) Dr. Robert Pastor, director of The Carter Center's Latin America and Caribbean Program; President Carter; and George Prince, former Prime Minister of Belize on a December 1990 election monitoring mission to Haiti sponsored by The Council of Freely Elected Heads of Government. Photo courtesy of The Public Information Office of The Carter Center.

President Carter observes the corn harvest in Zambia in 1986 as a part of the Global 2000, Inc. Agricultural Program. Photo courtesy of The Public Information Office of The Carter Center.

CHAPTER 6

CARTER MISSIONS TO KOREA, HAITI, AND BOSNIA

President Carter and representatives from the Carter Center were very active in trying to resolve several seemingly intractable conflicts during the latter half of 1994, including ones in the Korean Peninsula, Haiti, and Bosnia. The Korean Peninsula has been a potential hot spot ever since the Korean conflict in the mid-1950s. Tensions mounted on the Korean Peninsula over North Korea's nuclear program and threatened to escalate into a regional, if not international, conflict. In the Caribbean country of Haiti, free and fair elections, facilitated and monitored by the Carter Center, had moved the country toward democracy in 1991. The promise of democracy that the election of President Aristide provided was short-lived when a military coup forced him into exile eight months later. By the fall of 1994, pressure from the international community and several U.N. mandates had failed to return Aristide to office, and a threatened U.N.-sponsored U.S. invasion held the potential for a serious confrontation. Since the breakup of the former Yugoslavia, the Balkans had witnessed several devastating civil wars resulting in significant military and civilian casualties. While drawing world attention and diplomatic efforts, the Bosnian conflict, and those in Korea and Haiti, seemed destined to either continue their carnage or further escalate. President Carter's personal involvement in these conflicts demonstrated his commitment to peacemaking and his ability to get parties in conflicts to seek peaceful, nonviolent means of conflict resolution.

DEFUSING TENSIONS ON THE KOREAN PENINSULA

President Carter's involvement in the tensions between North Korea, South Korea, and the international community during the summer of 1994 began with his acceptance of an invitation from North Korean President Kim Il Sung to visit his country. The Carters had been invited to visit North Korea on several occasions since 1991 ("Carter trip paves the way," 1995, p. 6). For example, in

1992 Carter had been invited by both North and South Korea to help ease tensions in the region, but at the urging of the Bush administration, had declined the invitation (Stone, 1994, p. A4). Under the State Departments of Presidents Reagan and Bush, Carter was twice refused permission to travel to North Korea.

As the simmering tensions threatened to boil over during the summer of 1994 and erupt into an armed regional conflict, the invitation was renewed, and the visit of the Carters took on very visible, public, and immediate dimensions. At issue in the conflict was the United States' and the international community's objective to get the North Koreans to accept full and regular inspection of their nuclear facilities, and the desire of the North Koreans to establish full diplomatic relations with the United States as well as to modernize their nuclear program (Burns, 1994a, p. 3A). In announcing that he would travel to North Korea, President Carter stated, "We will be going as private citizens, representing The Carter Center. The invitation for this trip has been from Korea, not Washington, and I will have no official status relating to the U.S. government. My hope is to discuss some of the important issues of the day with leaders in the area" ("Carter takes offer," 1994, p. A3). The Clinton administration helped to facilitate the Carter trip to North Korea (Jehl, 1994b, p. A3). Three weeks prior to his trip, Carter was in contact with Clinton administration officials including Robert Gallucci, assistant secretary of state for political-military affairs, who flew to Atlanta to discuss Carter's concern over the mounting tensions on the Korean Peninsula. These talks and the administration's focus on the pursuit of economic sanctions against North Korea left Carter "distressed to realize we were approaching the possibility of a major confrontation . . . and that there was no avenue of communication that I could ascertain that might lead to a resolution" (quoted in Smith and Devroy, 1994, p. A12). Following these talks, Carter contacted Vice President Gore and told him that he was "strongly inclined" to travel to North Korea. Gore relayed these concerns to President Clinton, who gave his approval for the trip (Jehl, 1994b, p. A3). Representatives of the Carter Center had maintained an active dialogue with both North and South Korea in the years preceding this latest escalation ("Carter trip paves the way," 1995, p. 6). In fact, the Korean Peninsula was one of several conflict situations that was the focus of the first INN consultation in January 1992 ("Resolving intra-national conflicts," 1992).

Though Carter was "officially" traveling as a private citizen, the White House was supportive of the trip. President Carter was briefed by National Security Adviser Anthony Lake, White House staff, and members of the State Department. In qualifying the administration's support, Michael McCurry, State Department spokesperson, said that while Carter was briefed, he "is not carrying any formal message from the United States" even though he was accompanied by a career foreign service officer (quoted by Stone, 1994, p. A4). A senior White House official expressed the hope that Carter's visit would be an opportunity for "a face-saving resolution" to the tensions (Jehl, 1994a, p. 7).

Tensions on the Korean Peninsula had come to a head in June 1994 when

North Korea refused to allow inspectors from the International Atomic Energy Agency (IAEA) to inspect parts of its nuclear program. On June 11, the IAEA suspended its technical assistance to the North Korean nuclear program, at which time the North Koreans asked the two remaining IAEA inspectors to leave the country (Jehl, 1994a, p. 7). North Korea withdrew from the IAEA on June 13, saying that it would "not be bound to any rules or resolutions" of the IAEA (Smith and Reid, 1994, p. 1). The fear among those in the international community was that the North Korean nuclear program was moving toward the construction of nuclear weapons, a development that could seriously destabilize an already-tenuous relationship between the North Koreans and the international community. The international community, led by the United States, responded to these events by calling for U.N. economic sanctions against North Korea in an effort to force compliance with IAEA inspections and to ensure a peaceful North Korean nuclear program. In addition to the obvious threat to South Korea from the North, the Japanese were drawn into the situation when they expressed their willingness to support U.N. sanctions. The North Korean Foreign Ministry declared that such support would be regarded "as a declaration of war, and Japan would be unable to evade a deserving punishment for it" (Hamilton, 1994, p. A6). China—one of North Korea's few allies, a vital economic trade partner, and a member of the Security Council—resisted the call for sanctions (Sun, 1994, p. A20).

Against the backdrop of these tensions, the Carters arrived in Seoul, South Korea, on June 14 for meetings with top South Korean officials, including President Kim Young Sam (Sanger, 1994a, p. A12). On June 16, the Carter delegation crossed into North Korea at the truce village of Panmunjom, which had separated the Korean Peninsula for forty years. It traveled to the capital, Pyongyang, for meetings with Foreign Minister Kim Young Nam and President Kim Il Sung ("Carter visits Pyongyang," 1994, p. A34).

The Carter mission sought to accomplish two primary objectives: to defuse the immediate tensions related to the North Korean nuclear program and to reopen talks between the United States and North Korea ("Carter trip paves the way," 1995, p. 6). Upon his arrival in Pyongyang, Carter stated that "the time has come to establish full friendship and understanding, open trade, exchange of visits and full diplomatic relations between our two countries" (quoted by Choe, 1994a, p. 2A).

Even as President Carter began his visit and talks with the North Koreans, the Clinton administration on June 16 outlined its plans for U.N. sanctions. As explained by Madeline Albright, U.S. ambassador to the United Nations, the sanctions called for restricting arms exports from North Korea, cutting U.N. aid to the country, and further diplomatic isolation. These sanctions would be followed by additional economic sanctions if North Korea failed to comply with IAEA inspection requirements (Lewis, 1994, pp. A1, A12).

While a wide variety of issues were discussed during the three hours of talks with President Kim Il Sung, the issue of the North Korean nuclear program was clearly kept in focus. When Carter reported on his meetings with President Kim Il Sung, he said that North Korea had agreed not to expel the remaining two IAEA inspectors from the contentious nuclear complex at Yongbyon so long as good-faith efforts between the parties continued (Choe, 1994a, p. 2A). Following his meetings, Carter told the Cable News Network (CNN) that "President Kim Il Sung has committed himself to maintain the inspectors on site at the disputed nuclear reactor positions and also to guarantee that the surveillance equipment would stay in good operating order." Carter concluded, "I look on this commitment of President Kim Il Sung as being a very important and positive step toward the resolution of this crisis" (quoted by Choe, 1994a, p. 2A). Kim reportedly also expressed a desire to establish a nuclear-free Korean Peninsula. According to CNN, President Kim Il Sung told Carter, "What is important between us is trust, confidence in each other" (quoted in Choe, 1994a, p. 2A). Carter described his talks with the eighty-two-year-old president of North Korea as "fairly definitive and important" and noted that Kim was "extremely sharp." President Carter offered his continued involvement "to help iron out a problem or discuss these matters," concluding that "I think the North Koreans have confidence in me" (quoted by Smith, 1994a, p. A20).

Following his first round of talks with the North Koreans, Carter contacted Assistant Secretary of State Robert Gallucci to report on the progress of his discussions (Burns, 1994a, p. 3A). In response to the reported developments, President Clinton said that his administration would be willing to participate in high-level talks if the North Koreans followed through and agreed to freeze their nuclear program. Clinton stated, "If today's developments mean that North Korea is genuinely and verifiably prepared to freeze its nuclear program while talks go on, and we hope that is the case, then we would be willing to resume high-level talks" (quoted by Gordon, 1994b, p. A1). In other comments, Clinton cautioned, "We want to know what they mean [the North Korean proposals] and if it represents a change in position" (quoted in Sanger, 1994b, p. A10). What Clinton was seeking was "an ironclad guarantee" that no more nuclear fuel would be diverted to weapons research (quoted in Sanger, 1994b, p. A10).

While the Clinton administration would continue to pursue sanctions, this announcement marked a policy shift, if not a change in policy goals. Originally the administration had insisted that talks would continue only if the North suspended efforts to develop nuclear weapons, and if it could be determined that no diversion of plutonium had taken place in the past (Gordon, 1994c, p. A1). While plans for U.N. sanctions continued and the military options were explored, the Clinton administration reportedly opted to stress the diplomatic approach because of the uncertainty of Security Council approval and the obvious risks of war. According to press reports, "Indications that North Korea is prepared for a diplomatic accommodation came when former President Carter reported on his talks in Pyongyang" (Gordon, 1994d, p. A10). In commenting on the administration's continued push for sanctions, Carter stressed that "nothing should be done to exacerbate the situation now," adding that "the reason I came here was to try to prevent an irreconcilable mistake" (quoted by Sanger, 1994b, p. A10). Carter called on the United States to suspend the imposition of sanctions pending the consideration of North Korean "compromise proposals" (quoted by Sanger, 1994b, p. A10). In commenting on the use of sanctions following his trip, Carter remarked, "If I had thought the sanctions were a good idea, I never would have gone over there" (quoted by Jehl, 1994b, p. A3).

Among the proposals resulting from the Carter talks were offers by the North Koreans to allow IAEA monitors to remain so long as good-faith efforts continued, and the renewal of an offer by the North to scrap several older plutonium-producing reactors if the United States and other industrialized nations would assist in constructing light-water energy-producing reactors (Gordon, 1994d, p. A10). In response to these proposals, Assistant Secretary of State Gallucci said that in addition to allowing for IAEA inspection and monitoring of their nuclear facilities, the United States would insist that the North Koreans not proceed with plans to refuel and operate a key reactor suited for the production of plutonium and that they cease reprocessing spent nuclear fuel rods (Smith, 1994a, p. A20).

The results of President Carter's talks with the North Koreans were promising and positive, yet appeared to create some confusion and ambiguity in terms of how the United States and the international community should respond. Had the North Koreans agreed to suspend their nuclear program and submit to international verification? Had the Clinton administration changed its policy regarding the North Koreans? Had President Carter misrepresented the U.S. position and/or that of the North Koreans? These and other questions were raised as Carter left North Korea. On the positive side, the Carter talks held out the hope that a confrontation could be avoided if the North Koreans followed through on the reported commitments. The ambiguity resulting from the talks stemmed from the perception that the Clinton administration was shifting its policy to accommodate the North Koreans. The issues were further confused when CNN reported on June 17 that Carter had told Kim Il Sung—and wrongly asserted—that the Clinton administration was prepared to conditionally suspend the push for U.N. sanctions and restart negotiations ("U.S. clarifies N. Korea policy," 1994, p. 3A; Gordon, 1994b, p. A1). Carter later clarified the issue by noting that he was expressing his personal view, rather than that of the Clinton administration (Smith and Devroy, 1994, p. A12).

The lack of direct lines of communication between the Clinton administration and President Carter while he was in North Korea made clarification of the issues difficult. This lack of direct communication caused considerable speculation and commentary over the weekend of June 18 and 19. As the policies and positions were clarified, one report on Saturday, June 18, noted that "Administration officials say they are merely exploring new signs of flexibility on the part of the North Koreans and argue that any agreement in which they would freeze their nuclear weapons program while high-level talks proceed would be a good deal for the United States" (Gordon, 1994c, p. A1). Another report noted that "Clinton, Vice President Gore, national security advisor Anthony Lake and Assistant Secretary of State Robert Gallucci each went to considerable lengths yesterday [June 17] to say Washington is still pursuing its sanctions drive even as it explored new prospects for dialogue with the hard-line communist state" (Smith and Graham, 1994, p. A1). As the speculation and clarification continued, President Carter completed his trip, calling it "a good omen" (quoted by Sanger, 1994c, p. A6). It would take additional time for the details and positions of all parties to become clear.

Another measure of the success of the Carter mission came on Sunday, June 19, when for the first time since the peninsula was divided by war, the presidents of North and South Korea agreed to hold a summit meeting. President Carter delivered the offer from the North Korean president to his South Korean counterpart. President Kim Young Sam responded by saying, "The sooner the better" (quoted by Sanger, 1994d, p. A1). On June 20, the South Koreans asked the North for a meeting [as early as June 28] to discuss plans for the summit meeting between their leaders (Smith and Devroy, 1994, p. A12). Even as they apparently welcomed the positive moves and said that they would explore ways to arrange the summit, the South Koreans on June 19 moved three hundred troops and heavy weapons into the Demilitarized Zone that divides the two Koreas. These troop movements prompted the North to accuse the South of escalating a "war atmosphere" between the two countries (Roche, 1994, p. A12). There were certainly issues yet to be resolved. Yet the fact that direct talks had taken place and that additional talks and a possible unprecedented summit were proposed was certainly preferable to the escalation of tensions and the lack of dialogue that had existed prior to the Carter mission.

As an interesting side development, Carter reported that at the urging of President Kim's wife, Kim accepted proposals for joint U.S.–North Korean searches for the remains of U.S. servicemen buried in the North (Gordon, 1994a, p. A1; Smith and Devroy, 1994, p. A12). This development is interesting to note because it would be the wife of General Raoul Cedras, Haiti's leader, who would be instrumental in the resolution of the Haitian crisis several months later. Also of interest was the unique common ground established between Presidents Carter and Kim Il Sung. During a boat trip following their meetings, the two discussed trout fishing, and Kim Il Sung told Carter (an avid outdoorsman) of his efforts to save the rainbow trout in North Korean streams ("Fish deal," 1994, p. 14). While such common ground had little to do with the immediate nuclear issues, it helped to build the trust President Kim referred to as having developed during the meetings.

Carter took the opportunity of a news conference following the announcement of the North–South Korean summit to criticize the Clinton administration's sanction drive and the confusion that surrounded his talks. According to Carter, sanctions would be doomed to failure and would, in fact, heighten tensions. Carter stated, "The declaration of sanctions by the U.N. would be regarded as an insult by them, branding it as an outlaw country" and would be interpreted as "a personal insult to their so-called Great Leader" (President Kim Il Sung) (quoted by Sanger, 1994d, p. A1). In commenting on his trip in more general terms, Carter remarked that he found it "inconceivable" that Clinton had not taken the initiative to send his own administrative delegation to North Korea to attempt to resolve the crisis (quoted by Jehl, 1994b, p. A3). In clarifying the confusion that followed Carter's trip, and especially his comments on the lifting of sanctions, it was reported that "Mr. Carter insisted today that his words had been misinterpreted. The sanctions, he said, would be held in abeyance only if Mr. Kim agreed to open the nuclear program to full inspection" (Sanger, 1994a, p. A12).

Upon his return to the United States, President Carter briefed President Clinton on the results of his trip. After meeting with Clinton, Carter told reporters, "I personally believe that the crisis is over" and remarked that President Clinton was "very grateful that I had gone and thought it was a very fine accomplishment" (quoted by Gordon, 1994c, p. A3). In commenting on Carter's mission, President Clinton removed some of the confusion surrounding Carter's comments about sanctions by saying that "President Carter was very faithful in articulating the policy of our government" (quoted in "Carter trip paves the way," 1995, p. 6). Robert Gallucci, Clinton administration point man on North Korea, was more cautious in his assessment of the mission, stating that "there may be an opening here. But at this point our posture is one in which we really do need to follow up on what he [Carter] has brought back to see just exactly how much is there" (quoted by Gordon, 1994c, p. A1). There would obviously be numerous details to be worked out and clarified by all the parties involved as future talks took place.

The Clinton administration pursued the opening provided by the Carter mission. On Monday, June 20, a letter was sent to the North Koreans saying that the administration would agree to resume high-level talks (as early as July) if the North Koreans took steps to confirm that they were willing to freeze their nuclear program. According to President Clinton, "We expect and hope to hear back within a couple of days about whether President Carter's understanding of what they said is correct" (quoted by Gordon, 1994d, p. A10). The administration also acknowledged that it was postponing a Pentagon-recommended troop buildup in South Korea, concluding that it could jeopardize prospects for a peaceful settlement (Jehl, 1994d, p. A6).

While the North did not immediately respond, it did renew the visas of the IAEA monitors. Noting the tie between a resumption of talks and the U.S. drive for U.N. sanctions, Secretary of State Christopher said, "If we get the kind of confirmation that I've outlined, it's clear that sanctions would have to be held in abeyance at that time" (quoted by Gordon, 1994d, p. A10). Specifically, Washington wanted three things: an agreement by the North Koreans not to reprocess additional plutonium, for the North Koreans to allow international inspection, and for the North Koreans not to refuel the reactor at Yongbyon (Gordon, 1994d, p. A10). The North Korean Foreign Ministry did, in fact, send a letter that, according to President Clinton, contained assurances that North Korea would not reprocess recently removed fuel rods or reload the contentious reactor at Yongbyon and would submit to IAEA inspections (Jehl, 1994d, p. A6).

On June 22, President Clinton announced that he was satisfied that the North Koreans were willing to freeze their nuclear program and agreed to open a new round of talks in Geneva. According to Clinton, "It is the beginning of a new stage on our efforts to pursue a non-nuclear Korean Peninsula," and he concluded that "this does not solve the problem, but it certainly gives us the basis for seeking a solution" (quoted by Jehl, 1994d, p. A1). On Friday, July 8, talks between the United States and the North Koreans opened in Geneva ("U.S., North Korea begin talks," 1994, p. 7A). Details were also worked out for the North–South Korean summit planned for July 25–27 in the North Korean capital of Pyongyang (Choe, 1994b, p. 7A).

Against the backdrop of these positive developments growing out of the Carter mission to North Korea, President Kim Il Sung died on Saturday, July 9 ("North Korea's leader dies," 1994, p. 1A). Kim's death raised doubts as to the future of both sets of talks, which were immediately suspended. Following the official mourning period and political realignments in North Korea, renewed activity to follow up on the initial agreements made during the Carter mission took place during the fall of 1994. In an effort to help renew the talks, President Carter met with ambassadors from both North and South Korea at the Carter Center in late September following his trip to Haiti. While no specific arrangements resulted from his meetings with the South Korean ambassador to the United States and the North Korean ambassador to the United Nations, Carter said that he was willing, if necessary, to return to the Korean Peninsula to facilitate the resumption of talks (Putnam, 1994, p. 3A).

The South Korean ambassador delivered a letter from President Kim Young Sam thanking Carter for helping bring the countries together, while the North Korean ambassador delivered a letter from North Korean President Kim Il Sung—written before his death—confirming the June agreements. Following these meetings, Carter said, "I think that both the North and South Korean people would like to see steps resumed at an early date that would lead to the complete reconciliation and understanding between North and South Korea" (quoted by Putnam, 1994, p. 3A).

Talks between North Korea and the United States continued throughout the fall of 1994 ("Korean nuclear talks resume," 1994, p. 2A). On October 21, 1994, the United States and North Korea signed an agreement designed to resolve the long-standing tensions over the North's nuclear program ("U.S., North Korea sign nuke program pact," 1994, p. 2A). The chief North Korean negotiator stated, "We believe that this agreed framework is a very important milestone . . . of historic importance" ("U.S., North Korea sign nuke program pact," 1994, p. 2A). Chief U.S. negotiator Robert Gallucci was more cautious in his assessment, saying, "We left each other with the thought that we have a long road ahead of us" (quoted in "U.S., North Korea sign nuke program pact,"

1994, p. 2A). This agreement provided the framework for talks that would continue well into 1995 to resolve the details and specifics of the accord (Lippman, 1994a, p. A17). In recognizing President Carter's part in facilitating these talks, Secretary Gallucci said, "President Carter played a key role" in averting sanctions and in reopening the dialogue between Washington and Pyongyang (quoted in "Carter trip paves the way," 1995, p. 6).

REESTABLISHING DEMOCRACY IN HAITI: THE CARTER MISSION

Haiti is one of the oldest independent nations in the hemisphere, and by most accounts, it is one of the poorest and most oppressed. When the dictatorship of the Duvalier family (which had controlled Haiti for decades) finally collapsed in February 1986, there were several attempts made at establishing democracy in Haiti. Elections were attempted in November 1987 but resulted in widespread violence and election fraud. Haiti eventually elected its first president in free and fair elections in December 1990. In February 1991, Jean-Bertrand Aristide was inaugurated as the first democratically elected president of Haiti. At his inauguration, Aristide observed, "It took 200 years to arrive at our second independence. At our first independence we cried 'Liberty or Death!' We must now shout with all our strength, 'Democracy or Death!'" (quoted in French, 1991, p. A3). The transition from dictatorship to democracy was a rocky and violent one, and unfortunately, it was short-lived. In September 1991, just eight months after he was inaugurated, Aristide was forced to flee into exile in the United States following a bloody military coup. During the period from September 1991 to September 1994, numerous unsuccessful attempts were made by the United Nations and the United States to return Aristide to power. For example, less than a year before the crisis came to a head in September 1994, U.N. Special Envoy Dante Caputo tried unsuccessfully to enlist the help of Carter and other leaders to "witness who is responsible for the violence" that had almost daily been perpetrated on the Haitian people by the military government (quoted by Downie, 1993). Caputo and the United Nations were attempting to implement an agreement signed in July 1993 that called for the return of Aristide (Murray, 1993).

After ousting Aristide from power, three military officers—Lt. Gen. Raoul Cedras, Lt. Col. Michel Francois, and Brig. Gen. Philippe Biamby—and Emile Jonassaint, their hand-picked president, defiantly clung to power in the face of crippling international economic sanctions imposed by the United Nations. During the period from September 1991 to September 1994, "Human rights groups estimate[d] that Haitian soldiers and their leaders [had] killed at least 3,000 people" (Farah, 1994b, p. 6A).

In September 1994, as still another U.N. deadline for him to step down approached, General Cedras defiantly stated that he "would rather die" than surrender to the mounting international pressure (quoted in Farah, 1994a, p.

A32). One day earlier, on September 15, in a speech to the nation, President Clinton warned the Haitian military leaders to "leave now or we will force you from power" (quoted in "Clinton sends Carter," 1994, p. A1). With the United States poised to invade Haiti under U.N. mandate and with the defiant Haitian military leaders refusing to return control of the country to Aristide, the two sides had arrived at a dangerous standoff by Friday, September 16, 1994.

President Carter was familiar with the Haitian situation because of his involvement with the earlier failed election in 1987 and with the successful elections of 1990 that had brought Aristide to power. Having followed the developments in the situation over the months and years and having remained in contact with several of the principal players, President Carter knew the issues, the country, and the principal leaders in the pending confrontation.

On Thursday evening, September 15, President Clinton addressed the nation on the deteriorating situation and evolving standoff between the Haitian military and the United States and the United Nations. Clinton was very direct: "The message of the United States to the Haitian dictators is clear: Your time is up." Following the speech, Clinton called Carter to accept the former president's offer to mediate in the situation ("Dateline NBC," 1994, p. 3). Carter, who had just returned days earlier from a trip to five African nations and Russia, agreed to travel to Haiti (Sewell, 1994, p. 9A). Even as Clinton administration national security officials were saying that an invasion of Haiti was imminent, President Clinton announced on Friday afternoon that he was dispatching a delegation led by Carter to try to persuade the military leaders to relinquish power peacefully.

Whether Clinton dispatched Carter or Carter persuaded Clinton that a diplomatic settlement might be possible is not entirely clear. Press reports at the time suggested that Clinton and Carter had been conferring on Haiti for some time ("Clinton sends Carter," 1994, p. 1A). The White House described the initiative as an outgrowth of talks between Carter and Cedras. Indeed, there were reports that Carter had been in recent contact with Cedras in the days preceding the standoff, and that as early as Thursday, Carter had informed Clinton that Cedras might agree to meet with him ("Clinton sends Carter," 1994, p. A1). According to one report, it was President Carter's reputation as a nonpartisan peacemaker "that caused Haitian strongman Raoul Cedras to call him and open negotiations" (Walters, 1994, p. 9A). Other reports suggested that Carter had been working behind the scenes for two months to establish contacts with Cedras, whom he knew from earlier election-monitoring missions (Kramer, 1994, p. 35).

Both Clinton and Carter realized that there was the potential for a peaceful diplomatic settlement. President Clinton, in explaining his decision to dispatch the Carter delegation, said, "It is the responsibility of an American president to pursue every possible alternative to the use of force" (quoted in Beard, 1994a, p. 6A). The delegation that departed for Haiti on Saturday, September 17, was headed by President Carter and included retired General Colin Powell (former chairman of the Joint Chiefs of Staff), Senator Sam Nunn (chairman of the

Armed Services Committee), and several members of the Clinton national security team. Carter was chosen because of his extensive diplomatic experience and his credibility as an international mediator, Powell because of his military background and the fact that he had an established relationship with Cedras, and Nunn, who opposed Clinton administration policy in Haiti, because he could impress upon Cedras the fact that the lack of congressional approval would not prevent an invasion of Haiti from occurring. Further, Nunn could give Cedras assurances that minority parties would be protected in the transition to an Aristide administration ("Clinton sends Carter," 1994, p. 1A; Walters, 1994, p. 9A).

The Carter mission was reportedly authorized only to arrange for the departure of the Haitian military leaders or, as one administration official bluntly phrased it, to make "travel arrangements" (Beard, 1994a, p. 6A). Carter was more diplomatic when he explained, upon his arrival in Haiti, that "we have a very simple, but very important mission in Haiti: to work with Haitian officials to devise a peaceful implementation of the policies of the United States government and the resolutions passed by the Security Council of the United Nations" (quoted by Beard, 1994a, p. 6A). From the Haitian perspective, Chief of Staff General Biamby stated unequivocally that it was "absolutely false" that a compromise agreement had been negotiated by which he, Cedras, and police chief Lt. Col. Francois would step down if the American invasion were called off. The negotiations were obviously going to be complicated and, unknown to Carter, would take place against the backdrop of the tightly scheduled pending U.S. military operation.

Upon their arrival in Port-au-Prince, the Carter delegation met for three hours with Cedras and top Haitian military leaders. While Carter refused to comment on the first round of talks, a Haitian source characterized the talks as "more positive than negative," and a U.S. official reported that a working document was being discussed (quoted and reported by Beard, 1994a, p. 1A). Following the initial meeting with Cedras and the military leadership, the Carter delegation held meetings on Saturday evening with political leaders from all sides, including Aristide supporters. Even as talks were proceeding in Haiti, President Clinton, in his weekly Saturday radio broadcast, said of the Haitian leaders, "Their time is up. The remaining question is not whether they will leave but how they will leave," alluding to the pending U.S. invasion (quoted in Beard, 1994a, p. 6A). The talks dragged on until the early morning hours of Sunday, September 18.

When the first round of talks ended, no one was optimistic. Carter said at the time, "We're doing the best we can" ("Dateline NBC," 1994, p. 4). The Carter delegation was scheduled to leave Haiti by noon on Sunday. Meanwhile, two of the final key elements of the invasion force arrived in Haitian waters, the aircraft carriers *Eisenhower* and *America* with their complements of army and special operations forces and helicopters. According to Pentagon spokesman Dennis Boxx, with their arrival, "Everything is in place. The gun is cocked" (quoted in Burns, 1994b, p. 4A).

Following the first round of talks, Carter reportedly called Rosalynn. According to Rosalynn Carter, "We had heard that she [Yanick Cedras] was a very strong woman, a very religious woman, and I just thought that if Jimmy saw her and got together with the family, that it might make the difference" ("Dateline NBC," 1994, p. 4). Senator Nunn reported that a World Bank official had informed the delegation that Yanick Cedras would become key to a peaceful resolution of the conflict (Kramer, 1994, p. 35). The opportunity for a meeting with Yanick Cedras came when the Carter delegation was invited by Cedras to his home on Sunday morning, just four hours prior to the delegation's original noon deadline.

In recounting this key meeting, Senator Nunn reported that on Saturday night, Yanick Cedras had gathered her children to her bed because she felt that it was going to be their last night alive together. Yanick Cedras was convinced that their house had already been targeted, that they were not going to leave, and that they were determined to die. Yanick Cedras reportedly said, "We will die before we leave Haiti, and my husband will do the same" (quoted in Kramer, 1994, p. 36). According to the "Dateline NBC" account, Carter was despondent at hearing this, but the third member of the team, General Powell, who Nunn felt was "indispensable" to the mission, kept the talks going (quoted in Walters, 1994, p. 9A). As Senator Nunn recalled, General Cedras "was relying on Colin Powell to convince his wife that it was not the duty of the general and his family to die" (quoted in Kramer, 1994, p. 36). Devroy, in reporting on Powell's congressional briefing on the mission, said that Powell and the Cedras family spent a lot of time talking about honor, country, and the military code of conduct (Devroy, 1994, p. A12; Raum, 1994, p. 3A). Cedras was quoted as having told Powell that he and his wife "would rather take an American bullet in the chest than a Haitian bullet in the back" (quoted in Devroy, 1994, p. A12). Because of his exceptional military career, and the fact that he is an African American of Caribbean ancestry, Colin Powell appears to have had special significance and credibility with the Haitians. According to Nunn, "He [Powell] did a beautiful job explaining that sometimes the commander has a duty to preserve his military force and preserve his people and avoid senseless slaughter" (quoted in "Dateline NBC," 1994, p. 4). Powell was apparently successful in persuading Cedras and his wife that there was a peaceful way out of the situation.

During the morning and early afternoon hours of Sunday, September 18, the Carter delegation, Clinton administration officials, and the Haitians negotiated the resignation and departure deadline for the three military officials identified by the U.N. resolution. While the Haitian military leaders resisted firm commitments, Clinton administration officials were insistent on their immediate departure or on a firm deadline for their departure. The Carter delegation was placed squarely in the middle. According to Carter, forcing Cedras to resign was a part of the agreement, but "it is a serious violation of human rights for a citizen to be forced into exile" (quoted by Devroy, 1994, p. A12). Carter had to find the diplomatic middle ground between the two parties. According to

Carter, Cedras feared that his departure would plunge the country into civil war (Devroy, 1994, p. A12). The original White House policy of a final ultimatum for Cedras to accede and immediately leave the country was reconsidered, and officials began to "rethink our policy." They concluded that Cedras should remain in office until the U.S. military could secure the country (Devroy, 1994, p. A12). This plan would prevent a gap or a power vacuum between the departure of Cedras and the arrival of the U.S. invasion force.

As the original departure deadline for the Carter delegation of Sunday noon passed, the timetable was moved back to 3:00 P.M. to allow more time for negotiations. One o'clock on Sunday afternoon was a crucial time because it was the deadline for President Clinton to either give the order to begin or suspend the impending invasion of Haiti. Defense Secretary William Perry reportedly gave Clinton two options, to dispatch the troops (scheduled to arrive in Haiti at 12:01 A.M., September 19) or cancel the military strike. Clinton's response was "Pack 'em," a decision that meant that the invasion of Haiti was on at the same time that a negotiating team was actively negotiating in Port-au-Prince (quoted by Fournier, 1994, p. 1A). Timing would obviously become critical to avoid having the negotiating team caught in the middle of a major military operation.

At the same time that Clinton was issuing these orders, the Carter delegation had apparently reached agreement with Cedras and Biamby to resign, but had not established a firm deadline for their departure (Fournier, 1994, p. 5A). The Clinton administration was insisting that a firm date be set for their departure, but the Haitian leaders refused to budge. Reportedly, against this background, the Carter delegation was repeatedly told to "get out" by the Clinton administration. According to an anonymous administration source, the invasion would have taken place as scheduled "if not for the sheer stubbornness of former President Carter" (Fournier, 1994, p. 1A).

The Carter delegation and the Haitians were unaware of Clinton's decision to launch the invasion until late Sunday afternoon. When the delegation and the Haitians learned that planes were in the air, the negotiations almost fell apart. Seven hours prior to the invasion (approximately 5:00 P.M.), General Biamby received word via fax from "Haitian Americans" that the 82nd Airborne was in route (Devroy, 1994, p. A12) and accused the U.S. delegation of setting a trap ("Dateline NBC," 1994, p. 5). Biamby advised Cedras that the talks must end so that military preparations could be made (Devroy, 1994, p. A12). Upon learning that the invasion was on, Carter said, "I was distressed about it" and feared that all hope of reaching an agreement was lost (quoted in Devroy, 1994, p. A12). Carter appealed to the Haitians to continue talking, and they agreed to move the talks to the more secure offices of President Emile Jonassaint, where they were assured that the military action could be called off if an agreement was quickly reached (Devroy, 1994, p. A12).

It was at this point that Carter apparently demonstrated his sincerity to continue the negotiations and won the trust of the Haitians by telling them that he "was ashamed by the suffering that the kids [of Haiti] had suffered under our [and the U.N.'s] embargo" ("Dateline NBC," 1994, p. 5). Carter was reportedly very moved by the sick and hungry Haitian children he had seen during his trips to the country. While acknowledging that he had not carefully considered the diplomatic niceties and implications, Carter stated later, "I never was ashamed of my nation" (quoted in "Dateline NBC," 1994, p. 5).

In addition to being moved by Carter's sincerity, the Haitian military was convinced in the final hours by Colin Powell of the futility of resistance. According to a U.S. official, Powell said, "Look, I have not been all that supportive of an invasion, but I've got to tell you: This is what's going down" and then proceeded to detail what the Haitians could expect in terms of the pending invasion's overwhelming force and troop strength (Raum, 1994, p. 3A). Following the final agreements, Powell told a White House press conference upon his return that he tried to "appeal to their sense of honor and to appeal to their sense of what was wrong at this particular point in their history" (quoted by Raum, 1994, p. 3A).

While Carter thought that the move to the Haitian Presidential Palace was a waste of negotiating time, events progressed quickly after the change of venue. At 7:00 P.M., President Clinton informed Carter that the invasion was on, which meant that the agreement must be finalized or the delegation must leave ("Dateline NBC," 1994, p. 6). The move to the offices of President Jonassaint could have been problematic. Because he had been installed by the Haitian military, the Clinton administration did not recognize his authority and demanded that Cedras and Biamby personally sign any accord (Devroy, 1994, p. A12). While President Jonassaint was dismissed as a "puppet" of the Haitian military by the Clinton administration, Carter described him as the "civilian leadership" who "laid down the law" to the military as the negotiations came to a close (Devroy, 1994, p. A12). The de facto president of Haiti became a key player in finally resolving the conflict.

The agreement that was in place would require the three Haitian military leaders to step down by October 15 and to cooperate with the U.S. forces that would enter the country to oversee the peaceful transition of power to Aristide. In exchange, the Haitian Parliament would declare a general amnesty for all members of the military (Beamish, 1994, p. 5A). The sticking point at this last-minute negotiating session involved who would be allowed to sign and finalize the agreement. In recounting the final moments leading up to the signing, Senator Nunn recalled, "When he [Jonassaint] finally made his decision, and he said so very emphatically, very majestic kind of gestures, he basically said, 'Our backs are against the wall. Haiti accepts peace, not war'" (quoted in "Dateline NBC," 1994, p. 6). The question remained whether Cedras and the other two military leaders would accept the decision of Jonassaint. When asked the question, Carter recalled that Cedras responded something to the effect, "It's an insult for me to have to answer that question" ("Dateline NBC," 1994, p. 6). At that moment, General Powell told Cedras, "You have got to answer this question.

You know that the American military forces are on their way" (quoted in "Dateline NBC," 1994, p. 6). According to Carter's recollection, "Cedras stood extremely erect, at attention, and he said, 'On my word of honor as an officer of the Haitian military, I will accept the decision made by my president'" (quoted in "Dateline NBC," 1994, p. 6). Following the agreement, the American invasion force, which had been airborne and en route to Haiti since 6:47 P.M., was recalled seventy-three minutes into its mission (Beamish, 1994, p. 5A).

When Carter briefed congressional leaders on his mission to Haiti on Monday, September 19, he reported that his perception of Cedras was significantly different from that of the administration. He suggested that it was "plain wrong" to call Cedras a dictator; rather, Carter observed that Cedras had not led the coup against Aristide but had saved his life during the coup (Devroy, 1994, p. A1). Perhaps, as Carter had observed several days earlier, Cedras's motivation was that "not of a ruthless killer but of a military leader concerned with his country" (quoted by Devroy, 1994, p. A12). In one press account's description of the more than twenty hours of negotiations, "The Clinton policy became Carterized, its edges rounded, its demands softened, its rhetoric muted" (Devroy, 1994, p. A1). In any case, the arrival of American troops on Haitian soil was considerably different and safer for the troops as a result of the work of the Carter delegation.

President Clinton announced the result of the breakthrough negotiations late on Sunday evening when he told the nation, "From the beginning, I have said the Haitian dictators must go. And tonight I can say that they will go. This is a good agreement for the United States and Haiti." He also noted that Aristide would return "when the dictators depart" (quoted by Schafer, 1994, pp. 1A, 6A). The seven-paragraph agreement signed by President Jonassaint called for "certain military officers" to step down by October 15 (Schafer, 1994, p. 1A). While not mentioning them by name, the agreement clearly called for Cedras and Biamby to relinquish power, but did not require them to leave the country. Under the agreement, the dictators agreed to leave power as soon as the Haitian Parliament passed an amnesty law to protect the coup leaders (Schafer, 1994, p. 6A). However, as Secretary of State Warren Christopher observed, "I can't imagine they'd want to stay" considering the thousands of American troops that would soon be on the ground securing the country and paving the way for the return of Aristide (quoted by Schafer, 1994, p. 1A). Christopher also noted that "this is one instance where power has served diplomacy in an absolutely classic way" (quoted by Schafer, 1994, p. 1A). An Aristide spokesman expressed qualified optimism when he said, "It seems that was our coming out of a long, long dark night. Let's hope that what we expect will happen [the departure of Cedras], will happen" (Schafer, 1994, p. 6A). On October 13, Cedras and his family accepted the September 16 offer of asylum from Panama's President Ernesto Perez Balladares and left Haiti (Dorning, 1994, p. 6A; Hamm, 1994, p. 1A).

The agreement brokered by the Carter delegation averted the invasion of Haiti. According to Secretary of Defense Perry, instead of the planned nighttime paratroop drop, U.S. troops would enter Haiti on Monday morning and secure key strategic locations. The first U.S. troops did arrive on Monday morning, September 19, aboard fifteen helicopter-gunships to secure the Port-au-Prince airport (Valbrun, 1994, p. 9A). In characterizing the arrival of U.S. troops in Haiti to congressional leaders, President Clinton observed, "This is a very different and a much better day than it would have been had we not been able to successfully combine the credible threat of force with diplomacy" (quoted in "Haiti operation," 1994, p. 1A). The second phase of the operation called for establishing a secure situation in Haiti over a period of months. The third phase would involve handing over control of the situation to U.N. peacekeeping forces (Schafer, 1994, p. 6A).

Upon what some described as his triumphant return to Haiti on October 15, 1994, President Aristide declared, "Today is the day that the sun of democracy rises, never to set. Today is the day that the eyes of justice open, never to close again. Today is the day that security takes over morning, noon, and night" (quoted by Beard, 1994b, p. A1). Several days later, the Haitian Parliament, which had been closed for months by the now-deposed military leaders, reopened to take up the issue of amnesty for the very military leaders who had effectively held it hostage for the period of Aristide's exile ("Haitian Parliament meets," 1994, p. 3A). This was one of the first steps toward implementing the agreement negotiated by President Carter.

In assessing and explaining the role and success of the Carter delegation, Marion Creekmore, director of programs at the Carter Center and a veteran diplomat, noted that "President Carter was able to help the United States avert war in Haiti because of The Center's long history of involvement there" (quoted in "Jimmy Carter leads delegation," 1995, p. 4). The involvement of Carter and the Carter Center dates from the unsuccessful 1987 attempt by the Council of Freely Elected Heads of Government to arrange free and fair elections in Haiti, and the later involvement by Carter and the center to arrange and monitor the elections that brought Aristide to power. Even following the coup that deposed Aristide in September 1991, Carter and the center actively sought the restoration of democracy by meeting with and working with the United Nations, the Organization of American States, and President Aristide. According to the Carter Center, Carter and Aristide remained in contact throughout the latter's exile from office ("Jimmy Carter leads delegation," 1995, p. 4).

Following the dramatic events of September 1994, President Carter continued to be interested and involved in Haiti. In December 1994, a mission of the Council of Freely Elected Heads of Government, an organization based at the Carter Center, traveled to Haiti at the invitation of President Aristide to explore what the council could do in terms of consolidating democracy and furthering economic development ("Assessment mission to Haiti," 1995). President Carter returned to Haiti in February 1995 at the invitation of Aristide to monitor progress on security and economic issues and the movement toward democracy in Haiti. Specifically, he was invited to help prepare for elections set for June

1995 ("Haiti gives Carter cold reception," 1995, p. 2A). Lest Carter and the Carter Center be criticized for their unconditional support of Aristide, the election-monitoring team that observed the 1995 elections was very critical of the Aristide government's efforts at ensuring free and fair elections (Greenhouse, 1995, p. A5).

In the long term, defusing the immediate conflict situation in Haiti and returning the democratically elected Aristide may prove to be an easier challenge than creating any sense of stability and prosperity for the Haitian people. One U.S. aid official, noting that the government of Haiti was literally flat broke, characterized the future of Haiti by saying, "We found the money to run this country into the ground over the past three years. Will we have the money and the will to rebuild it?" (Farah, 1994c, p. 1A). According to the U.S. Agency for International Development, the Haitian situation is indeed dismal. For example, 70 percent of the urban population is unemployed, the literacy rate is less than 50 percent, the health-care system is in ruins, and there is little or limited infrastructure (Farah, 1994c, p. A30). The challenge of building democracy in Haiti, while not as immediate as the crisis the Carter delegation defused, will require the long-term committed attention of the United States and the international community. In expressing the goals of the Carter Center for Haiti, President Carter stated, "We believe that with the United States forming a partnership with Haiti, the most poverty-stricken nation in our hemisphere will grow into one based on economic progress, democracy, freedom, and respect for human rights" (quoted in "Jimmy Carter leads delegation," 1995, p. 5).

CARTER IN BOSNIA

The region of the Balkans has been in turmoil and has witnessed several different civil wars since the breakup of Yugoslavia. In particular, in 1992 the Bosnian Muslim government declared its independence from Serbian-dominated Yugoslavia. The civil war that erupted between the Bosnian Muslims and the Bosnian Serbs has claimed tens of thousands of lives—some reports mark the number of military and civilian dead as high as 200,000 (Squitieri, 1994, p. A6).

In February 1993, the Conflict Resolution Program (CRP) and the International Negotiation Network (INN) at the Carter Center held a discussion session regarding the various conflicts in the Balkans region and has since monitored ongoing developments in these conflicts ("Carter Center jump starts peace efforts," 1995, p. 3). These discussions and the policy research generated by the CRP and the INN helped to provide President Carter and representatives of the Carter Center with the background knowledge and analysis necessary to become involved with these conflict situations.   Similar policy research, discussion, and analysis have preceded Carter's missions to Ethiopia and the Sudan and, more recently, to Korea and Haiti.

In mid-December 1994, President Carter received an invitation to travel to the region from Dr. Radovan Karadzic, the leader of the Bosnian Serbs. The invitation was reportedly preceded by meetings with Karadzic's representatives at the Carter Center (Jehl, 1994e, p. 24) and by extensive contacts between Carter aides and Charles Thomas, the Clinton administration's Bosnian specialist (Sciolino, 1994, p. A3). On December 14, President Carter and Karadzic conducted back-to-back telephone interviews with the Cable News Network in which Carter described a six-point plan of promised concessions by Karadzic that, upon their implementation, would clear the way for Carter to travel to Bosnia and to meet with Karadzic (Sciolino, 1994, p. A3). The concessions included pledges of a cease-fire around Sarajevo, the freeing of U.N. peacekeepers, and human rights guarantees. These developments were greeted with skepticism by the European Community, the Clinton administration, and the United Nations. The Europeans were distrustful of Karadzic and the promised concessions, the Clinton administration neither endorsed nor discouraged the proposed trip by Carter, and a senior U.N. official paraphrased U.N. Secretary General Boutros-Ghali as warning against "a proliferation of mediators" in the Bosnian situation (Sciolino, 1994, p. A3).

In describing the invitation, President Carter said, "He called me. I didn't call him" (quoted by Lippman, 1994b, p. A39). When Karadzic asked Carter to mediate, Carter responded, "Of course I was willing to do this as a goodwill gesture" (quoted by Lippman, 1994b, p. A39). One day following the public announcement of the invitation, and perhaps with the intent of demonstrating good faith, Karadzic and the Bosnian Serbs opened the Sarajevo airport and allowed a U.N. convoy to travel to the Muslim town of Bihac. These moves on the part of the Bosnian Serbs implemented, in part, the preconditions for the Carter trip. However, at the same time, reportedly there were still forced expulsions of Muslims taking place in northeastern Bosnia (Cohen, 1994a, p. A3).

Before making final plans to travel to Bosnia, President Carter was briefed extensively by representatives from the White House, the National Security Agency, the Central Intelligence Agency, the U.S. State Department, and the United Nations. These briefings were intended to ensure that Carter was well versed on U.S. policy and could emphasize the administration's position that the Contact Group plan be the basis for negotiations. They also stressed to Carter the importance of meeting with leaders from all sides in the conflict to minimize the emphasis of his proposed meeting with Karadzic (Jehl, 1994e, p. 24).

Following these briefings, the Carter mission sought and received the approval of President Clinton to travel to the region as private citizens representing only the Carter Center ("Carter Center jump starts peace efforts," 1995, p. 1). Prior to the final announcement of his trip, Carter clearly stated, "I don't have any portfolio. . . . If I should go to Sarajevo, it would be representing The Carter Center, not representing the United States government" (quoted by Lippman, 1994b, p. A39). Some administration officials privately expressed their concern and doubts about the mission. Publicly, Leon Panetta, White House chief of staff, said, "If he can find a way to solve some of these problems, fine. But we're skeptical about his ability to do that" (quoted by Jehl, 1994e, p. 24). The Clinton administration did provide military aircraft for the delegation, and the United States and the United Nations assisted with transportation and logistical support for the trip. President Carter was tentatively scheduled to meet with Croatian President Franjo Tudjman, Bosnian Prime Minister Haris Silajdzic, and Bosnian President Alija Izetbegovic prior to deciding whether the situation warranted a meeting with Karadzic (Jehl, 1994e, p. 1). While in the Balkans, Carter also held talks with the U.N. special representative to the former Yugoslavia, representatives of the Contact Group, and various human rights groups.

The Carter mission was preceded by months of negotiations by the United Nations and representatives of the Contact Group, composed of the United States, Britain, France, Germany, and Russia. These negotiations had been unsuccessful in getting the Bosnian Serbs and the Muslim-dominated Bosnian government to accept territorial concessions designed to end the civil war. Under the Contact Group plan, which was proposed in the summer of 1993, the Serbs would receive 49 percent of the disputed territory rather than the 72 percent they had succeeded in acquiring by force of arms (Squitieri, 1994, p. A6). These territorial disputes and the Contact Group plan and percentages were important early on and would remain the fundamental point of contention and possible resolution as Carter's involvement in Bosnia developed. Land and control of territory have been central issues throughout the conflict (Rohde, 1994, p. 1). While Carter had no mandate to change the terms of the Contact Group plan, his mission would seek to get the adversaries to negotiate a mutually acceptable adjustment to the plan.

When President Carter departed for the region on December 18, some of the pledges made by Karadzic had been met; others could not be verified, thereby preventing Carter from confirming that he would, in fact, meet with Karadzic. The Carter delegation arrived in Sarajevo for talks with the various parties involved amid Serb mortar and sniper fire. Carter reiterated the goal of his mission and the position of the Contact Group when he said, "There is no other basis for future negotiations than the Contact Group plan." He also stated that he hoped that he could encourage "negotiations based on the Contact Group proposals" (quoted in Cohen, 1994c, p. A12).

In addition to talks with various factions and leaders in the region, Carter did hold more than eight hours of talks with Karadzic and the Bosnian Serbs in Pale, the Serb headquarters outside Sarajevo. As he was greeted by Karadzic in Pale on December 19, Carter said that his talks with Karadzic "will be the key to success or failure of my mission. It may be that today is one of the rare chances to let the world know the truth and to explain the commitment of the Serbs to a peace agreement. There are some difficult decisions to be made" (quoted in Kovacic, 1994). As a result of his talks with Carter, Karadzic reportedly said that new American interpretations of the Contact Group plan had transformed it into "a basis for further development" (quoted by Cohen, 1994d, p. A1). While not an acceptance of the plan, this statement by Karadzic was not the flat rejection of the plan that the Serbs had issued when it was first proposed in July 1994. According to a U.N. spokesperson, "This is the first time the Serbs have shown a willingness to even consider the plan." The spokesperson also noted that Carter's visit "was a very positive development" (Pomfret, 1994, p. A27). The Serbs also agreed to a proposed cease-fire for the region.

President Carter read the following statement following his talks with Karadzic: "We agree that while a cessation of hostilities is in effect we shall negotiate a complete peace agreement with the proposals of the Contact Group as the basis for negotiations of all points" (quoted in Cohen, 1994d, p. A1). This statement fell short of the Serbs fully accepting all parts of the Contact Group plan that Bosnian President Izetbegovic had insisted be the basis for negotiations. The points of contention remained the percentages of territory to be granted to each party. Even as a White House spokesperson reiterated the administration's position that "the Bosnian Serbs are the aggressors in this war," the Clinton administration raised no objections to the Serbian statement (Cohen, 1994e, p. A14). Reportedly, this marked a slight shift in U.S. policy away from its strong past support for the Bosnian government toward exerting equal pressure on both sides to stop the fighting (Cohen, 1994e, p. A14). This apparent policy shift was welcomed by Karadzic, who said, "If the Clinton Administration puts pressure on the Bosnian Government, real pressure, and approaches this conflict in a fair way as Mr. Carter has, then we may be able to start negotiations" (quoted by Cohen, 1994e, p. A14). In characterizing this phase of his mission, President Carter said that "if good faith is demonstrated by the Serbs on the cease-fire, on keeping the Sarajevo airport open, on United Nations convoys and on human rights, then in my opinion the United Nations can quickly lift sanctions on the Serbian side" (quoted by Cohen, 1994e, p. A14).

By December 20, Carter had succeeded in securing mutual agreements from the Bosnian Muslims and the Bosnian Serbs on the following points: a nationwide, seventy-two-hour cease-fire following Carter's departure, to be followed by a four-month cease-fire yet to be negotiated; the resumption of peace talks under the auspices of the Contact Group; unrestricted movement of relief convoys; the safe delivery of humanitarian aid; access to the Sarajevo airport during the cease-fire; access by the U.N. Commission on Human Rights to observe compliance with human rights standards; and prisoner exchanges under the direction of the International Committee of the Red Cross ("Carter Center jump starts peace efforts," 1995, p. 3). The long-term cease-fire was to be negotiated as the initial seventy-two-hour cease-fire, which would begin on December 23, was observed. While the agreement on a cease-fire was a significant accomplishment, this cease-fire had been preceded by at least thirty others since the beginning of the civil war (Cohen, 1994e, p. A1). On December 23, the details of the cease-fire were negotiated by U.N. diplomat Yasushi Akashi, and the warring parties did in fact sign the agreement.

President Carter characterized the results of his trip by saying, "There are many difficult issues and questions that still need to be resolved. It is my hope that these issues can be resolved peacefully, using the services of the Contact Group and UNPROFOR [U.N. forces] as appropriate" (quoted in "Carter Center jump starts peace efforts," 1995, p. 3).   The Clinton administration was somewhat skeptical of the results of the Carter mission because Carter had in fact emerged from his talks with two agreements.   One agreement was signed by Karadzic for the Bosnian Serbs, and one was signed by President Izetbegovic for the Bosnian government (Jehl, 1994g, p. A14).   While Carter described the differences between the agreements as "semantics," the basic issue of whether Bosnia would remain one country or be divided and partitioned between the Serbs and the Bosnian Muslims remained a fundamental difference separating the warring parties (quoted by Cohen, 1994d, p. A14).   The final acceptance or modification of the Contact Group plan would be key to resolving this issue. The territorial percentages outlined in the Contact Group plan were an issue with the Bosnian government's accepting the territorial concessions outlined in the plan, while the Serbs resisted any reference to "acceptance" of the plan, seeking rather to use the plan as the beginning point for renewed negotiations (Cohen, 1994e, p. A14).

As with other negotiation missions by President Carter, the results of his trip to the former Yugoslavia were somewhat mixed.   While he did not succeed in resolving all of the issues, he did secure a cease-fire and a pledge that negotiations would continue.   Before he left on his mission, Carter said, "I don't intend to become a permanent negotiator in Bosnia" (quoted by Lippman, 1994b, p. A39).   Rather, what Carter achieved, or what had been pledged, was movement in the stalled and stalemated peace talks.   According to one report, "Carter is seen as a neutral, open-minded envoy" by the parties involved, and, in particular, "To the Bosnian Serbs, former President Jimmy Carter is the first U.S. leader who will really listen to them" (Squitieri, 1994, p. A6).   According to the director of the Bosnian Serb news agency, "Mr. Carter has the moral stature to get peace talks going again.   Up to now, America has damaged peace prospects by not treating the two sides equally and by encouraging the Muslims in their offensives" (Cohen, 1994b, p. 24).   Another report noted, "Indeed, that has been Carter's greatest strength as he has sought to mediate one conflict after another. By not taking sides, but by listening with seemingly endless patience even to those viewed by others as villains, Carter has built an unrivaled reputation for creative diplomacy" (Lippman, 1994b, p. A39).

If there was to be a negotiated settlement to the conflict in Bosnia, the parties had to communicate with each other.   However, under a U.N. resolution passed in the summer of 1994, only the United Nations was supposed to have contact with the Bosnian Serbs.   This resolution had prevented the United States and others from having direct public contact with the Serbs since that summer (Allen, 1995, p. 4A).   Complicating any negotiations was the perception of the Bosnian Serbs as the aggressors in the conflict and the reports of human rights abuses perpetrated by the Serbs against the Muslim population.   While there was considerable evidence to support these perceptions, the fact remained that

Karadzic was a force who had to be included in any negotiated settlement. One criticism of the Carter mission by Clinton administration officials was the fact that Carter agreed to meet with Karadzic, who was perceived to be and was charged by the international community as a war criminal. Carter's meeting with Karadzic appeared to legitimize the position of the Serbs (Jehl, 1994f, p. A11). While such criticism may be justified and the characterization of Karadzic probably is accurate, if the Carter mission facilitated more direct lines of communication among the parties (which it apparently did), perhaps the conflict could be moved closer to resolution.

In January 1995, the United States notified the Bosnian government that U.S. officials would pursue contacts with the Serbs despite their rejection of the Contact Group's peace plan (Allen, 1995, p. 4A). This move marked a change, if only slight, in U.S. policy. According to one report, "[Secretary of State] Christopher's letter [to the Bosnian government] appears to represent at least a change in U.S. tactics, and an effort to build on informal links to the Bosnian Serbs that were opened by the visit of former President Jimmy Carter in December" (Allen, 1995, p. 4A). Other reports suggested that "there is some hope among U.S. and U.N. officials that Karadzic will use Carter's visit as a way to save face and accept a cease-fire" (Squitieri, 1994, p. A6). If the Serbs would accept the peace plan as the basis for negotiations—rather than as an end in itself—perhaps all parties could return to renewed negotiations designed to resolve the civil war. In the months that followed the Carter mission, a shaky cease-fire was periodically observed, fighting was renewed in several areas, and proposals for negotiations on several fronts were made.

By late spring 1995, the situation in Bosnia had again deteriorated, and the conflict appeared to be poised for renewed escalation. President Carter once again called for a renewal of peace talks. In a rare appearance by a former president before a congressional committee, Carter told the Senate Armed Services Committee in June that "we face a horrible tragedy in Bosnia. Before we go any further, let's have good-faith talks forced on the parties" by the United States and the international community (quoted by Deans, 1995, p. 20A). According to Carter, the Serbs had presented him with a compromise proposal to the original Contact Group plan under which they would retain 53 percent of the country (instead of the 72 percent they controlled by force) as the basis for renewed peace talks. In exchange for this concession, the Serbs would require specific territorial guarantees. These included access to the Adriatic Sea, control over parts of Sarajevo, some of Bosnia's eastern cities, and a wide corridor in northern Bosnia (Deans, 1995, p. 20A). According to Carter, "They've come back with an alternative proposal with some excessive modifications, but reducing their 70 percent down to 53 percent, which is not all that far from 49 percent," the figure demanded by the original Contact Group plan (quoted by Deans, 1995, p. 20A). Under the proposal, the Serbs guaranteed Carter that they would agree to yet another cease-fire, permit the delivery of humanitarian aid, and allow unrestricted movement of U.N. peacekeepers in exchange for the lifting of economic sanctions on Serbia by the international community.   In characterizing the situation at a press conference following his testimony, Carter conceded, "It may be hopeless. But if it [the new proposal] is not tried, will be a real tragedy, and the failure will be in not trying it" (quoted by Deans, 1995, p. 20A).

The fighting and talking continued throughout the summer of 1995. As fall approached, air strikes by the U.N. and NATO forces were once again used to try to force the Bosnian Serbs to the peace table. As he had done in December 1994, President Carter once again facilitated the exchange of proposals between Karadzic and the United Nations, NATO, and negotiators from the Contact Group (Cohen, 1995, p. A9). While lacking the high profile of his December trip, President Carter's continued involvement was important in the ultimate resolution of the conflict. In the wake of the air strikes, renewed talks in Geneva on September 8, 1995, resulted in what was promised to be a framework for the final resolution of the conflict ("Agreement reached," 1995, p. 2A).

The second half of 1994 was a very busy time for President Carter considering that the three missions described here were in addition to his already-busy schedule. Each mission resulted in developments toward peace and the prevention of continued violence. None of the three missions could be described as a complete success.

Hostilities were defused on the Korean Peninsula, but concessions were made, and policies were modified. Forty years of isolation had failed significantly to change North Korea's international behavior. The proposed sanctions, while further isolating North Korea, would probably not have changed the direction of its nuclear program. President Carter addressed the problem by talking directly to the North Koreans. While his mission was not designed to solve the problems involved with the North Korean nuclear program, the talks he initiated furthered the process and possibly averted the escalation of the conflict from a war of words and sanctions to a regional armed conflict.

The military dictators who had ousted President Aristide were themselves forced to leave Haiti. However, demands were softened and positions were changed, but a forcible invasion of Haiti was averted. The military dictators in Haiti had been demonized and branded as murderers and criminals by the United States and the international community. While they were certainly not guiltless, President Carter agreed to talk directly to them rather than to continue to escalate the verbal hostility. The United States was poised and capable of taking Haiti by force. President Carter's mission made this use of force unnecessary.

Even in the face of several cease-fires, the fighting in Bosnia continued. However, perhaps lives were saved during the tenuous cease-fires, and ultimately, perhaps, a negotiated settlement will be possible. As is true of most negotiation situations, the parties involved rarely receive everything they seek. In Bosnia, the results of the Carter mission are not clear-cut. While there were agreements signed, the fighting continued. While Karadzic was charged with war crimes, he remained a key leader to be dealt with in Bosnia. President Carter was probably not anxious to talk to Karadzic, yet he was willing to do so in an effort to resolve the conflict.

Perhaps the most significant conclusion to be drawn from the three peacemaking missions undertaken by President Carter during 1994 is that he was willing, if not eager, to talk to the leaders of these countries whom the international community had sought to sanction, to force from power, or simply to ignore. Equally important, the leaders of North Korea, Haiti, and the Bosnian Serbs actively sought out President Carter because of his reputation as a neutral third party and skilled mediator. From Carter's perspective, there were problems shared by the parties involved in each of these conflict situations that could only be resolved if meaningful dialogue and communication took place between the parties.

REFERENCES

Agreement reached at Bosnian peace talks. (1995, Sept. 8). *Erie Daily Times* (Associated Press), p. 2A.

Allen, A. (1995, Jan. 22). U.S. overture to Bosnian Serbs angers government. (Erie) *Times News* (Associated Press), p. 4A.

Assessment mission to Haiti, December 11–14, 1994. (1995, Jan. 5). Working paper series, the Council of Freely Elected Heads of Government. Available from the Carter Center, One Copenhill, Atlanta, GA 30307.

Beamish, R. (1994, Sept. 19). Dramatic breakthrough halts invasion. *Erie Daily Times* (Associated Press), pp. 1A, 5A.

Beard, D. (1994a, Sept. 18). Peace: Delegation tries to stop invasion. (Erie) *Times News* (Associated Press), pp. 1A, 6A.

_____. (1994b, Oct. 16). Aristide returns in triumph. (Erie) *Times News* (Associated Press), p. A1.

Burns, R. (1994a, June 17). Clinton needs details of North Korea offer. *Erie Daily Times* (Associated Press), p. 3A.

_____. (1994b, Sept. 18). Pentagon says U.S. forces now set for invasion. (Erie) *Times News* (Associated Press), p. 4A.

Carter Center jump starts peace efforts in Bosnia-Herzegovina. (1995, Winter). *Carter Center News*, pp. 1, 3.

Carter takes offer to visit North Korea. (1994, June 10). *Pittsburgh Post-Gazette* (Reuters News Service), p. A3.

Carter trip paves the way for U.S.–North Korean pact. (1995, Winter). *Carter Center News*, pp. 6, 11.

Carter visits Pyongyang; Seoul practices air raid. (1994, June 16). *Washington Post* (Washington Post Foreign Service), p. A34.

Choe, S. (1994a, June 16). Carter says North Korea plans to keep inspectors in country. *Erie Daily Times* (Associated Press), p. 2A.

_____. (1994b, July 2). Korean envoys work on details of summit. (Erie) *Times News Weekender* (Associated Press), p. 7A.

Clinton sends Carter to Haiti in peace effort. (1994, Sept. 17). (Erie) *Times News Weekender* (reprinted from *Los Angeles Times*), p. 1A.

Cohen, R. (1994a, Dec. 17). Seeking Carter visit, Bosnia Serbs ease up. *New York Times*, p. A3.

_____. (1994b, Dec. 18). Carter visit instills hope among Serbs. *New York Times*, p. 24.

_____. (1994c, Dec. 19). Carter is in Sarajevo, but no progress is reported. *New York Times*, p. A12.

_____. (1994d, Dec. 20). Serbs, meeting with Carter, agree to Bosnia cease-fire. *New York Times*, pp. A1, A14.

_____. (1994e, Dec. 21). Bosnia foes agree to 4-month truce, Carter reports. *New York Times*, pp. A1, A14.

_____. (1995, Sept. 5). A NATO deadline in Bosnia passes without attack. *New York Times*, pp. 1A, 9A.

Dateline NBC. (1994, Sept. 23). Minute by minute. Transcript by Burrelle's Information Services, Box 7, Livingston, NJ 07039.

Deans, B. (1995, June 15). Carter says rebel Serbs will swap land for peace. *Cleveland Plain Dealer* (Cox News Service), p. 20A.

Devroy, A. (1994, Sept. 20). Carter swayed Clinton into bending in talks. *Washington Post*, pp. A1, A12.

Dorning, M. (1994, Sept. 18). Fearful Haitians leave their homes. (Erie) *Times News* (reprinted from *Chicago Tribune*), p. 6A.

Downie, A. (1993, Oct. 25). U.N. negotiator seeks to help resolve Haiti crisis. Reuters News Service (available through CD NewsBank 1995 Comprehensive).

Farah, D. (1994a, Sept. 16). Leaders defiant as U.S. warships mass for attack. *Washington Post*, pp. A1, A32.

_____. (1994b, Sept. 18). Thorny societal conflicts await U.S. forces; however, they eventually arrive. (Erie) *Times News* (reprinted from *Washington Post*), p. 6A.

_____. (1994c, Sept. 23). Tough task in Haiti: Reviving Economy. *Washington Post*, pp. A1, A30.

The fish deal that got away. (1994, Nov. 20). *Parade Magazine*, p. 14.

Fournier, R. (1994, Sept. 19). Carter ignores "give up" order. *Erie Daily Times* (Associated Press), pp. 1A, 5A.

French, H. W. (1991, Feb. 8). Haiti installs democratic chief, its first. *New York Times*, p. A3.

Gordon, M. R. (1994a, June 17). Clinton may add G.I.'s in Korea while remaining open to talks. *New York Times*, p. A1.

_____. (1994b, June 18). U.S. shift on Korea. *New York Times*, pp. A1, A6.

_____. (1994c, June 20). Back from Korea, Carter declares the crisis is over. *New York Times*, pp. A1, A3.

_____. (1994d, June 22). U.S. offers North Korea a chance to resume talks. *New York Times*, p. A10.

Greenhouse, S. (1995, July 21). Election monitor criticizes Haitian vote for widespread fraud. *New York Times*, p. A5.

Haiti gives Carter cold reception. (1995, Feb. 24). *Erie Daily Times* (Associated Press), p. 2A.

Haiti operation to last months. (1994, Sept. 20). *Erie Daily Times* (Associated Press), pp. 1A, 9A.

Haitian Parliament meets in first step toward democracy. (1994, Sept. 28). *Erie Daily Times* (Associated Press), p. 3A.

Hamilton, D. P. (1994, June 10). North Korea threatens war against Japan. *Wall Street Journal*, p. A6.

Hamm, L. M. (1994, Sept. 13). Cedras flees to Panama. *Erie Daily Times* (Associated Press), pp. 1A, 10A.

Jehl, D. (1994a, June 11). U.S. is pressing sanctions for North Korea. *New York Times*, p. 7.

_____. (1994b, June 20). Carter, his own emissary, outpaces White House. *New York Times*, p. A3.

_____. (1994c, June 21). Clinton is hopeful yet cautious about Carter's North Korea trip. *New York Times*, p. A6.

_____. (1994d, June 23). Clinton finds North Koreans really may be ready to talk. *New York Times*, pp. A1, A6.

_____. (1994e, Dec. 18). Carter takes off for Bosnia on broadened peace mission. *New York Times*, pp. 1, 24.

_____. (1994f, Dec. 20). U.S. cautious on new offer by the Serbs. *New York Times*, p. A11.

_____. (1994g, Dec. 21). U.S. officials voice doubts on truce pact. *New York Times*, p. A14.

Jimmy Carter leads delegation to negotiate peace with Haiti. (1995, Winter). *Carter Center News*, pp. 4-5.

Korean nuclear talks resume. (1994, Sept. 23). *Erie Daily Times* (Associated Press), p. 2A.

Kovacic, J. (1994, Dec. 19). Carter says Bosnian Serbs want peace. Reuters News Service. (Available through CD NewsBank 1995 Comprehensive).

Kramer, M. (1994, Oct. 3). The Carter connection. *Time*, 30–38.

Lewis, P. (1994, June 16). U.S. offers a plan for U.N. sanctions on North Koreans. *New York Times*, pp. A1, A12.

Lippman, T. W. (1994a, June 25). Clinton may meet with N. Korean leader. *Washington Post*, p. A17.

_____. (1994b, Dec. 15). The mediator's strength: "I'm not taking sides." *Washington Post*, p. A39.

Murray, K. (1993, Oct. 26). Haitian political standoff thrown into Parliament. Reuters News Service. (Available through CD NewsBank 1995 Comprehensive).

North Korea's leader dies. (1994, July 9). (Erie) *Times News Weekender* (Associated Press), p. 1A.

Pomfret, J. (1994, Dec. 22). Carter's down-home style eased way for accord. *Washington Post*, p. A27.

Putnam, W. (1994, Sept. 21). Carter returns to Korean peace effort. *Erie Daily Times* (Associated Press), p. 3A.

Raum, T. (1994, Sept. 21). Colin Powell may be the Eisenhower of the '90s; courted by Dems and GOP. *Erie Daily Times* (Associated Press), p. 3A.

Resolving intra-national conflicts: A strengthened role for non-governmental actors. (1992, Jan.). Conference Report Series, vol. 3, no. 2. Available from the Carter Center, One Copenhill, Atlanta, GA 30307.

Roche, A. (1994, June 20). South Korea moves soldiers into DMZ. *Washington Post*, p. A12.

Rohde, D. (1994, Dec. 22). A Bosnia cease-fire may depend on Serb intentions in land swap. *Christian Science Monitor*, p. 1.

Sanger, D. E. (1994a, June 14). North Korea quits atom agency in wider rift with U.S. and U.N. *New York Times*, pp. A1, A12.

_____. (1994b, June 17). Carter optimistic after North Korea talks. *New York Times*, p. A10.

_____. (1994c, June 18). Carter visit to North Korea: Whose trip was it really? *New York Times*, p. A6.

_____. (1994d, June 19). Two Koreas agree to summit meeting on nuclear issue. *New York Times*, pp. A1, A12.

Schafer, S. (1994, Sept. 19). Invasion averted: Haiti's rulers to step down. (Erie) *Morning News* (Associated Press), pp. 1A, 6A.

Sciolino, E. (1994, Dec. 16). Carter's Bosnia effort provokes skepticism. *New York Times*, p. A3.

Sewell, D. (1994, Sept. 25). Jimmy's world: Haiti mission spotlights ex-president's new role. (Erie) *Times News* (Associated Press), p. 9A.

Smith, R. J. (1994, June 17). "Promising" signs seen in N. Korea. *Washington Post*, pp. A1, A20.

Smith, R. J. and Devroy, A. (1994, June 21). U.S. debates shift on North Korea. *Washington Post*, pp. A1, A12.

Smith, R. J., and Graham, B. (1994, June 18). Carter faulted by White House on North Korea. *Washington Post*, pp. A1, A20.

Smith, R. J., and Reid, T. R. (1994, June 14). North Korea quits U.N. nuclear body. *Washington Post*, p. 1.

Squitieri, T. (1994, Dec. 19). Both sides have high hopes for Carter's mission to Bosnia. *USA Today*, p. A6.

Stone, A. (1994, June 15). Citizen Carter, the statesman. *USA Today*, p. A4.

Sun, L. H. (1994, June 17). North Korea presents China with dilemma. *Washington Post*, p. A20.

U.S. clarifies N. Korea policy. (1994, June 18). (Erie) *Times News Weekender* (Associated Press), p. 3A.

U.S., North Korea begin talks. (1994, July 9). (Erie) *Times News Weekender* (Associated Press), p. 7A.

U.S., North Korea sign nuke program pact. (1994, Oct. 22). (Erie) *Times News Weekender* (Associated Press), p. 2A.

Valbrun, M. (1994, Sept. 20). Haitians seem reserved, happy as peace-keeping force arrives. *Erie Daily Times* (Knight-Ridder Newspapers), p. 9A.

Walters, N. (1994, Sept. 20). Carter, Powell, Nunn are heros. *Erie Daily Times* (Knight-Ridder Newspapers), p. 9A.

CHAPTER 7

PEACEMAKING THROUGH DEMOCRATIZATION

President Carter is well known for, and has received considerable media attention as a result of, his efforts to arrange and monitor free and fair elections in developing countries. As was suggested in chapter 3, peace requires more than the absence of war and hostility; it requires the cultivation of the processes of agreeing. One aspect of such cultivation takes the form of enhancing and furthering the cause of democracy worldwide. If people are to live in peace, they must have the freedom and power to ensure and determine their own futures. Carter's election-monitoring efforts are related to both the necessary and sufficient conditions for peace. Elections can be a vehicle for ending conflicts between parties in a country and can help ensure future peaceful relations by empowering citizens to determine and chart their own futures. Since leaving the White House, President Carter and the Carter Center have worked to spread democracy through his election-monitoring activities in Latin America and the Caribbean and in several African countries.

THE COUNCIL OF FREELY ELECTED HEADS
OF GOVERNMENT

In November 1986, ten current and former presidents and prime ministers of Western Hemisphere countries gathered at the Carter Center to participate in a consultation entitled "Reinforcing Democracy in the Americas," which was cochaired by former Presidents Carter and Ford. The conference explored the meaning of democracy, why it had failed in the past and how it could succeed in the future, and what could be done to further democracy in developing countries ("Latin American and Caribbean Program," 1987, p. 6). These leaders formed the Council of Freely Elected Heads of Government, so that, individually and collectively, they could strengthen and reinforce democracy throughout the Western Hemisphere. The council formally announced its existence in a telegram to the heads of government in the region and the secretaries general of the United Nations and the Organization of American States. The telegram stated, in part, "We would be on call to existing international organizations or to those democratic heads of government who need help in alleviating threats to their democracies" (quoted in "Latin American and Caribbean Program," 1987, p. 6). The council has been very active throughout the region since its inception.

President Carter's election-monitoring activities have been conducted under the auspices of the council, which he chairs, and which operates as a part of the Latin American and Caribbean Program at the Carter Center. The council is composed of some twenty current and former freely elected heads of state from Western Hemisphere countries ("Carter Center at a glance," 1992, 1994). More recently, Carter has expanded his election-monitoring efforts to include emerging democracies in Africa in conjunction with the African Governance Program at the Carter Center. In the pages that follow, several of these election-monitoring efforts will be profiled, in addition to a long-term program of the council to strengthen democracy in Mexico.

WORKING TOWARD DEMOCRACY IN LATIN AMERICA AND THE CARIBBEAN

Elections in Panama (1989, 1994)

In May 1989, President Carter was invited by the parties involved in organizing the Panamanian elections to lead an international delegation from eight different countries in the region to monitor the elections (Applebome, 1989, p. A9). Carter's efforts were sanctioned by and coordinated with the Bush administration.

The elections were marked by violence directed by then Panamanian President Manuel Noriega against other candidates, political parties, and the Panamanian people. Carter observed, "He [Noriega] had no concept of the possibility that the people were going to vote against him" (quoted in "Election that wasn't," 1989, p. 47). While President Carter was cordially received by Noriega the day before the election, he refused to talk with Carter after the results became clear (Doerner, 1989, p. 42). One reporter observed that "Noriega underestimated Carter" (Galloway, 1989, p. 31).

Following the elections, and in spite of Noriega's claims of victory, independent polls by the Catholic church indicated that the hand-picked Noriega presidential candidate had lost the election by a three-to-one margin to opposition candidate Guillermo Endara. Based on his team's monitoring efforts, President Carter declared, "The government is taking the election by fraud. It's robbing the people of their legitimate rights," and further challenged, "I hope there will be a world-wide outcry against a dictator [Noriega] who stole this election from his own people" (quoted in Grunson, 1989, p. A1). Noriega declined efforts by Carter and the Spanish prime minister to mediate an honorable transition from power (Galloway, 1989, p. 30). Carter notified the Organization of American States of the election results and asked it to take action against Noriega, whose activities it subsequently condemned ("Waging peace," 1993, p. 19). Ultimately, it would take the U.S. military and Operation Just Cause to remove President Noriega from power and to establish an elected government for the Panamanian people. Following the U.S. invasion of Panama, Guillermo Endara, who was projected to have won the election had Noriega not intervened, was sworn into office on a U.S. military base.

Presidential elections in Panama would not be held again until May 1994. These elections were also monitored and observed by President Carter and 1,200 other international and Panamanian observers ("Candidate with links to Noriega," 1994, p. 1). Ernesto Perez Balladares, a millionaire banker and businessman with ties to the ousted General Noriega, was the victor in the 1994 elections. In assessing the elections, President Carter noted that "reports from the various observers and officials all suggest that everything is going well" (French, 1994, p. A5). President Carter compared the 1989 elections with those in 1994: "In the 1989 elections, the Panamanian people were denied their democratic right to choose their leaders. Today, we must congratulate the Panamanian people, President Endara, the Electoral Tribunal, and all the leaders in the political arena for their extraordinary expression of civic participation" ("Council witnesses," 1994, p. 5). Carter Center representatives were invited by both the winners and losers to assist with the transition of power from President Endara to President-elect Balladares.

Elections in Nicaragua (1989, 1990)

President Carter and the council played an instrumental role in arranging for elections in war-torn Nicaragua, organizing and monitoring those elections, and mediating the peaceful transfer of power from the Sandinista regime to the newly elected government. At the February 1989 inauguration of Carlos Andres Perez, the newly elected president of Venezuela, Nicaraguan President Daniel Ortega discussed his plans to move up the date for Nicaraguan elections from November to February 1990 with President Carter and other leaders in the area. He also proposed reforms in Nicaraguan electoral policies ("Observing Nicaragua's elections," 1990, p. 14). On February 15, 1989, the Central American Accord, which described the electoral processes to be followed and President Ortega's agreement to invite international observers, was signed in El Salvador, thereby paving the way for the elections to proceed.

In September 1989, the Carter Center established an office in Managua, Nicaragua, to act as the council's representative in Nicaragua for the duration of the election process ("Observing Nicaragua's elections," 1990, p. 11). The presence of the council during the planning process, voter registration, and the campaign phases of the elections helped to ensure that free and fair elections would take place in February 1990. During the period from September 1989 to

February 1990, several trips by President Carter and Carter Center delegations reinforced the commitment of President Carter and the council to promote democracy in Nicaragua.

The stature of President Carter and the council as impartial election monitors was demonstrated by the fact that they were simultaneously invited to monitor the elections by the Sandinistas, the Nicaraguan Electoral Council, and the United Nicaraguan Opposition ("Role likely for Carter," 1989, p. A8). In all, 1,300 election observers representing the council, the United Nations, the OAS, and the U.S. government monitored the elections (Uhlig, 1990, p. A3). While these groups worked to ensure free and fair elections, media accounts at the time suggested that President Carter "played a crucial role in paving the way for the Sandinistas to hand over power to President-Elect Chamorro" ("Jimmy Carter's second chance," 1990, p. 35).

By 9:30 P.M., February 25, the evening of the election, the U.N. ballot count provided a clear indication that President Daniel Ortega would be defeated. At 11:30 P.M., President Ortega invited President Carter and other international observers to Sandinista headquarters to discuss the results (Babbit, 1990, p. 18). As the results became clear, a series of early morning meetings between Carter and the key players paved the way for the peaceful transition of power (Hockstader, 1990, p. A19). During these meetings, President Carter convinced President Ortega to release the election results. At the same time, he persuaded President-elect Violeta Chamorro to give Ortega the time he needed to prepare his administration for the announcement of the results. Carter also convinced Chamorro to call for the immediate demobilization of the contras, which required Chamorro to break a campaign promise to keep the contras as a military force ("Jimmy Carter's second chance," 1990, p. 35). Following these meetings, Carter coordinated his efforts in the country by contacting U.S. Secretary of State James Baker regarding a constructive U.S. response to the results. According to Carter, Secretary Baker "said all that we asked him to say" ("Jimmy Carter's second chance," 1990, p. 35). Following the announcement of the results, the key groups who had arranged and monitored the elections remained to work with the winners and the losers during the transition period from the elections until the inauguration of President Chamorro in April 1990.

While Carter critics charged that he failed as president to prevent the Sandinistas from taking power in 1979, it was his persistence and commitment to peaceful principles that resulted in his efforts to assure free and fair elections, the peaceful transfer of power, and the promise of democracy in Nicaragua. Former Arizona Governor Bruce Babbit, who served as one of the election observers, commented following the elections that "for the first time in history, a Communist leader who had seized power by force was relinquishing it, peacefully and more or less voluntarily, to the opposition" (Babbit, 1990, p. 18).

Following the elections, President Carter's continued personal involvement in consolidating and furthering democracy in Nicaragua included a March 1991 trip to encourage international support for the newly elected government's economic recovery program.   These efforts included personal appeals to the leaders of Japan, Canada, and Germany to assist Nicaragua with its large international debt. Commenting on this trip, Carter said, "Our efforts to facilitate a free election in Nicaragua were fruitful, but the process of consolidating democracy will take more time" (quoted in "Democracy takes root," 1991, p. 11).

Elections in Haiti

Haiti is the second-oldest independent nation in the Western Hemisphere and the oldest black republic in the world. Almost two hundred years of Haitian history have been characterized by poverty and oppression and most recently by a brutal dictatorship. Modern Haitian history, at least until February 1986, was dominated by the Duvalier family, who ruled the country for twenty-eight years. When the dictatorship of Jean-Claude Duvalier finally collapsed in February 1986, the country was plunged into several years of political turmoil and a succession of military leaders.

In October 1986, following the ouster of Duvalier, the provisional military junta held elections for a commission that was to write a new Haitian constitution.   This commission was to be the first step toward presidential elections in November 1986. Old political habits intervened, and the military junta ensured control of the commission by appointing one-third of its members. According to reports, less than 10 percent of the electorate voted for commission members, and the elections took place "in a Duvalierist climate of fear and insecurity that has been perpetrated by the army" ("After Duvalier," 1986, p. 476). The same report suggested that the U.S. State Department, eager for the Haitian government to succeed, sponsored programs by the U.S. Agency for International Development to reform the legal and judicial system, and the U.S. Information Agency brought prominent Haitians to witness U.S. elections in November 1986. The establishment of the Haitian election commission took place against the backdrop of an October 9, 1986, Americas Watch/National Coalition for Haitian Refugees report titled "Duvalierism since Duvalier." This report charged that little had changed under the military junta, and that Haitians continued to experience the same terror as they had under Duvalier ("After Duvalier," 1986, p. 476).

On November 29, 1987, presidential elections, mandated by the new Haitian constitution and scheduled by the military junta of General Henri Namphy, ended in widespread bloodshed and violence. The violence and bloodshed were, at worst, orchestrated by or, at best, ignored by the military junta. Haitian and international observers halted the elections in hopes of stopping the violence that would eventually claim more than fifty lives. At the same time, General Namphy dissolved the independent electoral commission, a move that was seen by Haitians and diplomats alike as a "coup d'etat against the constitution" (Smolowa, 1987, p. 38). When General Namphy appeared on Haitian television to explain why the elections had been suspended, he charged that the electoral commission had failed to maintain "law and order" and had been negotiating with foreign powers to "interfere in the internal affairs of the country" (quoted in Rodman, 1988, p. 48). Commenting on the election violence and the response of the government, a U.S. State Department official said, "They [the military junta] were simply unwilling to stop the violence. The army failed in its responsibilities" (Smolowa, 1987, p. 38). The violence and suspension of the elections were the culmination of the military junta's efforts, begun as early as June 1987, to derail any attempt at democracy in Haiti (Rodman, 1988, p. 48). Clearly, the attempts made at establishing democracy in Haiti following the departure of Duvalier, including the attempt to establish a free and independent Haitian electoral commission and the scheduled presidential elections, had ended in disaster and had moved Haiti closer to anarchy than to democracy.

Following the election violence, U.S. officials suspended $66 million in economic and military aid to Haiti and urged that new elections be scheduled as soon as possible. U.S. officials carefully avoided accusing the Namphy government of subverting the elections (Smolowa, 1987, p. 39). Though the failed election ended in disaster, an electoral commission member characterized the Haitian people's spirit and determination to establish a democracy when he said, "Even if we are massacred by the hundreds, we will never turn back" (Smolowa, 1987, p. 40).

Between the first attempt at democratic elections in 1987 and the elections of December 1990, several presidents, who were installed by the military, served in Haiti. In early 1988, the military junta conducted an election and installed a president. This election drew only 4 percent of the electorate and was boycotted by most candidates. Early in 1990, another interim government was formed with Supreme Court Justice Ertha-Pascal Trouillot serving as acting president. One of the goals of this interim government was to organize a successful presidential election, originally scheduled for November but later rescheduled for December 1990.

President Carter and the council became involved in these 1990 Haitian elections at the invitation of interim President Ertha-Pascal Trouillot and the major political parties in Haiti. The council's election-monitoring efforts were cosponsored by the National Democratic Institute for International Affairs. President Carter was accompanied on the December 1990 monitoring mission by Prime Minister George Price of Belize and former U.S. Deputy Secretary of State John Whitehead ("Haiti inaugurates first freely elected president," 1990, p. 6).

The work of President Carter and the council in helping to bring democracy to Haiti through free and fair elections began in July 1989 when Carter made the first of several visits to the Caribbean country. During a September 1990 trip, Carter reported that "the Electoral Council for the first time was receiving support from the colonels and other mid-level officers in all regions" (Carter, 1990, p. 2). He reported that despite attempts by the Council of State to declare the decisions of President Trouillot null and void, support from General Herard

Abraham, army commander-in-chief, enabled the efforts designed to lead to fair elections to continue.

Jean-Bertrand Aristide was elected president of Haiti on December 16, 1990. International observers, including the delegation from the council and the National Democratic Institute, concluded that the elections were free and fair. The council, the OAS, and the United Nations conducted a quick count to ensure the accuracy of the results ("Haiti inaugurates first freely elected president," 1990, p. 6).

On February 7, 1991, Jean-Bertrand Aristide, a thirty-seven-year-old Catholic priest from a small rural parish who had struggled against the Duvalier dictatorship, was sworn in as Haiti's first democratically elected president. Eudrice Raymond, the president of the newly elected Haitian Senate, said that the inauguration of Aristide represented "the overthrow of a system of repression and darkness" (quoted in French, 1991, p. A3). President Carter commented, "I hope that the inauguration of Jean-Bertrand Aristide will mark the beginning of a long democratic tradition in Haiti, a country that has suffered at the hands of brutal dictators throughout history. The people of Haiti chose Father Aristide in a free and fair election, and he has a clear mandate to bring his people together under the rule of law" (quoted in "Haiti inaugurates first freely elected president," 1990, p. 6). Dr. Robert Pastor, director of the Carter Center's Latin American and Caribbean Program, observed that "with the support of his people and that of the international community, President Aristide has a unique opportunity to build a just and democratic Haiti" ("Haiti inaugurates first freely elected president," 1990, p. 6). In looking toward the future, many Aristide supporters feared that the United States would be less than supportive of the Aristide administration because of his criticism of American foreign policy (French, 1991, p. A3). In attempting to reassure and calm such fears, Dr. Louis Sullivan, who represented the Bush administration at Aristide's inauguration, stated, "We want to work in every way we can, as desired by the new Haitian Government, on whatever we can do to help" (quoted in French, 1991, p. A3).

The election of Aristide marked the beginning of democracy in Haiti. However, several months after his inauguration, yet another military junta would force Aristide to flee the country. Just as President Carter had lent his support to the election that brought Aristide to office, it was President Carter who played an instrumental role in returning President Aristide to office in the fall of 1994, as was described in chapter 6. The Carter Center continues to be involved in furthering democracy in Haiti, for example, in monitoring parliamentary elections in 1995.

Elections in Guyana

In mid-October 1990, President Carter traveled to Guyana to assist with the first free and fair elections in more than twenty-five years for this Latin American country. Carter was invited to be an election monitor by President

Hugh Desmond Hoyte and the opposition political parties ("Carter to pay Guyana a visit," 1990, p. A4). Even before gaining its independence in 1966, Guyana had been ruled by a single political party, the People's National Congress (PNC).

In order to facilitate open elections, the government of President Hoyte agreed to major electoral reforms recommended by President Carter and Dr. Robert Pastor of the Carter Center. According to Pastor, the two major obstacles to free and fair elections were an outdated voter registration list, which omitted some names and contained the names of deceased citizens, and the centralized vote-counting method. Plans for an updated and accurate voter registration list and for accurate vote counts at the local level were negotiated by the council and accepted by both sides. In summarizing these negotiations, Pastor said, "President Carter helped bridge the differences between the government and the opposition, and both have now cheered these important reforms and anticipate a free and fair election" ("Council forges historic election reforms," 1990, p. 7).

On October 5, 1992, the people of Guyana participated in the country's first free and fair presidential election in twenty-eight years. The elections were originally scheduled for December 1991, but were postponed at the recommendation of the council to allow sufficient time to correct problems with the voter registration process ("Guyanese election postponed," 1991, p. 11). The elections were the culmination of two years of electoral reform work by President Carter and the council, including the establishment of an office in the capital of Georgetown ("Guyanese officials commit," 1992, p. 12).

While the elections were marked by some violence in Georgetown, overall they were declared free and fair by the international observation teams, including representatives of the council. At a news conference following the elections, President Carter said, "Ninety-eight percent of the polling sites were peaceful, and the elections were free and fair" (quoted in "Guyana moves closer to democracy," 1992, p. 4). The declaration of a free and fair election was the result of the presence of an international observation team. Joining President Carter in leading the international monitoring team were Prime Minister George Price of Belize and former Costa Rican President Rodrigo Carazo ("Guyana moves closer to democracy," 1992, p. 1). Reports by Robert Pastor of the Carter Center suggested that the presence of President Carter at the Election Commission helped to protect the commission's chairman, Rudolph Collins, from attack until police could arrive to secure the commission. Pastor concluded, "Electoral reforms set the foundation for a free election, but these three factors—the quick count, the observation forms, and the defense of the Elections Commission—made the difference between a stolen [election] and a fair one" (quoted in "Guyana moves closer to democracy," 1992, p. 4).

Monitoring teams visited polling sites throughout the country despite the danger and threats of violence. Initial counts indicated that the opposition People's Progressive Party (PPP) had clearly won the presidential election. The "quick count" by the monitoring teams was used as a means of checking the validity of the official count. Reports by the council indicated that the PPP won

52 percent of the national vote and thirty-two seats in Parliament, and President Hoyte and the PNC received 41 percent of the vote and thirty seats in Parliament ("Guyana moves closer to democracy," 1992, p. 4).

Elections alone cannot ensure the peaceful transition of power from an old administration to a new one, especially with such a close vote. Following the elections, defeated President Hoyte urged national reconciliation when he conceded the election to President-elect Cheddi Jagan. President Carter and Pastor met with the president and president-elect to discuss the transition of power to a new administration. Each side assured the other of its commitment to democracy in order to relax ethnic fears and encourage the nation to move forward together ("Guyana moves closer to democracy," 1992, p. 4). Noting the close vote and the hope for a democratic future in Guyana, Pastor suggested, "The benefit of a close vote is that all parties will have an incentive to work together" (quoted in "Guyana moves closer to democracy," 1992, p. 4). After President-elect Jagan was sworn into office on October 9, 1992, President Carter and the council offered their ongoing support as Guyana moved toward democracy.

In his most recent trip to Guyana in 1994, President Carter worked to consolidate the gains made possible by the 1992 elections. Noting the ongoing difficulties in establishing democracy in Haiti following recent elections there, President Carter and the council have come to recognize that elections alone do not guarantee economic stability, prosperity, or tranquility in a society. During the 1994 trip, Carter wanted to draw world attention to the fragile new democracy in Guyana, something that did not happen after the Haitian elections, and to establish or foster a dialogue between the new Guyanese government and development and economic assistance agencies that could support the new government. Extensive consultations took place between Carter Center representatives and President Jagan and officials from his government. An in-country conference of the economic development community, led by the World Bank, brought officials from Guyana together with potential backers from more developed countries in the region. The conference resulted in pledges of substantial resources for Guyana. The parties involved also urged the Carter Center to continue to work closely with the new government in order to ensure that existing aid funds would be used in a timely and proper manner.

Guyana would become a test case for the Carter Center's goal of fostering sustainable development in emerging democracies. Working in conjunction with the Environmental Initiative and the Global Development Initiative of the Carter Center, the Guyanese government formulated a comprehensive development plan for Guyana's future economic, political, and social life ("Waging peace," 1993, p. 14). President Carter summarized his 1994 trip to Guyana by noting, "By bringing all these groups together to develop a sound long-range plan, we are cutting the risks of an economic stalemate that could lead to violent conflict and the collapse of this beautiful country," and further, "After this visit, we are encouraged by the prospects of success and believe that Guyana truly has the opportunity to be a model of what all of us working together can do" (quoted in "Carter Center correspondence," March 15, 1994, pp. 3–4).

Elections in Paraguay

On May 9, 1993, the citizens of Paraguay elected Juan Carlos Wasmosy to be the country's first civilian president in four decades. This was the second election to be held in Paraguay following the fall of dictator Alfredo Stroessner in late 1989. President Wasmosy succeeded General Andres Rodriguez, who was elected in 1989 after he led the bloody coup that ended the lengthy dictatorship of Stroessner, who had ruled Paraguay since 1954.

Three main candidates vied for the presidency of Paraguay. Juan Carlos Wasmosy, a wealthy construction tycoon, represented the long-dominant Colorado Party. Domingo Laino, author of several books on corruption in Paraguay, outspoken critic of the Stroessner government, and winner of several prizes for his fight for democracy and human rights in Paraguay, represented the Authentic Radical Liberal Party. Finally, Guillermo Caballero Vargas, a wealthy textile industrialist, founded and represented the National Unity Alliance (Jarvie, 1993a, 1993b). Opinion polls prior to the election gave a clear lead to Caballero, but no party was expected to achieve a clear majority. This led Caballero to comment, "We will be forced to sit down at a negotiating table with the other parties to work out a durable policy" (quoted in Jarvie, 1993a). The differences between the candidates appeared to be ones of party rather than policy, given the similarity in the programs being advocated. All proposed a free-market economy and the overhaul of the education, health, social security, and judicial systems (Jarvie, 1993a).

President Carter became involved in the election process when opposition parties became concerned about ensuring the integrity of the elections. During the campaign, General Oviedo of the Paraguayan military reportedly stated that the military's alliance with the long-ruling Colorado Party would remain unbreakable ("Delegation's presence," 1993, p. 7). It was the Colorado Party that had been used by Stroessner to legitimize his thirty-four years in power. Such statements by military leaders were taken as threats by the three main presidential candidates, including the Colorado candidate, who then contacted President Carter and invited him to observe the elections. Opposition candidates said that they "expect[ed] attempts at fraud from Colorado factions reluctant to relinquish their 45-year stranglehold on power" (Jarvie, 1993b). Candidate Caballero told journalists, "It is frightening how the official [Colorado] party has such a well developed know-how when it comes to committing fraud" (quoted by Jarvie, 1993a). In responding to the request by the opposition parties and the potential for problems, President Carter said, "This kind of activity would not be so serious in most countries, but in one like Paraguay, just emerging tenuously from military dictatorship, it was truly intimidating and threatening" (quoted in "Delegation's presence," 1993, p. 7).

Between May 5 and May 11, 1993, President Carter led a thirty-one-person international delegation to observe the elections in Paraguay and to assure their integrity. The Carter team was among a reported two hundred foreigners invited to observe the elections (Jarvie, 1993b). The total number of observers, two hundred international and twenty thousand from the National Unity Alliance, were deployed at hundreds of polling stations to monitor procedures and check complaints of irregularities. The Carter monitoring team was jointly sponsored by the council and the National Democratic Institute for International Affairs. Joining President Carter on the monitoring team were the former president of Costa Rica, Rodrigo Carazo, and Canadian Senator Al Graham. Commenting on his mission, Carter said, "My task is to observe the elections and ensure that they take place in an orderly manner and accurately reflect the will of the people" (quoted in Jarvie, 1993b).

The council reported that overall, the elections went smoothly. However, in some areas there were reports of fraud, there was one incident of election sabotage that was directed at the communication systems of an independent vote-counting organization, and there was an attack on a radio and television station sympathetic to the opposition in which the building was strafed by machine-gun fire (Jarvie, 1993b). President Carter reported, "The overall voting process was satisfactory at 92.5 percent of the voting tables that we surveyed" (quoted in "Delegation's presence," 1993, p. 7). In commenting on the negative incidents that occurred, Carter stated, "There is no doubt our presence helped to stabilize the situation in moments of crisis and made it possible for all candidates to accept the results calmly and graciously" (quoted in "Delegation's presence," 1993, p. 7).

Between 70 and 80 percent of the country's 1.7 million electorate participated in this, the first truly democratic election in Paraguay's 182-year history, and the first election in which the country chose a nonmilitary president (Jarvie, 1993a). Juan Carlos Wasmosy of the Colorado Party, who was backed by outgoing President Andres Rodriguez and the armed forces, received 40 percent of the vote. Guillermo Caballero Vargas of the centrist coalition National Encounter Party received 25 percent of the vote, and Domingo Laino of the Authentic Radical Liberal Party received 33 percent of the vote ("Delegation's presence," 1993, p. 7). Voters also cast ballots for national and provincial governmental offices during this election.

The involvement of President Carter and the council in Paraguay spanned two years and culminated in the first verifiably free elections. Robert Pastor summarized these efforts by saying that Paraguay's election was "successful in being respected by all parties; every country in South America has now held free, competitive elections." Looking toward the future, Pastor noted, "The next step for the hemisphere is to forge new bonds to preserve, consolidate, and deepen the new democracies" (quoted in "Delegation's presence," 1993, p. 7). The same continued vigilance and involvement that were required in Guyana are necessary in Paraguay if the gains made at the ballot box are to be secured long term.

Strengthening Democracy in Mexico

President Carter, the Latin American and Caribbean Program, and the Council of Freely Elected Heads of Government have worked not only to establish democracies in the Western Hemisphere, but also to strengthen existing democracies, most notably in Mexico. While Mexican politicians and government officials historically have been resistant to any outside involvement in Mexican elections, the Carter Center has been involved with issues related to elections and electoral reform in Mexico since 1990, culminating in several exchanges of observer delegations in 1992 and 1994 ("Electoral reform in Mexico," 1993, p. 9).

In the spring of 1992, the council and Carter Center delegates were invited to observe elections in two Mexican states. They were asked to examine the ways in which Mexican groups were observing the elections, rather than the elections themselves ("Electoral reform in Mexico," 1993, p. 10). A reciprocal invitation from the council brought delegates from Mexico to observe the 1992 fall U.S. general elections. The delegates observed President Carter and voters in Georgia casting their ballots. The Mexican delegation also participated in a seminar on the U.S. electoral system, observation techniques, and U.S. political parties. As President Carter explained, "We invited leaders of observer groups and representatives of major political parties in Mexico because we wanted to work with them and explain how the U.S. system works" (quoted in "Mexicans observe U.S. elections," 1992, p. 11). Not only did the Mexican delegates learn about the U.S. electoral system, they provided their assessments and recommendations for improving the system, noting the problematic practice of the media's projecting winners prior to the close of the polls and the difficulty of registering to vote.

Since these early exchanges, Carter Center representatives have remained in contact with Mexican officials regarding electoral reform. In the fall of 1994, the council was included in an eighty-member, multinational group of international observers who were the first ever to monitor Mexican elections. Following the elections, the council delegation stressed that "the 1994 presidential election was the most secretive for voters, the most open for observation of the process, and the most competitive for political parties in the nation's history" ("Council helps make history," 1995, p. 8). The success of these Mexican elections was shaped, in part, by the ongoing efforts of the council and the Latin American and Caribbean Program to strengthen democracies in the Western Hemisphere.

DEMOCRACY IN AFRICA:
THE AFRICAN GOVERNANCE PROGRAM

As described in chapter 4, the African Governance Program works to promote democracy in the countries of sub-Saharan Africa. According to the African

Governance Program, democracy is on the move in Africa, with the number of countries the Carter Center classifies as having pluralist democracies increasing from four in 1989 to fifteen in 1993 ("Waging peace," 1993, p. 9). Two of these countries are Zambia and Ghana, where free and fair elections were monitored by representatives of the Carter Center. The African Governance Program also has been at work in Liberia, where it has been providing technical assistance on arranging elections as a means of resolving a civil war.

Elections in Zambia

On October 31, 1991, twenty-five years of one-party rule came to an end in the African country of Zambia. Kenneth Kaunda, who had ruled Zambia since its independence from Britain in 1964, was defeated by Frederick Chiluba, a former trade-union leader. President Carter characterized the people of Africa in general, and Zambia in particular, as "demanding more open and democratic systems" (quoted in "Zambia holds first democratic elections," 1991, p. 7). The October 31 elections were the result of six months of effort to arrange and monitor the elections by Carter Center representatives. During their preliminary work, delegates advised election officials on registration and polling procedures and on the means of ensuring the credible conduct of the elections ("Zambia holds first democratic elections," 1991, p. 9). These efforts were similar to other election-monitoring efforts that have been carried out by the council.

President Carter led the twenty-five-member election-monitoring team, cosponsored by the Council of Freely Elected Heads of Government and the National Democratic Institute for International Affairs, to cover the elections in Zambia. The team included parliamentarians, political leaders, election experts, and representatives from thirteen countries in Africa, Europe, and North America. On the day of the elections, the group was divided into teams that witnessed the balloting in eleven regions of the country. Voters reportedly tolerated long lines and extremes in temperature to cast their ballots in this historic election. In spite of some administrative confusion, President Carter reported, "The balloting was carried out calmly, with great care and pride in the process" (quoted in "Zambia holds first democratic elections," 1991, pp. 7, 9). Prior to the elections, President Kaunda reminded his fellow Zambians that the elections are "a means to an important end—a good government for the people" (quoted in "Zambia holds first democratic elections," p. 9).

Following the balloting, Chiluba reportedly received 80 percent of the vote, and his Movement for Multiparty Democracy Party received 90 percent of the vote for legislative seats ("Zambia holds first democratic elections," 1991, p. 7). President Carter commented on the victory, "The expression of popular will in Zambia proves that a peaceful transition of power is possible, and that even long-standing rulers will give way to the power of the ballot box" (quoted in "Zambia holds first democratic elections," 1991, p. 7). President Chiluba was sworn into office on November 2, 1991, by Chief Justice Annel Silungwe, with former

President Carter at his side. In characterizing the transfer of power, Dr. Richard Joseph, director of the African Governance Program, noted that President Kaunda's willingness to step down was a tribute to his statesmanship. Newly elected President Chiluba acknowledged former President Kaunda's contribution as the leader who had led Zambia to independence ("Zambia holds first democratic elections," 1991, p. 9). As the new democracy in Zambia moved toward a free society, Joseph assured the people of Zambia that the efforts at democratization by the Carter Center and the National Democratic Institute would continue through efforts to strengthen the judiciary and the election and registration process and to establish a free press.

As is the case in all emerging democracies, an ongoing effort will be required to consolidate the gains made through elections. The African Governance Program continues to work with the government of Zambia to strengthen its emerging democracy ("Waging peace," 1993, p. 8). In April 1992, the Carter Center and the Zambian Election Monitoring Coordinating Committee held a workshop in Zambia on "The Role of Civil Society in a Plural Democracy" from which emerged the Foundation for Democratic Process. This organization assists with democratic reforms, elections, and the promotion of human rights and civil liberties in the country. Zambian government officials have also visited the Carter Center for a conference on democracy, growth, and business opportunities in the country ("Waging peace," 1993, p. 9). Joseph observed that as the country anticipates national elections in 1996, "Zambia continues to enjoy considerable peace and stability in a troubled region" (quoted in "Waging peace," 1993, p. 9).

In his analysis of the Zambian elections entitled "Zambian Democracy Movement: A Model for Africa," Richard Joseph suggested three important lessons for democracies in Africa (1991, p. 2). First, the institutions of democratic accountability, namely, an independent judiciary and election bureaucracy, are essential. The courts are instrumental in facilitating the demands for political change in a country. Reportedly, in Zambia, journalists were successful in gaining court injunctions that removed political appointees from key positions at the broadcasting network and at a major newspaper, and the election commission had enough statutory autonomy and leadership to help assure the fairness of the elections.

A second lesson, one that has been demonstrated repeatedly in each election-monitoring effort in which President Carter has been involved, is the importance of international observers, especially in transitional elections. Joseph reported, "On election day, the Zambian voters told local and foreign monitors that without their presence they would not have had faith in the elections" (1991, p. 2). When respected eyes, like those of President Carter and the eminent persons assembled by the council and the Carter Center, observe the elections and certify the results, the potential for fraud and deceit are lessened.

A final lesson to be drawn from the Zambian elections is the importance of media coverage and an open and free press. This lesson confirms the importance of international observers in that the presence of prominent individuals in a country draws international media attention to the country. Joseph observed that the dominant media in Zambia were owned, operated, and controlled by the government of President Kaunda. Further, he stated that as international observers added their criticism to the one-party control of the media, "the government began allowing greater coverage of the views and activities of the opposition parties" (1991, p. 2). One of the prerequisites of a pluralistic democracy is an informed electorate. While Joseph concluded that complete openness and access were not achieved in Zambia, "enough of an opening had been introduced to allow Zambians to hear all sides of the debate" (1991, p. 2).

A final conclusion to be drawn from the Zambian elections and from efforts at democratization throughout Africa is that one-party systems and monopolistic political practices are neither inherent nor inevitable in Africa. When given the opportunity, the Zambian people voted for change. Joseph observed that the 1991 vote for change "cut across regional, ethnic and class lines," suggesting that "the barriers to pluralistic democracy in Africa can no longer be said to reside in ethnic divisions, underdevelopment, illiteracy, traditions of chieftaincy, and all the other familiar arguments that have been used to deny the people the right to choose freely who should govern them" (1991, p. 2).

Elections in Ghana

In 1957, Ghana was the first sub-Saharan country to achieve independence from colonial rule. Following independence, the country was ruled by a series of military and civilian governments. Since December 1981, the country has been ruled by Flight Lieutenant Jerry Rawlings and the Provisional National Defence Council (PNDC) ("Ghana holds democratic elections," 1992, p. 10). Ghana held its first democratic presidential elections on November 4, 1992. The elections were monitored by a team of eighteen international observers from the Carter Center working in association with the African-American Institute and the National Democratic Institute for International Affairs ("Ghana holds democratic elections," 1992, p. 10) and groups from the Commonwealth, the OAU, the European Community, and the countries of Canada and Switzerland.

The November elections were the result of several years of political mobilization against the PNDC calling for a return to a constitutional multiparty democracy. In the transition to a multiparty democracy, opposition groups were concerned with the advantages enjoyed by the incumbent party, the PNDC. Richard Joseph noted that the four opposition parties in Ghana expressed these common concerns. In particular, they were concerned with the voter registration list, which was outdated and alleged to be inflated and inaccurate ("Ghana holds democratic elections," 1992, p. 10).

In spite of these problems, the elections went forward. After the balloting, Rawlings and the PNDC had received 58.3 percent of the vote, with the New Patriotic Party, the closest of the four opposition parties, receiving 30.4 percent of the vote ("Ghana holds democratic elections," 1992, p. 10). The results were not peacefully received by the opposition. Violence followed, and the government imposed a dusk-to-dawn curfew to restore order. According to Richard Joseph, "The four opposition parties vigorously protested the results of the presidential elections" and said that they would boycott future legislative elections ("Ghana holds democratic elections," 1992, p. 10).

In evaluating the elections, monitoring groups reached somewhat different conclusions. Reports by the Commonwealth and the OAU said that despite irregularities and voter registration problems, on balance the elections were free and fair. The Carter Center delegation took a somewhat more critical approach by diplomatically praising the government of Ghana, the election commission, and the people of Ghana "for the significant progress that had been made in laying the basis for a constitutional democracy" ("Ghana holds democratic elections," 1992, p. 10). The Carter Center report noted inconsistencies in implementing election procedures and logistical difficulties in the voter registration list. Having noted these problems, the Carter Center team concluded that it "did not encounter a systematic pattern that would suggest fraudulent conduct or the rigging of the elections" ("Ghana holds democratic elections," 1992, p. 10).

In following up on the elections, the Carter Center provided the government with a summary of the problems encountered during the elections and encouraged officials to correct the irregularities before legislative elections were held. Richard Joseph of the Carter Center remained in the country following the elections to encourage all parties to resolve their differences peacefully and to work toward ensuring the integrity of the legislative elections. Joseph summarized the Ghanian elections and looked toward the future by stating, "I hope Ghana will make an effort to consolidate the new democratic system and begin to generate the level of private domestic and foreign investment that is critically needed after years of comprehensive but painful economic reforms" (quoted in "Ghana holds democratic elections," 1992, p. 10).

Since their inception, the Carter Center, the council, and the African Governance Program have learned several important lessons regarding monitoring elections based on their experiences in several countries, and they have integrated these lessons into their ongoing efforts. These lessons include the following: Observers must be completely impartial, election monitoring should be at the invitation of all parties involved in a country's elections, observer teams should be composed of individuals representing a variety of nationalities, a physical presence in the country should be established well in advance of the scheduled elections, and the team should remain in the country following the elections—in some cases until inauguration—to conclude the work of the monitoring team ("International observation," 1992, pp. 12–13). The impartial and multinational makeup of the observation team, combined with the presence of respected leaders like President Carter, instills confidence in voters that the elections will be fair. Receiving invitations from all parties helps to ensure their cooperation with the monitoring effort. In the cases of Nicaragua and Guyana, establishing a headquarters in the capital helped to lay the groundwork for the monitoring team and to facilitate the work of the Carter Center. Maintaining a presence in the country following the elections is essential for final assessments to be made regarding the election and its results, as well as to provide advice and counsel during the transition period from the old to the new administration. Providing access to the media, primarily television, has also been noted as being important to the furtherance of democracy. Toward this end, the Carter Center established the Commission on Radio and Television Policy in 1990 to improve media access and to establish democratically oriented television policy, primarily in the countries of the former Soviet Union.

These lessons continue to shape the efforts of President Carter and the Council of Freely Elected Heads of Government as they work to establish and strengthen democracy in developing nations. Election-monitoring missions have enabled the peaceful transition of power to take place in Nicaragua and single-party governments to give way to the popular will of the citizens in Panama, Haiti, Paraguay, Guyana, Ghana, and Zambia. While each of these missions experienced unique problems and setbacks, the promise of democracy would not have been possible in these nations had the world community, including teams from the Carter Center, not become involved.

In the broader context of peacemaking, President Carter has observed of the work of the International Negotiation Network that "the INN has learned a lot in these last four years. One new principle of conflict resolution that bears great promise for the future is the holding of an internationally supervised election as an alternative to direct talks or direct mediation" (quoted in "Resolving intra-national conflicts," 1992, p. 12). Free and open elections, supervised by the international community, appear to be an effective means of resolving conflicts between and among political parties, in the same way that mediation and negotiation can resolve conflicts between parties experiencing armed conflict.

REFERENCES

After Duvalier. (1986, Nov. 8). *Nation, 243*, 476–477.

Applebome, P. (1989, May 11). Unofficial era of Carter is still here. *New York Times*, p. A9.

Babbit, B. (1990, Mar. 19). Poll position. *New Republic*, pp. 17–19.

Barrett, M. E. (1991, Mar. 15–17). How Jimmy will save the world. *USA Today Weekender*, pp. 4–5.

Candidate with links to Noriega leads Panama presidential vote. (1994, May 9). *Atlanta Journal*, p. 1.

Carter, J. (1990, Fall). The Haitian elections: Dreams of democracy. *Carter Center News*, p. 2.

The Carter Center at a glance. (1992, 1994). Summary of Carter Center programs, available from the Carter Center, One Copenhill, Atlanta, GA 30307.

Carter Center member correspondence. (1994, Mar. 15).

Carter to pay Guyana a visit to consider role in elections. (1990, Oct. 11). *New York Times*, p. A4.

Council forges historic election reforms in Guyana. (1990, Fall). *Carter Center News*, p. 7.

Council helps make history by observing Mexican elections. (1995, Winter). *Carter Center News*, p. 8.

Council witnesses "spirit of democracy" as voters elect new president of Panama. (1994, Summer). *Carter Center News*, p. 5.

Delegation's presence assures fair national elections in Paraguay. (1993, Spring). *Carter Center News*, pp. 1, 7.

Democracy takes root in Nicaragua. (1991, Spring). *Carter Center News*, pp. 10–11.

Doerner, W. R. (1989, May 22). Lead-pipe politics. *Time*, pp. 40–44.

The election that wasn't. (1989, May 13). *Economist*, p. 47.

Electoral reform in Mexico: Final report. (1993, Nov.). Occasional paper series, vol. 4, no. 1. Available from the Carter Center, One Copenhill, Atlanta, GA 30307.

French, H. W. (1991, Feb. 8). Haiti installs democratic chief, its first. *New York Times*, p. A3.

_____. (1994, May 9). Businessman appears to oust "old guard" in Panama election. *New York Times*, p. A5.

Galloway, J. (1989, May 22). Standoff in Panama. *U.S. News and World Report*, pp. 28–32.

Ghana holds democratic elections under CCEU's watchful eye. (1992, Fall). *Carter Center News*, p. 10.

Grunson, L. (1989, May 9). Noriega stealing election, Carter says. *New York Times*, p. A1.

Guyana moves closer to democracy. (1992, Fall). *Carter Center News*, pp. 1, 4.

Guyanese election postponed at suggestion of Carter Center. (1991, Fall). *Carter Center News*, p. 11.

Guyanese officials commit to breaking barriers to free elections. (1992, Spring). *Carter Center News*, p. 12.

Haiti inaugurates first freely elected president. (1990, Spring). *Carter Center News*, p. 6.

Hockstader, L. (1990, Feb. 27). Carter played pivotal role in hours after polls closed. *Washington Post*, p. A19.

The international observation of the U.S. elections. (1992, Nov.). Occasional Paper Series, vol. 3, no. 1. Available from the Carter Center, One Copenhill, Atlanta, GA 30307.

Jarvie, R. (1993a, May 8). Paraguayans warned about fraud in Sunday's landmark elections. Reuters News Service (available on CD News Bank Comprehensive 1995).

_____. (1993b, May 9). Three candidates end neck and neck in Paraguay elections. Reuters News Service (available on CD News Bank Comprehensive 1995).

Jimmy Carter's second chance. (1990, Mar. 12). *U.S. News and World Report*, p. 35.

Joseph, R. (1991, Fall). Zambian democracy movement: A model for Africa. *Carter Center News*, p. 2.

Latin American and Caribbean Program: Reinforcing democracy. (1987, Summer). *Carter Center News*, p. 6.

Mexicans observe U.S. elections. (1992, Fall). *Carter Center News*, p. 11.

Observing Nicaragua's elections, 1989–1990. (1990). Special Report no. 1 of the
    Council of Freely Elected Heads of Government. Available from the Carter Center,
    One Copenhill, Atlanta, GA 30307.
Resolving intra-national conflicts: A strengthened role for non-governmental actors.
    (1992). Conference Report Series, vol. 3, no. 2 of the International Negotiation
    Network. Available from the Carter Center, One Copenhill, Atlanta, GA 30307.
Rodman, S. (1988, Jan. 22). The election that wasn't. *National Review*, pp. 48–50.
Role likely for Carter in Nicaragua elections. (1989, Aug. 8). *New York Times*, p. A8.
Smolowa, J. (1987, Dec. 14). Blood in the ballot box. *Time*, pp. 38–40.
Uhlig, M. A. (1990, Feb. 23). Nicaragua vote monitors confident. *New York Times*, p.
    A3.
Waging peace around the world. (1993). Available from the Carter Center, One
    Copenhill, Atlanta, GA 30307.
Zambia holds first democratic elections in history. (1991, Fall). *Carter Center News*, pp.
    7, 9.

CHAPTER 8

PEACEMAKING THROUGH HUMANITARIAN DEVELOPMENT ABROAD

Peace requires more than the absence of armed conflict. If people are to live in peace, they must be well nourished, enjoy good health and be free from disease, and live in a safe society. These ideals are among the goals being pursued by various international programs operating through the Carter Center. One of the most significant programs directed at accomplishing these goals is Global 2000, Inc., an independent organization mandated to improve agricultural, health, and educational services in developing countries. Other similar programs and initiatives include the Task Force for Disease Eradication, the Task Force on Child Survival and Development, and the Environmental and Global Development initiatives, which address a variety of humanitarian needs in target countries from the perspective of sustainable development. The protection and promotion of human rights, which was a central issue throughout the Carter administration, continues to be a vital concern advanced through the Human Rights Program (HRP) and the Carter-Menil Human Rights Foundation.

The various international development programs of Global 2000, Inc., are designed to translate academic and technical knowledge into practical application. These programs work toward peace by helping to create the sufficient conditions that are a prerequisite for peace. They assume that people in a developing country are better able to reap the benefits of peace if they are well fed, healthy, and productive, and that improving conditions in these countries removes potential causes for unrest and conflict. Advancing human rights is perhaps the most fundamental of all humanitarian needs if the possibilities of peace are to become a reality.

GLOBAL 2000, INC.: AGRICULTURAL, HEALTH, AND EDUCATION PROGRAMS

Origins and Approach

Global 2000, Inc., is one of several independent nonprofit organizations operating through the Carter Center. Global 2000 was established in 1985 as an action program to implement recommendations derived from studies at the Carter Center ("Action program," 1987, p. 10) and is funded by grants from individuals, corporations, foundations, and governments. The mandate of Global 2000 is to improve health and agricultural services in developing countries. The work of this organization is the result of a report commissioned in 1977 entitled "Global 2000" and prepared during the Carter administration. This long-range study was designed to assess the future of the world environment ("Action program," 1987, p. 10) and projected trends in population growth and environmental degradation into the twenty-first century. This report predicted "a spiral of poverty, disease, hunger, and social injustice in rural areas of developing countries that could seriously threaten economic stability and world peace" ("Global 2000, Inc.," p. 1). Global 2000 addresses this downward spiral through programs that "motivate and support the governments of these countries to promote food self-reliance, improve health standards, and address environmental problems" ("Global 2000, Inc.," p. 1). President Carter serves as the chair of Global 2000, which has benefited from two major sponsors, Ryoichi Sasakawa, a Japanese philanthropist, and Agha Hasan Adedi, an international banker ("Action program," 1987, p. 10).

The problems of food self-sufficiency, improving health standards, and environmental degradation are addressed from the perspective of technology transfer. In many cases, it is not that the knowledge or technology to alleviate human suffering does not exist; it is more often the case that such knowledge and technology are not available to those in need. Global 2000 bridges the gap between research and application, and between the developed world and the developing world. Bridging this gap requires a combination of political will, financial support, and technical expertise. These elements are combined through the leadership of President Carter, who helps provide the political will; organizations like the Sasakawa Africa Association and the United Arab Emirates/Abu Dhabi Investment Authority, as well as government and nongovernmental organizations, which provide the financial support; and Nobel laureate–caliber scientists and health experts, who provide the technical expertise.

Global 2000 follows the development principle of helping people to help themselves by providing long-term support for development efforts in the pursuit of sustainable development. Former President Carter acts as a catalyst for change by working with the heads of government in host countries to create necessary policy changes. To assure cooperation from a country, President Carter often personally negotiates with the heads of government in target countries prior to the establishment of Global 2000 programs. Coalitions are built, and where necessary, conflicts are resolved in order to facilitate development programs.   Programs are integrated with existing government services to promote self-reliance and sustainable development and to avoid duplication of existing programs.

By following these principles and strategies, Global 2000 has made considerable progress in humanitarian development in the last ten years, including the following achievements: increases in maize and wheat production in target countries; training thousands of farmers in basic food-crop production, thus doubling, tripling, and even quadrupling crop yields; the virtual elimination of Guinea worm disease in Pakistan and significant reductions of its incidence in African countries; and training special-education teachers and building and staffing a prosthetic center in China ("Global 2000, Inc.," p. 1).   While Global 2000 is headquartered and administered through the Carter Center in Atlanta, it maintains offices in Ghana, Togo, Benin, the Sudan, Tanzania, Nigeria, Pakistan, and Uganda.

Increasing Agricultural Production

The 1980s saw famine strike numerous countries, in particular those of sub-Saharan Africa.   While the populations of developing countries continue to increase, in some cases doubling every twenty-four years, the ability of developing countries to feed their people has failed to keep pace.   Much of African agriculture, up to 75 percent, still depends on rather primitive hand tools and simple subsistence farming ("Global 2000, Inc.," p. 3).   Global 2000's concern for Africa was heightened in light of the famine conditions that several African countries had experienced in 1984.   Japanese philanthropist Ryoichi Sasakawa responded to the immediate crisis by helping to provide emergency food supplies, but more importantly, he forged a relationship with Nobel laureate Dr. Norman Borlaug, who is credited with India's "Green Revolution" in the 1960s ("Global 2000, Inc.," p. 3).   Sasakawa agreed to fund similar programs in Africa in conjunction with Global 2000.

One of the first target countries for Global 2000 agricultural programs was Ghana.   In 1986, under the direction of Borlaug, the program began with twenty demonstration plots of maize and sorghum and yielded two-, three-, and fourfold increases in production ("Feeding the future," 1988, p. 14).   Because of the success of the program's first year, banks in Ghana, which had been reluctant to loan money for seed and fertilizer to village farmers the first year, financed 200 farmers the second year.   The banks received a 100 percent payback and subsequently financed 8,000 farmers during the third year ("Feeding the future," 1988, p. 14).   The proven success of the programs solidified this essential coalition between Global 2000, local farmers, and banking officials. Interestingly, Borlaug pointed out that the success of the early programs created crop surpluses, which created crop-storage problems, which necessitated new collaborative programs with the Ghanian government ("Feeding the future," 1988, p. 14).

The successful three-part strategy of Global 2000 of leadership, financing, and expertise led to the formation of the Sasakawa Africa Association (SAA), designed to transfer existing food-crop-production technologies to other countries. The collaboration between Global 2000 and the SAA supported initiatives designed to increase cereal-crop production in Africa through the distribution of the best available technologies to resource-poor farmers. These programs have sparked a grass-roots movement among village farmers to improve agricultural technology ("Global 2000, Inc.," p. 3).

The grass-roots movement begins with farmers in rural villages who work with highly trained extension agents under the leadership of Borlaug to produce test plots. The extension agents supply the necessary seed and fertilizer, which the village farmer repays after harvest. Test plots are planted beside traditionally planted plots to allow for easy comparison of the differences in crop yields. The test-plot farmers then share their experience with other farmers in the region. In this strategy, the new technology is transferred from the extension agent to test-plot farmers and then to farmers throughout the region. SAA and Global 2000 staff function as technology-transfer agents but also attempt to fully integrate their efforts with government agriculture ministries to ensure that indigenous capacity is developed ("Global 2000, Inc.," p. 4; "Feeding the future," 1988, p. 15).

The results of these Global 2000 efforts have been quite impressive. The 40 farmers in four countries in 1985 increased to 75,000 participants in 1989 who reported fourfold crop-yield increases (Cloud, 1989, p. 63). Since 1986, village farmers in Ghana, the Sudan, Zambia, Tanzania, Benin, and Togo have grown 140,000 test plots using traditional hand tools and better seed and have reported increased yields of up to 400 percent ("Action program," 1987, p. 11).

Looking toward the future, "A major goal of SAA–Global 2000 is to bring the small-scale food producer into the world of modern commercial agriculture" ("Global 2000, Inc.," p. 5). In coming years, SAA and Global 2000 hope to continue their programs in existing host countries, expand to new countries, facilitate food-storage and marketing efforts, organize farmers into associations to purchase seed and fertilizer, and teach them to market their surplus production.

Following the successes of Global 2000 agricultural programs, in July 1989 President and Rosalynn Carter traveled to six African counties to launch Project Africa: Strategies for Food Security. The goal of this collaborative effort by the Carter Center and international development experts was to reduce hunger substantially in sub-Saharan Africa by the turn of the century ("Project Africa," 1989, p. 15). In announcing the program, President Carter said, "Hunger is a problem with a solution. Our job is to replicate the success of a few food enhancement programs currently in place in Africa with the help of African governments, international development organizations, and non-governmental agencies" (quoted in "Project Africa," 1989, p. 15).

Recent initiatives of Global 2000 and Norman Borlaug have worked in cooperation with the SAA (forming SG 2000) and the World Bank to promote further sustainable agricultural development in Africa. According to Borlaug, "I am confident that by more closely coordinating their efforts in support of national extension services in Africa, the World Bank and SG 2000 can help to accelerate significantly the process of agricultural development" (quoted in "Global 2000 joins World Bank," 1995, p. 14). This effort continues Global 2000's efforts to work in cooperation with and to coordinate the efforts of various organizations, rather than duplicate existing programs. This initiative is designed to fully utilize existing agricultural extension services in target countries. As explained by President Carter, "SG 2000 has great operational flexibility to test new ideas for agricultural development on a pilot scale, while the World Bank can finance the much larger scale capital investments needed to strengthen African governmental institutions. This is the kind of international collaboration needed to get agriculture moving in Africa" (quoted in "Global 2000 joins World Bank," 1995, p. 14).

Preventing Disease and Improving Health

Several organizations and programs operating through the Carter Center, including the Task Force for Disease Eradication (TFDE) and the Task Force for Child Survival and Development (TFCSD), have addressed the issues of the health and well-being of the people in developing countries. One of the most significant initiatives of the TFDE, which was founded in 1988, has been to eradicate Guinea worm disease, polio, measles, yaws, and rabies and to target other diseases for worldwide eradication efforts ("Polio, Guinea worm," 1989, p. 9; "Disease eradication task force formed," 1988, p. 10). The TFDE acts as a catalyst for these eradication efforts and works with the Carnegie Corporation of New York, the Centers for Disease Control, the Institute of Medicine, the Swedish Academy of Sciences, and the Dana Foundation. According to Dr. William Foege of the Carter Center, "To date, the only total success we have had in public health has been the eradication of smallpox from the world" (quoted in "Polio, Guinea worm...," 1989, p. 9), but he and the TFDE predict the eradication of Guinea worm disease and polio in the next decade. In addition to the eradication of Guinea worm disease, programs at the TFCSD, which was founded in 1984, have targeted the eradication of several other preventable childhood diseases.

The "Fiery Serpent." Dracunculiasis, or Guinea worm disease, is unknown in the developed world, yet millions of people in developing countries like India, Pakistan, and seventeen African nations are at risk of contracting this highly preventable disease, and up to three million people per year have suffered from its effects ("Global 2000, Inc.," p. 7). People contract the disease, also known as the "fiery serpent," by drinking water contaminated with the worm's larvae. Following ingestion, the larvae develop and emerge painfully a year later as yard-long threadlike parasites. Victims are left incapacitated during the emergence period—children are unable to attend school and adults are unable to work. The negative impact of the disease on farming, for example, has been significant. Following successful eradication efforts, Dr. Donald Hopkins of the Carter Center reported, "In one heavily-affected district of Ghana's northern region, the production of yams reportedly increased by 33 percent in the first nine months of 1991 because so many farmers were restored to full productivity by the sharp reduction of Guinea worm" (quoted in "Guinea worm reduced," 1991, p. 14).

In 1986, the World Health Organization (WHO) targeted Guinea worm disease for eradication and established 1995 as a target date. In collaboration with the U.S. Centers for Disease Control, early Global 2000 programs worked to eradicate the disease in Pakistan ("Action program," 1987, p. 10). Since the technology for eradicating the disease is simple and readily available, disseminating the technology became the challenge. The technology for eradication involves the use of a nylon or cloth mesh filter to strain the larvae from the water, boiling the water, or using a larvicide to purify the water.

Global 2000 and the TFDE have worked through village health agents in thousands of communities to promote the use of these techniques. Agents identify villages where the disease is a problem, monitor the problem, and distribute the filters and teach safe water-management techniques ("Global 2000, Inc.," p. 7). By using these techniques, Ghana and Nigeria (two of the most severely affected countries in Africa) reduced the number of cases of the disease by more than one-third during 1990, and similar efforts have left Pakistan on the verge of eradicating the disease ("Global 2000, Inc.," p. 7).

In a way similar to Global 2000 agricultural programs that work from the grass-roots to the national level, Guinea worm eradication programs depend on coordinating local through national efforts in target countries. At the local level, the eradication programs train at least one health worker in each affected community as a Guinea worm educator. These health-care workers educate the local population on the causes of the disease and on techniques for its eradication ("Guinea worm reduced," 1991, p. 14). At the national level, the Ministry of Education in Ghana, for example, distributed teachers' manuals in order to educate about Guinea worm disease, while the Nigerian government committed $1 million for disease eradication and targeted improving rural water-supply projects. Local through national efforts are coordinated under the auspices of development agencies such as Global 2000 ("Global 2000, Inc.," p. 8).

The experiences of Global 2000 in India, Pakistan, Ghana, and Nigeria between 1986 and 1991 led Global 2000 to spearhead the Target 1995 plan to eradicate the parasite from the world. This effort will depend on a combination of political will in the target countries, financial support, and technical training and expertise. President Carter has been personally involved in eradication efforts by participating in fund-raising drives, visiting affected villages, and maintaining regular contacts with political leaders in target countries to promote awareness of the problem ("Global 2000, Inc.," p. 9).

The conference "Target 1995: The Global Eradication of Guinea Worm" was held in Lagos, Nigeria, and sponsored by Global 2000, the Bank of Credit and Commerce International, the United Nations Development Programme, and Nigeria's Federal Ministry of Health ("International community pledges $10 million," 1989, p. 14). This conference was attended by dozens of participants and raised $10 million to support eradication efforts in Africa. According to Global 2000's Donald Hopkins, "Apart from the direct pledges made at the conference, we are aware of additional support of about $20 million which is likely to be made available soon. Another important result of the conference has been the enormous international and national awareness of the problem of Guinea worm in Nigeria, the world's most endemic country, and in other key areas of the world" (quoted in "International community pledges $10 million," 1989, p. 14). Hopkins noted that $76 million will be needed to rid the world of the disease.

President Carter's personal involvement in Guinea worm eradication has also included working with the Du Pont and Precision Fabrics corporations in the development of an effective water filter ("Unusual donation aids war," 1990, p. 13). In late 1989, President Carter and representatives of Guinea worm eradication programs contacted the Du Pont Company to enlist the company's help in developing a filter to fight the Guinea worm. Following these meetings, Du Pont CEO Edgar Wollard, Jr., stated, "We are committed to assisting President Carter in his efforts to rid the world of this painful and often crippling disease" (quoted in "Unusual donation aids war," 1990, p. 13). Scientists and researchers at Du Pont, in collaboration with Precision Fabrics, worked to develop an ultrafine nylon monofilament fiber that could be used in a reusable water filter. Lanty Smith, president and CEO of Precision Fabrics, said, "This is a unique opportunity for us to help people lead a better life" (quoted in "Unusual donation aids war," 1990, p. 13). According to Global 2000, "At Du Pont, we were greeted by enthusiastic employees from all divisions of the company who were anxious to reinforce their commitment to this project. And when President Carter toured the Precision Fabrics plant, a worker stopped him to explain how careful everyone was being because they realized a mistake in the fabric could cause a child in Africa to get Guinea worm" (quoted in "Unusual donation aids war," 1990, p. 13). By October 1990, the fabric filter had been developed, manufactured, and shipped to the African country of Ghana, with additional shipments going to Nigeria, Cameroon, Benin, Burkina Faso, and Mali ("Guinea worm reduced," 1991, p. 14). Du Pont and Precision Fabrics agreed to donate a total of nine million filters over the next five years. Additional private corporate support has come from the Bank of Credit and Commerce International and from the American Cyanamid Company, which has provided the larvicide Abate, from Georgia-Pacific, which has donated the paper needed for educational materials, and from Communicorp, which has donated printing services ("Global 2000, Inc.," p. 9; "International community pledges $10 million," 1989, p. 14). In acknowledging the $2 million worth of the chemical Abate donated in March 1990, President Carter said, "American Cyanamid has a product that is necessary to eliminate a debilitating disease, and when presented with an opportunity, they chose to give all that was needed for our worldwide eradication campaign. This generous gift will be instrumental in ending the unnecessary suffering of millions of people" (quoted in "Guinea worm eradication efforts," 1990, p. 13). All of these financial resources were raised, coordinated, and channelled through development agencies including Global 2000.

Under the leadership of Global 2000, significant progress is being made toward reaching the WHO target date of December 1995 for eradication. Early results from Ghana indicate a 31 percent decrease in the disease between 1989 and 1991, while Nigeria experienced a 38 percent decrease in the number of cases during the same period ("Guinea worm reduced," 1991, p. 14). As of 1995, officially reported cases of the disease in affected countries dropped from 900,000 in 1989 to about 125,000 cases in 1994—an 86 percent decrease ("USAID joins Carter Center," 1995, p. 9). As Global 2000 eradication programs succeed in targeted countries, additional programs are initiated in the remaining affected African countries. In 1994, Norway contributed $1.5 million to Global 2000 and the United Nations International Children's Education Fund to help meet the targeted eradication date of 1995 ("Norway contributes $1.5 million," 1994, p. 13). In 1995, the U.S. Agency for International Development awarded a $3.5-million grant to the Carter Center to continue Guinea worm eradication efforts ("USAID joins Carter Center," 1995, p. 9).

In the spring of 1995, President Carter and a delegation from the Carter Center traveled to several African countries to monitor and facilitate the Guinea worm eradication program and to attend the National Conference on Guinea Worm in the Sudan ("Carter sets four-nation Africa trip," 1995). It is significant to note that on this trip, President Carter negotiated a temporary cease-fire in the Sudanese civil war to allow for disease-eradication and immunization efforts to take place (Ciabattari, 1995, p. 7). This case is an excellent example of President Carter's working to stop conflict and to facilitate humanitarian development efforts, both of which are required for peacemaking.

Preventing River Blindness. In 1988, the TFCSD and Merck and Company formed a partnership to target the eradication of river blindness by supervising the distribution of the drug Mectizan ("Polio eradication," 1988, p. 13). River blindness is a parasitic disease spread by black flies that affects up to 15 percent of the populations of eastern and western African countries and also affects parts of the Americas. Annually, the disease threatens 90 million people, infects an estimated 18 million people, blinds up to 355,000, and creates serious visual impairment in 1 million more ("Merck & Co. donates sight-saving drug," 1991, p. 13; "Mectizan and the control of river blindness," 1992, p. 12). A single yearly dose of Mectizan can prevent the loss of sight. Merck has agreed to donate lifetime supplies of the drug to ensure that all affected countries have access to the drug regardless of their ability to pay ("Polio eradication," 1988, p. 13). By 1991, efforts to eradicate this disease had treated 3 million people in twenty-seven African and Latin American countries ("Merck & Co. donates sight-saving drug," 1991, p. 13). At the fifth anniversary of the program, P. Roy Vagelos, CEO of Merck, stated, "We are committed to making Mectizan available without charge for as long as there are people suffering from river blindness who need this drug" (quoted in "Mectizan and the control of river blindness," 1992, p. 12). By 1995, Merck had donated $80 million worth of the drug and by 1994 had treated 11 million people ("Carter Center and Merck step up efforts, 1995, p. 12).

As is the case with Guinea worm disease, river blindness is a socioeconomic disease. Dr. Michael Heisler, who directs the river blindness eradication program for the Carter Center, explained, "When you fix the medical problem, which is easy to do with Mectizan, these villages become repopulated, cash crops begin to grow again, and families can come back together" (quoted in "Carter Center and Merck," 1995, p. 12). According to the Carter Center's Dr. William Foege, "This program means there is now hope to save the sight of thousands of people" (quoted in "Merck & Co. donates sight-saving drug," 1991, p. 13).

Health care and disease prevention have been central concerns of the TFCSD and the TFDE since their founding in the mid-1980s. Their accomplishments and those of Global 2000 have been impressive. As it marked its fifth anniversary, the TFCSD had helped thirty countries vaccinate 80 percent of their children under one year of age, had assisted thirty-eight countries in meeting Universal Child Immunization goals, had launched a polio-eradication effort, and had conducted research and development efforts on vaccine technology ("Task Force celebrates fifth anniversary," 1989, p. 13). As Foege summarized the task force's work as of 1989, he said, "This year 2.5 million children will *not* die because of measles, whooping cough, diphtheria or tetanus. Five hundred thousand will *not* develop polio, and one million will *not* die because of diarrhea" (quoted in "Task Force celebrates fifth anniversary," 1989, p. 13).

These Global 2000, TFDE, and TFCSD programs continue today, and additional areas have been targeted as new needs and problems are identified. For example, in 1991 and 1992, hunger in general and micronutrient deficiencies in particular, acute respiratory infections, and parasitic infections were targeted for attention by the TFCSD and other development agencies ("Hidden hunger kills," 1991, p. 13; "Task force takes aim," 1992, p. 13). Neonatal tetanus is another preventable disease being eradicated by Carter Center programs ("Global 2000," p. 11; "Feeding the future," 1988, p. 15). Other Carter Center programs in the early 1990s addressed the problems associated with the proliferation of tobacco use in developing countries. In 1990, the Carter Center joined with the WHO and international health groups to discourage tobacco use around the world ("CCEU, WHO join," 1990, p. 10; "Center works to reduce tobacco use," 1991, p. 8). These international programs to discourage tobacco use are in addition to domestic programs sponsored by the Carter Center to curb tobacco use and to shape legislation designed to improve the long-term health of people at home and abroad.

Helping the Mentally and Physically Disabled

In conjunction with the United Nations Decade of Disabled Persons (1983–1992), the People's Republic of China adopted the philosophy that society should understand, respect, and help the physically challenged. This philosophy was translated into action in 1987 when President and Rosalynn Carter met with Chairman Deng Xiaoping and Prime Minister Zhao Ziyang to discuss improving the quality of life for China's physically and mentally challenged citizens.

A 1987 survey found that fifty-one million Chinese suffered from disabilities that left them unable to participate fully in society because of a lack of special-education services ("Helping China," 1989, p. 15). According to the Center for Effective Performance—an Atlanta-based organization that provided much of the special-education expertise for this Global 2000 effort—China lacked sufficient numbers of qualified special-education teachers to provide handicapped children with basic skills and vocational instruction ("Helping China," 1989, p. 15). Responding to this need, Global 2000 launched a new phase in its humanitarian activities when President Carter signed letters of intent with China to initiate two projects. The first aimed at increasing the number of special-education teachers for the mentally challenged, and the second sought to enhance the quality, production, and use of artificial limbs for the physically challenged ("Carter legacy," 1991, p. A2; "Carters take Global 2000 to China," 1987, p. 4; "Global 2000, Inc." p. 13). Commenting on these new programs and their broader importance to international relations, President Carter said, "I am delighted that Global 2000 is launching two projects in the area of public health. Such activities should help to remove lingering fragility in Sino-American relations" ("Carters take Global 2000 to China," 1987, p. 4).

When Global 2000 became involved with special-education efforts in China in 1987, only 5 percent of China's thirty-five million visually and hearing-impaired children were enrolled in school. Global 2000 agreed to coordinate its efforts with the China Disabled Persons Federation, which was chaired by Deng Pufang, the physically disabled son of Chairman Deng Xiaoping, and the China Fund for the Handicapped ("Carters take Global 2000 to China," 1987, p. 4). Global 2000 made the commitment to train three hundred special-education teachers and to assist China in its goal of doubling or tripling the enrollment of visually and hearing-impaired children over the next five years ("Global 2000, Inc.," p. 13). The five-year training effort drew upon the expertise of American special-education professors in conjunction with the Atlanta-based Center for Effective Performance. The Chinese government provided the facilities, American professors designed the courses and served as trainers, and Global 2000 financed the visiting teachers and the necessary equipment for the courses.

In order to facilitate special-education self-sufficiency in China, the Center for Effective Performance sent thirty-five American special-education teachers to present a ten-month course for special educators who would become the "teachers of teachers" and pass their newfound knowledge on to others ("Teachers and technology," 1991, p. 14). These courses were conducted in

China from September 1988 to July 1989 ("Helping China," 1989, p. 15). In the first phase of the project, ninety students completed the course and returned to their homes in twenty-eight different provinces to establish local special-education training programs ("Global 2000," 1995, p. 14). The success of the project is demonstrated by the fact that three hundred Global 2000 educated teachers have trained an additional three hundred teachers in provinces throughout China and are building a growing community of special-education teachers in China ("Global 2000, Inc.," p. 14; "Teachers and technology," 1991, p. 14). In other developments associated with the program, specialists in hearing impairment were trained in diagnostic and intervention techniques, and factories in China are preparing to manufacture amplification devices ("Teachers and technology," 1991, p. 14).

The Global 2000 special-education project, through media and public information campaigns, has helped to increase public awareness of the needs of mentally and physically challenged Chinese. In April 1991, President Carter made a three-day trip to China, including visits to a Chinese school for the deaf and the capital of Beijing, to follow up on the progress of these programs. During the trip, Carter commented, "We hope that this project . . . will spread its beneficial influence to every handicapped person in the entire country" ("Carter legacy," 1991, p. A2).

Until ten years ago, prosthetic care for China's three million amputees depended on relatively crude fifty-year-old technology, with the situation in rural regions of the country being even worse. In 1987, a three-year project sponsored by Global 2000 was initiated to establish and improve technologies for the fabrication and manufacture of artificial limbs ("Carters take Global 2000 to China," 1987, p. 4). It is interesting to note that in addition to the program in China, President Carter also signed a letter of intent with President Moi of Kenya (who would later play a key role in the Ethiopian-Eritrean peace negotiations) for Global 2000 to collaborate with Kenya's Ministry of Health to assess current technology and manufacturing techniques for artificial limbs in Kenya ("Expansion of health initiatives," 1988, p. 15).

The Global 2000 China project involved the construction of a new factory that would be built and staffed by the Chinese government, with equipment and training to be provided by Global 2000 ("Global 2000, Inc.," p. 15). In 1988, Global 2000 sent a team of specialists, including representatives from J. E. Hanger, Southwest—the largest provider of prosthetic and orthotic services in the United States—to assist the Chinese in the design of the new factory ("Teachers and technology," 1991, p. 15). Global 2000 advisers worked with their Chinese counterparts on improving the design, manufacture, and delivery of services. Ted Thranhart, president of J. E. Hanger, also arranged for Chinese prosthetic technicians to tour American companies to study new methods and technology ("Teachers and technology," 1991, p. 15).

The project culminated in the dedication in April 1991 of the Beijing Prosthetic Center, the Prosthetic Research Institute, and the Model Making and

Testing Center. This center includes two six-story buildings for patient evaluation and care facilities and includes facilities for short-term housing for patients receiving services and housing for the 250 staff members. Speaking at the dedication, President Carter said, "We hoped to provide China with self-sustaining special education and prosthesis development programs that would continue long after Global 2000 ceased to be directly involved" (quoted in "Teachers and technology," 1991, p. 14).

The Global 2000 special-education and prosthetics projects in China are providing immediate benefits to their target populations and will continue to provide long-term benefits because they were designed to encourage self-sufficiency. Commenting on the projects, Andy Agle, director of operations for Global 2000, said, "The Global 2000 project did not provide a single prosthesis to a single individual. Instead, it helped the Chinese with something infinitely more valuable: acquiring the tools they needed to help themselves" (quoted in "Teachers and technology," 1991, p. 15). According to Global 2000, "The ultimate goals [of the special-education and prosthetics projects] were never to provide individual solutions to individual problems . . . but rather to develop systems, knowledge, and tools to address these problems for years to come. China's clearly demonstrated capacity to sustain these programs into the twenty-first century leaves us with the best evidence of a successful model for international collaboration" ("Global 2000, Inc.," pp. 15–16).

Global Development and the Environmental Initiative

In 1991, the mandate of Global 2000 to improve health and agricultural services in developing countries was expanded to include consideration of the problem of global deforestation, in particular, and sustainable environmental development issues in general. Recognizing that each year more than fifty million acres of forest disappear from the world, forestry experts, including environmentalists and timber-company executives, gathered for a conference at the Carter Center in September 1991 ("New program seeks," 1991, p. 15). One result of the conference was the establishment of the Forestry Technical Advisory Group, which would follow the Global 2000 tradition of working with local community groups as well as enlisting the support of heads of state and world leaders to deal with the unique environmental problems of different countries.

This advisory group focused much of its attention on preparing for the 1992 United Nations Conference on the Environment and Development, "the Earth Summit," which was to be held in Rio de Janeiro in June 1992. According to Andy Agle of the Carter Center, "This conference [had] the potential to set the global environmental agenda" (quoted in "New program seeks," 1991, p. 15). This agenda held the potential to mobilize the world's attention to the environmental problems of the world, but also to further polarize those countries favoring environmental protection from those supporting further development of the earth's resources. John Spears of the Forestry Technical Advisory Group believed that Global 2000 "has the potential to be a neutral forum for resolving such disputes and for developing new models of cooperation and partnership" (quoted in "New program seeks," 1991, p. 15). Commenting on the opportunities provided by the Rio de Janeiro conference, President Carter challenged, "We must seize the tremendous potential in a post–Cold War world to turn away from the constant confrontation that evolves into war and toward an improvement in quality of life for all of us" (Carter, 1992, p. 2). President Carter's involvement in this effort included speaking at the Earth Summit in June 1992 and, in cooperation with the Turner Broadcasting Service, helping to orchestrate a global television campaign to promote environmental awareness and to urge international support for the Earth Summit ("New program seeks," 1991, p. 15).

The initial concerns regarding deforestation evolved into the Environmental Initiative and the Global Development Initiative. These initiatives have as their goals the prevention and reversal of environmental degradation, the promotion of environmentally sound public policy, and the encouragement of sustainable population policies ("Carter Center Programs," 1994–1995, p. 7). These initiatives are designed to coordinate development efforts in such a way as to achieve the goal of sustainable development.

The Global Development Initiative developed out of a 1992 conference on ways to improve the development aid process that was chaired by President Carter and U.N. Secretary General Boutros-Ghali ("Conference for global development cooperation," 1992). This conference explored ways for emerging democracies to utilize their limited resources effectively and the external aid currently available. According to President Carter, in emerging democracies, "You have to make sure that a new democratic government, if it has little experience in governing, is capable; that its long-range plans are comprehensive; and that it works in harmony with other elements within the country" (quoted in "Guyana tests new partnerships," 1994, p. 10). The emerging democracy of Guyana, where Carter Center programs had worked to ensure democratic elections in 1992 and to facilitate international aid efforts, has become a successful test case of the Global Development Initiative. The Carter Center has made long-term efforts to work with the government, private industry, environmental groups, and citizens to coordinate plans for sustainable development in Guyana.

A SAFE SOCIETY: THE PROTECTION OF HUMAN RIGHTS

When President of the United States Jimmy Carter met with a foreign leader, human rights issues were almost always on the agenda. Critics at the time suggested that his administration focused too much attention on human rights, but this did not deter President Carter from working to protect and enhance basic human rights. Human Rights has continued to be a central concern for President Carter since his departure from the White House and helps to shape the work of several Carter Center programs. The Carter Center Human Rights Program

(HRP) provides "technical assistance to help countries establish human rights safeguards and engages in action-oriented interventions, policy research, and public education" ("Carter Center Programs," 1994–95). The HRP has also targeted efforts at emerging democracies and transitional governments seeking to incorporate human rights protection into new government structures. These formal programs are in addition to the personal intervention work by President and Rosalynn Carter on behalf of persecuted individuals and human rights activists. In 1986, President Carter and Dominique de Menil established the Carter-Menil Human Rights Foundation to promote the protection of human rights and annually award a $100,000 gift to individuals and organizations who work on behalf of human rights.

The Human Rights Program

Since its inception, the HRP has regularly gathered human rights organizations and governmental representatives to discuss issues related to the protection and promotion of human rights. The HRP in 1988 hosted citizens from Eastern- and Western-bloc countries to plan for the De Burght Conference. This conference would ultimately urge the implementation of the Universal Declaration of Human Rights ("East/West meet on human rights," 1988, p. 10). Government officials from Caribbean countries gathered for a 1988 conference called "The English-Speaking Caribbean and the Inter-American Human Rights System," which familiarized them with the American Convention on Human Rights and succeeded in convincing representatives to urge the adoption and ratification of this convention in their respective countries ("Caribbean leaders re-examine human rights commitment," 1988, pp. 1, 7).

In 1990, the director of the HRP traveled to Guatemala to meet with human rights activists and organizations to discuss conditions in that country and to raise awareness of human rights abuses ("Guatemalan violence," 1990, p. 11). On a return trip to Guatemala and El Salvador in 1991, HRP staff continued their dialogue with human rights activists, labor, peasant, and government leaders, and U.S. embassy personnel to identify ways in which President Carter and the Carter Center could support human rights in these countries, which have experienced a long history of human rights abuses at the hands of military governments ("Human rights violations," 1991, p. 9). Following this trip, the HRP staff noted that "although there continue to be serious human rights violations in both countries, there is at least some movement toward change in El Salvador" ("Human rights violations," 1991, p. 9).

Human Rights Program staff traveled to several African countries in 1990 to follow up on several human rights initiatives and met with Walter Sisulu (leader of the African National Congress and recipient of the 1988 Carter-Menil Human Rights Award) to discuss how the Carter Center could support human rights in South Africa ("Human rights in South Africa surveyed," 1989, p. 11). The HRP also facilitated the creation of the Human Rights Program on the Horn of Africa in order to document human rights abuses, to advocate human rights, and to educate for human rights in the countries of the Horn of Africa ("New group to defend human rights," 1990, p. 10). The programmatic work and the policy research of the Human Rights Program have been ongoing since the program was established.

Most recently, with the help of a $750,000 grant in 1995 from the John D. and Catherine C. MacArthur Foundation, the Carter Center and the HRP launched the International Human Rights Council. This twenty-seven-member council will seek to further the cause of human rights by increasing collaboration among national and international nongovernmental organizations and world leaders and by working to prevent violations of human rights rather than react to such violations ("International council," 1995, p. 7).

The work of the HRP has also been coordinated with other Carter Center programs like the African Governance Program and the International Negotiation Network to assist emerging democracies and transitional governments in guaranteeing the protection of their citizens' human rights. These transitional governments face two related human rights problems: coming to terms with past repression and preventing future violations. According to HRP director Dr. Jamal Benomar, "Every new elected government is going to have to cope with repressive powers and with human rights violations," Benomar asked, "What sort of structures are the new governments going to create to prevent these abuses from ever happening again?" (quoted in "Profile: Jamal Benomar," 1991, p. 3). A 1992 international symposium at the Carter Center entitled "Investigating Abuses and Introducing Safeguards in the Democratization Process" addressed these issues ("Investigating abuses," 1992). Representatives to the symposium discussed whether national reconciliation was best accomplished through declarations of amnesty for past abuses or by seeking justice and punishment for those who had abused human rights. The consensus among participants was that while justice is difficult to implement, it is preferable to amnesty ("Coming to terms," 1992, p. 7). President Carter summarized the results of the symposium when he said, "The most significant opportunity available to us today is the chance to coordinate our efforts on an international level to build a new culture of human rights throughout the world" (quoted in "Coming to terms," 1992, p. 7).

These dual goals of overcoming human rights abuses and ensuring future human rights protection were first targeted in HRP activities in Chad and later in Ethiopia and Liberia. As President Carter and the INN became involved in mediating the Ethiopian-Eritrean civil war, human rights considerations helped shape their work. Prior to a 1988 meeting with then President Mengistu, HRP staff briefed President Carter on the human rights situation in Ethiopia and suggested specific recommendations Carter could make during his meetings ("Development of protection program," 1988, p. 11). Among the tangible outcomes of these talks were agreements to facilitate relief aid and to allow for independent monitoring of relief operations, and the later release of several prisoners detained by the Mengistu government. Following the end of the civil war in 1991, President Carter and HRP staff members traveled to Ethiopia and assisted the new Ethiopian government in developing a comprehensive plan to ensure human rights safeguards and protection and in incorporating these plans into the new Ethiopian constitution ("Program helps establish human rights protection," 1992, p. 11). These efforts are ongoing as this emerging democracy struggles to overcome the legacy of thirty years of civil conflict and military oppression.

Personal Interventions by President Carter

On several occasions, President Carter has become personally involved in trying to protect the victims of human rights violations or to have them released from confinement. During negotiations intended to mediate the Ethiopian civil war, President Carter intervened with President Mengistu on behalf of several political prisoners who were subsequently released by the Mengistu government ("Carter's intervention results in prisoner releases," 1989, p. 11). At the same time, the HRP identified prisoners and recommended personal action on the part of President Carter on their behalf in Nigeria, Ghana, Zimbabwe, Zambia, the Sudan, Ethiopia, Nicaragua, Cuba, and China.

In the same way that President Carter's brand of personal diplomacy has been successful, when he intervenes on behalf of political prisoners and the victims of human rights abuse, the leaders of countries that have violated such rights have difficulty ignoring his efforts. According to President Carter, "When there is a threat of exposure, when there is a threat of focusing world-wide attention on a human rights abuse, it is a devastating threat to the country" (quoted in "Investigating abuses," 1992, p. 10).

Acknowledging that silence does nothing to promote human rights, President Carter has publicly spoken out regarding his concern for human rights in general, as well as addressing specific issues and cases. Following the abduction of a Guatemalan human rights worker in October 1990, President Carter sent a personal letter to Guatemalan President Marco Vinicio Cerezo calling for an immediate investigation of the incident ("Carter calls for inquiry," 1990, p. 6). While on a 1991 trip to China to monitor Global 2000 programs, and in the aftermath of China's efforts to silence prodemocracy students in 1989, President Carter publicly raised the issue of human rights at a speech to the College of Foreign Affairs in Beijing. He emphasized the commitments of the Chinese government to the protection of human rights and said, "My hope is that the Chinese government will decide to grant amnesty to all nonviolent dissidents" (quoted in "Carter to Chinese students," 1991, p. 2). In the same speech, Carter recognized that the United States also has human rights issues that are of concern. Interestingly, Carter agreed to the China trip only after the Chinese government agreed that human rights issues would be on the agenda for his talks with Chinese leaders ("Human rights tops agenda," 1991, pp. 1, 4). In October

1991, President Carter again personally contacted the president of Guatemala on behalf of several human rights workers who had reportedly been abducted by the government ("Carter asks Guatemala," 1990, p. 11). As the United States in 1993 was still struggling with the lingering question of what to do with detainees from the 1980 Mariel boatlift, President Carter reminded the nation of the human rights issues related to their detention and urged that the remaining cases be quickly and justly resolved (Gavzer, 1993, p. 6). Also in 1993, as the International Olympic Committee evaluated sites for the games of the year 2000, President Carter briefed the committee on the human rights record of China, which had bid for the games (Roughton, 1993, p. D3). In March 1995, he appealed successfully for the release from detention of a former military leader in Nigeria ("Military leader released," 1995, p. A5). President Carter's personal intervention on behalf of human rights abuses has made a positive difference.

The Carter-Menil Human Rights Foundation and Prize

In addition to the programmatic human rights work of the Carter Center and President Carter's personal involvement in human rights issues, the Carter-Menil Human Rights Foundation was established in 1986 to promote the protection of human rights. The foundation not only supports the human rights work of the center, but recognizes and celebrates the human rights efforts of individuals and organizations through an annual $100,000 prize. These awards have not only brought international attention to the recipient, but have allowed these individuals and groups to continue their vital work.

The individuals and organizations who have received the award have come from broad and diverse backgrounds, but all have demonstrated a commitment to the protection and preservation of human rights. Each year the award is presented on December 10, the anniversary of the United Nations Declaration on Human Rights. The annual awards ceremony also provides President Carter with the opportunity to deliver his annual "State of Human Rights Address."

The first award was presented in 1986 to a Soviet physicist and dissident named Yuri Orlov and to the Group for Mutual Support of Guatemala ("Affirming the human spirit," 1987, p. 4). According to a representative of the Guatemalan group, the prize money "enabled us to buy an office building, secure rooms to temporarily house those fleeing violence, and establish a medical clinic" ("Human rights violations," 1991, p. 9). The 1987 recipient was the group La Vicaria de la Solidaridad, a human rights organization working in Chile. The family of Walter Sisulu, the long-imprisoned leader of the African National Congress, received the award in 1988 for their anti-apartheid work in South Africa. Several years after receiving the award, Sisulu was able to travel to the Carter Center and acknowledged that the award and recognition came at a time when "the situation was very grave" and served as an inspiration to his family and the anti-apartheid movement (quoted in "Carter-Menil winners," 1991, p. 10). Awards in 1989 recognized the work of two Middle Eastern human rights groups, Al-Haq, a Palestinian group that promotes human rights and documents abuses in the occupied territories, and B'Tselem, an Israeli group that monitors human rights on the occupied West Bank and the Gaza Strip ("Middle East groups," 1990, p. 7). The fifth annual award went to two groups, the Consejo de Comunidades Ethnicas Runujel Junam (CERJ) of Guatemala and the Civil Rights Movement (CRM) of Sri Lanka. In announcing these awards, President Carter stated that "the citizens of both Guatemala and Sri Lanka have for decades borne the brunt of grave violations of their rights and dignity with insufficient attention of assistance from the rest of the world" ("Sri Lankan, Guatemalan groups, 1990, p. 6). Dominique de Menil, the foundation's president, suggested that the CERJ and the CRM were "role models of courage and leadership in two countries whose governments have chosen to ignore the voice of truth" (quoted in "Sri Lankan, Guatemalan groups," 1990, p. 6).

The 1991 award was presented posthumously to six Jesuit priests who were killed in 1989 in El Salvador. Joining President Carter for this sixth annual presentation was anti-apartheid leader Nelson Mandela. Dominique de Menil presented Mandela with a special $100,000 award as "a token of our solidarity with your fight against apartheid, which has become today a universal concern of humanity" (quoted in "Latin American activists," 1992, p. 9). After having presented the award to organizations abroad since 1986, in 1992 the foundation honored two U.S. organizations, the Native American Rights Fund and the Haitian Refugee Center, for their work to protect the rights of Native Americans and refugees in the United States ("U.S., Haitian groups," 1993, p. 13).

The efforts of the people of Norway, in general, and the Institute of Applied Social Science (FAFO), in particular, at brokering peace between the Palestinian Liberation Organization (PLO) and Israel were recognized with a special prize in 1994. The so-called Oslo Channel, created by researchers at the FAFO and the Norwegian Foreign Ministry, paved the way for the breakthrough 1993 declaration of principles between the PLO and Israel ("Carter-Menil award," 1994, pp. 1, 7). Both Shimon Peres and Yasir Arafat traveled to Oslo to recognize Norway's contribution to peace in the Middle East. While the monetary prize went to the FAFO, the people of Norway were presented with a Tony Smith sculpture called *Marriage*, which, according to Dominique de Menil, stands as a "door to the world and at the same time a peaceful arch" symbolic of the Norwegians' contributions to peace (quoted in "Carter-Menil award," 1994, p. 7).

In a 1990 interview with the journal *Human Rights*, President Carter was asked what legacy he wished to leave. Carter responded, "I'd like the people to remember me 100 years from now because of peace and human rights, but I've still got to earn that reputation" (quoted in Quade, 1990, p. 52). The work of the HRP of the Carter Center, President Carter's personal involvement in human rights issues and cases, the efforts of the Carter-Menil Human Rights Foundation, and the successful record Carter and these organizations have established go a long way to solidifying the reputation of President Carter as a champion for the human rights of all people in the world.

Humanitarian concerns have shaped much of President Carter's post-presidential agenda, as they shaped the programs of his presidential administration. Global 2000 programs have resulted in tangible differences in the lives of people throughout the developing world. Global 2000's successful agricultural and health-care programs are improving the daily lives of tens of thousands of people. Working to ensure that people can live free from fear of their own governments through the advancement of human rights benefits not only those living in the country, but makes the world in general a better, more humane place in which to live. For true peace to exist, it is not enough that conflict cease. True peace requires that people be allowed to live in conditions of health and fundamental safety. The humanitarian development programs of the Carter Center work to establish these sufficient conditions for peace.

REFERENCES

An action program: Mobilizing international cooperation. (1987, Summer). *Carter Center News*, pp. 10–11.

Affirming the human spirit. (1987, Summer). *Carter Center News*, p. 4.

Caribbean leaders re-examine human rights commitment. (1988, Fall). *Carter Center News*, pp. 1, 7.

Carter, J. E. (1992, Spring). United States has responsibility to protect world's environment. *Carter Center News*, p. 2.

Carter asks Guatemala to investigate abduction of rights workers. (1990, Oct. 21). *New York Times*, p. 11.

Carter calls for inquiry into kidnappings, deaths. (1990, Fall). *Carter Center News*, p. 6.

Carter Center and Merck step up efforts to fight river blindness in Africa. (1995, Winter). *Carter Center News*, p. 12.

Carter Center programs. (1994–1995). Available from the Carter Center, One Copenhill, Atlanta, GA 30307.

Carter legacy. (1991, Apr. 14). (Erie) *Times News* (Associated Press), p. A2.

Carter-Menil award honors people of Norway for peace efforts. (1994, Summer). *Carter Center News*, pp. 1, 7.

Carter-Menil winners honored as human rights heros. (1991, Fall). *Carter Center News*, pp. 10–11.

Carter sets four-nation Africa trip. (1995, Mar. 17). Reuters News Service (available on-line through CD NewsBank 1995 Comprehensive).

Carter to Chinese students: Human rights a global concern. (1991, Spring). *Carter Center News*, p. 2.

Carter's intervention results in prisoner releases. (1989, Fall). *Carter Center News*, p. 11.

Carters take Global 2000 to China. (1987, Summer). *Carter Center News*, p. 4.

CCEU, WHO join to fight tobacco use worldwide. (1990, Fall). *Carter Center News*, p. 11.

Center works to reduce tobacco use in developing countries. (1991, Fall). *Carter Center News*, p. 8.

Ciabattari, J. (1995, July 30). Intelligence report: Wiping out disease. *Parade Magazine* (*Erie Times News*), p. 7.

Cloud, S. W. (1989, Sept. 11). Hail to the ex-chief. *Time*, pp. 60–63.

Coming to terms with the past. (1992, Fall). *Carter Center News*, p. 7.

Conference for global development cooperation. (1992). Conference Report Series, vol. 4, no. 2. Available from the Carter Center, One Copenhill, Atlanta, GA 30307.

Development of protection program. (1988, Fall). *Carter Center News*, p. 11.

Disease eradication task force formed. (1988, Fall). *Carter Center News*, p. 10.

East/West meet on human rights. (1988, Fall). *Carter Center News*, pp. 10–11.

Ex-military leader released in Nigeria. (1995, Mar. 24). *New York Times*, p.A5.

Expansion of health initiatives. (1988, Fall). *Carter Center News*, p. 15.

Feeding the future: A conversation with Nobel laureate Norman Borlaug. (1988, Fall). *Carter Center News*, pp. 14–15.

Gavzer, B. (1993, Dec. 12). Are human rights being abused in our country? *Parade Magazine* (*Erie Times News*), pp. 6–7.

Global 2000, Inc., promoting food self-reliance, improving health standards, and preventing environmental degradation around the world. (undated). Published by the Carter Center of Emory University and Global 2000, Inc. Available from the Carter Center, One Copenhill, Atlanta, GA 30307.

Global 2000 joins World Bank to support African agriculture. (1995, Winter). *Carter Center News*, p. 14.

Guatemalan violence prompts increased human rights efforts. (1990, Spring). *Carter Center News*, p. 11.

Guinea worm eradication efforts receive boost. (1990, Spring). *Carter Center News*, p. 13.

Guinea worm reduced by more than one-third in Nigeria, Ghana. (1991, Fall). *Carter Center News*, p. 14.

Guyana tests new partnerships to stimulate economic development. (1994, Summer). *Carter Center News*, pp. 10–11.

Helping China meet its special education needs. (1989, Fall). *Carter Center News*, p. 15.

Hidden hunger kills millions each year in developing world. (1991, Fall). *Carter Center News*, p. 13.

Human rights in South Africa surveyed. (1989, Fall). *Carter Center News*, p. 11.

Human rights tops agenda for Carter's China visit. (1991, Spring). *Carter Center News*, pp. 1, 4.

Human rights violations continue in El Salvador, Guatemala. (1991, Spring). *Carter Center News*, p. 9.

International community pledges $10 million to fight Guinea worm. (1989, Fall). *Carter Center News*, p. 14.

International council will focus on prevention of human rights violations. (1995, Winter). *Carter Center News*, p. 7.

Investigating abuses and introducing safeguards in the democratization process. (1992). Conference Report Series, vol. 6, no. 1. Available from the Carter Center, One Copenhill, Atlanta, GA 30307.

Latin American activists honored at human rights ceremony. (1992, Spring). *Carter Center News*, p. 9.

Mectizan and the control of river blindness: Making a global impact. (1992, Fall). *Carter Center News*, p. 12.

Merck & Co. donates sight-saving drug. (1991, Spring). *Carter Center News*, p. 13.

Middle East groups win human rights prize. (1990, Spring). *Carter Center News*, p. 7.

New group to defend human rights in war-torn Horn of Africa. (1990, Spring). *Carter Center News*, p. 10.

New program seeks to preserve the world's forests. (1991, Fall). *Carter Center News*, p. 15.

Norway contributes $1.5 million to combat Guinea worm disease. (1994, Summer). *Carter Center News*, p. 13.

Polio eradication: A fitting gift for the 21st century. (1988, Fall). *Carter Center News*, p. 13.

Polio, Guinea worm slated for eradication in the next decade. (1989, Fall). *Carter Center News*, p. 9.

Profile: Jamal Benomar, fellow, human rights program. (1991, Fall). *Carter Center News*, p. 3.

Program helps establish human rights protection in Ethiopia. (1992, Spring). *Carter Center News*, p. 11.

Project Africa: Food security for the 21st century. (1989, Fall). *Carter Center News*, p. 15.

Quade, V. (1990, Sept.). Jimmy Carter works the world. *Human Rights*, pp. 23–25, 52.

Roughton, B. (1993, June 25). IOC chief: Games should be free of political pressure. *Atlanta Journal*, p. D3.

Sri Lankan, Guatemalan groups win rights prize. (1990, Fall). *Carter Center News*, p. 6.

Task force celebrates fifth anniversary. (1989, Fall). *Carter Center News*, p. 13.

Task force takes aim at parasitic infections. (1992, Spring). *Carter Center News*, p. 13.

Teachers and technology: Reaching out to China's disabled. (1991, Spring). *Carter Center News*, pp. 14–15.

Unusual donation aids war on Guinea worm. (1990, Fall). *Carter Center News*, p. 13.

U.S., Haitian groups honored for human rights work. (1993, Spring). *Carter Center News*, p. 13.

USAID joins Carter Center for final assault on Guinea worm. (1995, Winter). *Carter Center News*, p. 9.

CHAPTER 9

PEACEMAKING THROUGH HUMANITARIAN DEVELOPMENT AT HOME

In order for people anywhere to survive and thrive, basic human needs must be met. These needs include health care, basic decent housing, and safe, thriving communities. People cannot fully participate in a society if they are sick or their children are threatened by illness or disease. The prospects for full participation in society are limited if individuals do not have decent housing in which to live and if they do not feel secure in their homes. Individuals and communities are threatened if inner-city neighborhoods are allowed to deteriorate and decay. President Carter spent much of his time during the early years of his post-presidency focusing on international issues. More recently, he has directed the same energy and attention he was able to bring to bear on humanitarian development issues abroad to domestic humanitarian concerns.

Several programs operating at or initiated by the Carter Center have sought to address these domestic humanitarian needs. Health, in the broadest sense of the term—physical, spiritual, emotional, and social—is essential for the peace and well-being of any person. People require not only health care, but to live healthy lives. To do so, the gap between what we know about health and how we live should be closed. Whether children live in the United States or a developing country, they require childhood immunizations in order to remain healthy. In the broadest sense, health care must also ensure the mental as well as the physical health of the individual. Preventing the spread of tobacco use at home and abroad helps to ensure the health of the individual and the nation. Providing decent housing for individuals and families in need helps provide the basis for economic and social participation. Community development and involvement programs can help to rehabilitate, stimulate, and revitalize long-neglected inner-city neighborhoods. These and other humanitarian concerns have shaped the domestic agenda of President Carter and several programs at the Carter Center. These programs include health-care initiatives and programs ranging from childhood immunization to tobacco control, President and Rosalynn Carter's

long-term involvement in and commitment to the organization Habitat for
Humanity, and community development initiatives like the Atlanta and America
projects.

A common thread that unites all of these efforts is that they translate what
is currently known about healthy living into practical programs that address real
needs and problems. Addressing basic humanitarian needs is often not a matter
of extensive research to discover a solution to a problem but of taking action
based on what is already known to be effective and workable. Stated more
simply, these programs involve doing what will work to address the problem,
whether the concern is health care, disease prevention, housing, or community
development and revitalization.

HEALTH-CARE INITIATIVES AND PROGRAMS

Background and Early Efforts

Health-care issues have long been a concern for several Carter Center
programs. These programs date from initiatives and programs begun during the
Carter administration. For example, in 1979, the surgeon general issued a report
on health risk factors entitled "Healthy People." In 1987, the Carter Center, in
collaboration with the U.S. Centers for Disease Control, launched a program to
develop a computer program that would provide individuals with health risk
appraisals based on their personal and lifestyle characteristics ("Health risk
appraisal project," 1987, p. 8). The computer health risk-appraisal program
draws upon the factors identified by the earlier surgeon general's report, analyzes
a confidential questionnaire completed by the individual, and provides a report
recommending specific preventive measures. This project, supported by grants
from the W. K. Kellog Foundation, Morgan Guaranty and Trust Company, and
Southern Bell, resulted in a 1987 conference at the Carter Center titled "Healthier
People."

Since its development and introduction in January 1987, the "Healthier
People" health risk-appraisal program has been disseminated to more than 1,500
agencies and organizations across the country. Agencies using the program
included the U.S. Army, which proposed using the program to evaluate 900,000
enlisted personnel in three years, the Indian Health Service, which provides
health services to a population of 1.2 million Native Americans, and the National
Rural Electric Cooperative Association ("Nearly 1,500 organizations," 1988, p.
9). Another 1987 Carter Center initiative worked with the Henry J. Kaiser
Family Foundation to develop programs to address preventable causes of illness,
disability, and death in the United States that were linked to risk-increasing
behavior ("Kaiser Family Foundation," 1987, p. 8).

The Interfaith Health Program

In October 1989, the Carter Center sponsored a three-day conference called "Striving for Fullness of Life: The Church's Challenge in Health" to address health-care reform—before it was politically expedient to do so—and launched an initiative designed to involve faith communities around the country in the health of their members. The conference, cochaired by President Carter and former Surgeon General C. Everett Koop and cosponsored with the Wheat Ridge Foundation (a Chicago-based Lutheran charitable organization), brought together religious leaders from a variety of denominations who explored how faith communities could become practically involved in improving the health of their members. The conference also addressed major health-care-reform issues in the United States ("Religious leaders call for reform," 1989, p. 8). In characterizing the nation's health-care situation, Koop told the audience of religious leaders that "we need to change the [health-care] system. We need to change it thoroughly, and we need to do it soon" because it does not respond to the needs of at least 15 percent of Americans—primarily the working poor (quoted in "Religious leaders call for reform," 1989, p. 8). President Carter took this opportunity to urge religious leaders to become more involved with the physical health of their communities, as well as to take strong stands against drugs, to minister to AIDS victims, and to help the working poor. In particular, Carter targeted the tobacco industry, noting that "the most addictive drug [tobacco] among the American people last year was responsible for the deaths of 390,000 Americans"—more lives than were claimed by cocaine (quoted in "Religious leaders call for reform," 1989, p. 8). Rosalynn Carter, a long-time advocate for mental health, urged religious groups to help in removing the stigma associated with mental illness.

This conference not only allowed participants to explore programs and health-related ministries for their own communities, but resulted in plans to form a coalition of eleven denominations to lobby Congress on health-care and insurance-reform legislation. James Mason, then assistant secretary for health and human services, told the religious leaders that "churches and synagogues are uniquely equipped to make a major difference in the health of the nation. They should articulate the health benefits from their various traditions in order to improve the health of their people" (quoted in "Religious leaders call for reform," 1989, p. 8). The key, according to Mason and the Carter Center's Dr. William Foege, is for education to close the gap between medical knowledge and the application of that knowledge for healthier living.

The 1989 "Striving for Fullness of Life: The Church's Challenge in Health" conference built upon two earlier Carter Center conferences, one in 1984 called "Closing the Gap" and one in 1986 called "Risks Old and New." These early conferences addressed the gap between what medical knowledge suggests about healthy living and the practice of healthier living by Americans. These interfaith initiatives were supported by a $1.5-million grant in 1992 from the Robert Wood Johnson Foundation to establish an Interfaith Health Resources Center at the Carter Center. At the time, Foege said, "The IHRC will be a catalyst within faith communities to promote their involvement with health issues and to help them respond more effectively to health needs" (quoted in "Helping churches bridge health gap," 1992, p. 5). It also helped to launch the Interfaith Health Program at the Carter Center. Anticipating the future, Foege said, "It's not impossible to dream of thousands of congregations that see health as a seamless whole–physical, mental, social, spiritual–that see poverty and illiteracy and addiction and prejudice and pollution and violence and hopelessness and fatalism and conflict as brokenness, diseases that require that redemptive force offered by the faith community" (quoted in "Challenges of faith and health," 1994, p. 9). President Carter articulated his vision and strong belief in the potential of faith communities to address health-care issues when he said, "I see commitment in all religions to alleviating human suffering and preventing and curing illness, to be a common ground on which faith communities can communicate. This is not a time to talk about theology; it is a time to discover and to assess things that actually work" (quoted in "Challenges of faith and health," 1994, p. 10). As an example of the kinds of things that work, Carter challenged faith communities to make sure that children in their immediate community are immunized, that no one goes hungry or homeless in their community, and that every person has access to basic medical care. The focus here is on small, local efforts that collectively would significantly improve the quality of life for the entire community. The Interfaith Health Program continues to identify effective strategies for health, to publish reports and a newsletter called *Faith and Health* for disseminating health information to faith communities, and actively to work with congregations in low-income areas of Atlanta, in conjunction with the Atlanta Project, in health-promotion and disease-prevention activities ("Challenges of faith and health," 1994, p. 71). While the Interfaith Health Program supports health care reform, it has concluded that with 145 million members, 60 percent of the American population, "U.S. faith groups have an opportunity to create inspired ways to give each individual the power to improve his or her own health" ("Faith leaders learn," 1994, p. 12; "In perspective," 1994, p. 2).

An antiviolence program sponsored by the Interfaith Health Program designed specifically to address gun violence is called Not Even One. This program recognizes, as the Centers for Disease Control has noted, that each year five thousand youths under age nineteen are killed by guns. In February 1994, the Interfaith Health Program held a consultation entitled "The Crisis of Children and Firearms" to address this problem. The consultation produced a report advocating community outreach programs, legislative and legal actions, greater media attention, and continued research on the problem ("Not Even One," 1994). As a part of the research effort, Atlanta was named the first target city for this project. President Carter suggested that following a shooting, an investigative team should examine the root cause of the shooting, how the gun became available, and what could have been done to prevent the shooting, the goal being to limit youth access to guns ("Jimmy Carter campaigns," 1995, p. 11). The

Interfaith Health Program recognizes that while the primary goal of faith communities is the spiritual welfare of their members, they also hold the potential for improving and contributing to their members' physical well-being.

Every Child by Two/All Kids Count

Every Child by Two and All Kids Count are two health-care programs affiliated with the Carter Center. Every Child by Two is a childhood immunization initiative begun primarily through the efforts of former First Lady Rosalynn Carter. All Kids Count is a domestic offshoot of immunization programs sponsored by the Task Force for Child Survival and Development, a program also affiliated with the Carter Center.

In response to a significant increase in the cases of measles in 1990–the worst epidemic in twenty years, with more than 27,000 reported cases–Rosalynn Carter and Betty Bumpers, wife of Arkansas Senator Dale Bumpers, initiated the Every Child by Two campaign. Rosalynn Carter and Betty Bumpers had worked together to set up immunization programs in Georgia and Arkansas in the 1970s and had helped to achieve a national immunization level of 96 percent during the Carter presidency ("Carter, Bumpers immunization goal," 1991, p. 12). According to Rosalynn Carter, "It is a shameful fact that children in this country suffer from diseases that are easy to prevent. It is imperative that we move quickly to increase our capacity to vaccinate children who are at risk for measles and other diseases, including mumps, rubella, and polio" (quoted in "Carter, Bumpers immunization goal," 1991, p. 12). This effort enlisted the help of governors' spouses and organizations nationwide to call attention to this public policy problem and to educate the public about the importance of early childhood immunizations. The goal of the program was to have every child receive the immunizations recommended by the Centers for Disease Control by the age of two. In the fall of 1991, Rosalynn Carter and Betty Bumpers traveled to several states to visit clinics and organizations and to meet with governors' spouses and congressional spouses to emphasize the importance of immunization efforts. In addition to the immediate response to the epidemic, Rosalynn Carter at the time urged the medical community and insurers specifically to reform the health-care system to include coverage of childhood immunization. According to Betty Bumpers, "It [childhood immunization] should be as much a public health matter as clean drinking water" (quoted in "Carter, Bumpers immunization goal," 1991, p. 12). In 1992, Rosalynn Carter and Betty Bumpers toured the South to enlist the support of Hillary Clinton (wife of President–elect Bill Clinton), Tipper Gore (wife of Vice President–elect Al Gore), Mary Sasser (wife of Senator Jim Sasser), and Rhea Chiles (wife of Governor Lawton Chiles of Florida) in this important campaign ("Southern tour promotes childhood immunizations," 1992, p. 13). In the last several years, campaigns have been initiated in thirty-six states, with plans to form a partnership with the American Nurses Association and seventy other national organizations to develop effective immunization programs nationwide ("Carter Center programs," 1994, p. 12; "Waging peace," 1993, p. 39). When Every Child by Two celebrated its third anniversary in 1994, Rosalynn Carter commented that the success of the program results from the fact that "the public and private sectors are working together, and that's the way it has to be if we're going to solve this problem" (quoted in "Healthy start for childhood," 1994, p. 14). Another goal of the Every Child by Two initiative was to develop a computer registry and tracking system for childhood immunization.

The Task Force for Child Survival and Development, a program begun in 1984 to coordinate and expand global immunization efforts, developed a program in 1992 called All Kids Count. The program was made possible by a $9-million grant from the Robert Wood Johnson Foundation ("All Kids Count goal," 1992, p. 13). The program is designed to track childhood immunization in children under the age of five. This program recognizes that while 95 percent of school-age children are immunized, the rates are much lower for preschool-age children—therefore the name "All Kids Count" ("All Kids Count goal," 1992, p. 13). Through the program, communities are provided with funding to develop computer systems to link hospitals, schools, public health agencies, and doctors' offices in an effort to ensure that all children at risk of preventable disease receive the recommended immunizations ("Carter Center programs," 1994, p. 11; "Waging peace," 1993, p. 39). The need for this tracking system became evident during the measles outbreak that occurred in 1990. Each of these programs complements the work of the other in an effort to ensure that all children get a healthy start on life and are protected from preventable disease.

Mental Health Program

Rosalynn Carter has been an advocate for the mentally ill of the country since her days as first lady of Georgia and later in 1977–78 as honorary chair of the President's Commission on Mental Health. This long-term commitment continues through the Mental Health Task Force at the Carter Center. Even before the formal opening of the center in 1986, Rosalynn Carter had formed a collaborative partnership with the Department of Psychiatry at Emory University to sponsor the Annual Rosalynn Carter Symposia on Mental Health Policy ("Children and families at risk," 1995, p. 65). These conferences provide the opportunity for mental health consumers, advocates, and professionals to meet to address mental health issues, to develop specific initiatives, and to encourage the implementation of mental health-care programs. Since their inauguration in 1985, these symposia have addressed issues such as the mental health of the elderly, emotional disorders in children, family support for the mentally ill, financing mental health services and research, mental health in health-care reform, and most recently, children and families at risk ("Children and families at risk," 1995, p. 65; "Carter Center programs," 1994, p. 9).

As the nation turned its attention toward health-care reform in 1992,

Rosalynn Carter was a strong advocate not only for such reform, but for the inclusion of mental health coverage in any health-care-reform proposal. She noted that "just as mind and body are one, equitable mental health benefits must be a part of health care reform." She further noted that "the failure to address mental health care reform will lead not only to unnecessary suffering, but also to extraordinary public and private expense" (quoted in "Healthcare reform must address mental health issues," 1992, p. 2). In 1992, the eighth annual Rosalynn Carter Symposium on Mental Health Policy addressed the issue of the need for equitable mental and physical health-care benefits. At that symposium, Rosalynn Carter argued that "we must recognize that to be healthy, one must be mentally healthy" (quoted in "Mental health should be part," 1992, p. 5). In March 1993, Rosalynn Carter addressed the U.S. House of Representatives' Working Group on Mental Illness to advocate for the inclusion of mental health-care coverage in national health-care reform. Her advocacy efforts and those of the Mental Health Program continued at a daylong conference in Washington, D.C., on the Clinton administration's health-care-reform package ("Mental health: Coverage," 1993, p. 10). In November 1993, amid the national debate on health-care reform, the ninth annual Rosalynn Carter Symposium on Mental Health Policy discussed issues of access to, and the quality of, mental health-care services in national health-care reform and again urged coverage of mental health treatment ("National organizations urge more coverage," 1993, p. 5). Former First Lady Betty Ford has worked with Rosalynn Carter to improve mental health care and for its inclusion in health-care reform. Both former first ladies argue that early treatment of substance abuse and mental illness saves money in the long term. As Betty Ford concluded, "The dollars we spend in providing treatment not only save lives but also develop responsible fathers, mothers, employers, and citizens who better our communities" (quoted in "Mrs. Carter and Mrs. Ford," 1994, p. 6).

Rosalynn Carter's concern for health care led her to write *Helping Yourself Help Others: A Book for Caregivers* (1994). In this book, she offered advice and documented the research of doctors, social workers, nursing-home supervisors, and family caregivers. This book is addressed to those who provide care for people with physical and mental illnesses. It is based on research conducted at the Rosalynn Carter Institute of Georgia Southwestern College. This research determined the needs of people who care for the elderly, the chronically ill, or disabled relatives ("New books by the Carters," 1995, p. 10).

The Tobacco Control Program

Perhaps the single most preventable cause of disease and death in the United States is the consumption of tobacco. According to the U.S. Centers for Disease Control, the use of tobacco kills 8,300 Americans each week, some 400,000 annually—more than double the total combined deaths caused by alcohol, car accidents, AIDS, suicides, homicides, fires, cocaine, and heroin (reported in

"Waging peace," 1993, p. 30). The Tobacco Control Program at the Carter Center takes both a global and a national focus in seeking to prevent tobacco-related disease and death and to promote smoke-free societies through education and legislation. In addition to the educational and legislative efforts of the Carter Center, President Carter has become a vocal advocate for a significant increase in the tobacco tax in order to fund health-care reform or deficit reduction. The issue hits close to home for President Carter, who noted, "I know the incalculable toll of suffering and human loss caused by tobacco use. My father, my mother, both sisters, and my brother died of cancer. Everyone of them smoked cigarettes" (1993, p. 2). According to Carter, a doubling of the tobacco tax would raise approximately $30 billion in new revenue that could be used to better fund health-care programs over and above those required to treat the victims of tobacco-related illness. He cited Canada as an example of a country that significantly raised its tobacco taxes and saw a 40 percent decline in smoking, including a two-thirds reduction in teen smoking. Speaking as a public policy advocate, President Carter said, "Especially for our children, I urge President Clinton and the new Congress to take this historic opportunity and boost the tobacco tax" (1993, p. 2). In cooperation with the U.S. Centers for Disease Control and the World Health Organization, the Carter Center has shared model tobacco-control legislation with developing African nations and has encouraged programs designed to teach children of the dangers of tobacco before they start to smoke ("Waging peace," 1993, p. 30).

HABITAT FOR HUMANITY

Habitat for Humanity formally began in August 1976 when twenty-six people met at Koinonia Farm, a Christian community located in southwest Georgia, to form a new organization to continue the work begun at Koinonia Farm. Koinonia Farm began as a Christian community in 1942 under the leadership of Clarence and Florence Jordan and Martin and Mabel England. It evolved into an organization designed to aid the poor through providing decent low-cost housing (Fuller and Fuller, 1990, p. 4).

In 1965, Millard and Linda Fuller, the founders of Habitat for Humanity, joined Koinonia Farm in its work with the poor. In 1968, the Fullers and others at Koinonia Farm launched a program called Partnership Housing that began building no-interest houses for those in need. The first of many houses built by this group was constructed in 1969. From these beginnings, Habitat for Humanity has grown and flourished from a local initiative to an international organization dedicated to providing simple, decent, no-interest housing for the working poor. Each local affiliate is ecumenical in orientation, raises money locally for local projects, and depends on local volunteers to build homes. (Those interested in a more detailed account of the founding and work of Habitat for Humanity should read Millard and Linda Fuller's *The Excitement Is Building* [1990], Millard Fuller and Diane Scott's *Love in the Mortar Joints* [1980], and

Millard Fuller's *The Theology of the Hammer* [1994] which explains the biblical foundations of the organization.)

By the early 1990s, there were 500 Habitat affiliates in thirty nations, and 5,000 homes had been constructed, with Habitat houses being built at a rate of approximately 6 per day. By the mid-1990s, Habitat was completing houses at an average rate of 35 per day. An explosion of activity by Habitat affiliates throughout the world has been seen in recent years. In 1994, Habitat completed and dedicated its 30,000th house in a building program in Americus, Georgia, the home of Habitat for Humanity International. By mid-1995, there were more than 1,100 affiliates worldwide, operating in thirty-five countries ("New affiliates approved by HFHI," 1995, p. 15). Habitat has grown since 1976 to be counted among the largest builders of single-family housing in the country ("HFHI ranked," 1995, p. 14).

As Millard Fuller recalled, he went to Plains, Georgia, in 1984 to ask the Carters to become involved with Habitat. At this meeting, President Carter asked how he could be helpful. Fuller put together a list of fifteen things he could do, and "he agreed to do all of them" (quoted in "Tribute to Jimmy Carter," 1995, p. 16). Fuller explained that "without a doubt, the single most significant factor in Habitat's explosive growth over the past few years has been the involvement of former President Jimmy Carter and his wife Rosalynn" (Fuller and Fuller, 1990, p. 41).

The Carters became actively involved with Habitat during the summer of 1984 when they worked with a Habitat group to renovate a six-story building in New York City into housing for nineteen families. Later in the year, Jimmy Carter joined Habitat's International Board of Directors, and Rosalynn became a member of the Habitat Board of Advisors. As a member of the board, Jimmy Carter agreed to chair the "10 Million Campaign Committee," which by December 1986 had raised $12 million, including honoraria donated by Carter, individual and corporate contributions, and donations of building materials (Fuller and Fuller, 1990, pp. 41–42). As he wrote in tribute to Jimmy Carter's twelve years of involvement with Habitat, Millard Fuller said, "Jimmy Carter has been, and continues to be, a tremendous blessing to this ministry. He is a skilled builder, an indefatigable worker and an eloquent spokesman for Habitat" (quoted in "Tribute to Jimmy Carter," 1995, p. 16).

Perhaps President Carter's most significant contribution to Habitat's work is the media attention he is able to draw during the annual Jimmy Carter Work Projects. The 1995 work project in the Watts/Willowbrook neighborhood of Los Angeles was the twelfth such blitz-build effort. One of the earliest Jimmy Carter Work Projects took place in July 1986 in the West Garfield neighborhood of Chicago. The building project started on Monday and concluded with homeowners moving into their houses on Friday. The Carters worked alongside other volunteers during the week and even celebrated their fortieth wedding anniversary in a run-down, three-dollar per night hotel (Fuller and Fuller, 1990, pp. 42–44). As Millard Fuller recalled, "The Carters, of course, were the focus of the media attention. A slew of reporters made the work project front-page prime-time news," and according to Fuller, "Habitat for Humanity got 'on the map' in Chicago and the whole Midwest during the week" (Fuller and Fuller, 1990, p. 44). In addition to the media attention generated by a former president pounding nails to build housing for those in need, Fuller said, "The Carters' presence alone makes things happen when they need to happen" (Fuller and Fuller, 1990, p. 45). He recounted a story from the Chicago build when additional funds were needed to complete the project. A prominent banker organized a luncheon for a "who's who" of Chicago. Commenting on the success of the luncheon, Fuller noted, "His [Carter's] presence made the difference. And that would be the story across the nation over and over in the years ahead" (Fuller and Fuller, 1990, pp. 45–46).

In 1987, the Jimmy Carter Work Project was a blitz-build project in Charlotte, North Carolina, where 350 volunteer builders erected 14 homes over the course of the week. This project, in conjunction with other Habitat House Raising Week projects around the country and throughout the world, succeeded in surpassing Habitat's goal of building 1,000 homes in 1987. In fact, 1987 saw more than 1,200 homes built under Habitat sponsorship. The ambitious goal of 1,000 houses was in part inspired by the fact that 1987 was declared the International Year of Shelter for the Homeless by the United Nations.

Building on the successes of 1987, Habitat House-Raising Walk 1988 was launched. The event would combine the Jimmy Carter Work Project and the House-Raising Week from previous years with a marathon walk designed to raise awareness of the need for decent housing, as well as to raise funds to support Habitat. The event celebrated the first twelve years of Habitat's work with a 1,200-mile walk from Portland, Maine, through fourteen states to Atlanta, Georgia. The walk raised $1.2 million for Habitat's work, and along the route, walkers built or renovated 120 houses. The goal for the summer was to build 400 houses nationwide. Jimmy Carter's efforts during this eventful summer included helping to renovate 5 apartments at a north central Philadelphia Habitat project, working on a large blitz-build of 20 houses in Atlanta (the site of the 1988 Jimmy Carter Work Project), and addressing the twelfth-anniversary celebration of the founding of Habitat at the end of the summer. In all, 30,000 people participated, and 154 houses were worked on or completed during the twelve-week event. While the 1988 Habitat goal of 2,000 houses was not reached, more than 2,000 houses were completed in 1989. Annual Jimmy Carter Work Projects have built houses in Milwaukee, Wisconsin (1989), Tijuana, Mexico (1990), Miami, Florida (1991), Americus, Georgia (1992), Kitchener-Waterloo, Canada (1993), Eagle Butte, South Dakota (1994), and most recently in the riot-devastated area of East Los Angeles, California (1995).

Why does a former president of the United States, who could easily retire quietly and live comfortably, choose to become so deeply involved in an organization like Habitat for Humanity? Speaking at the twentieth-anniversary celebration of the founding of Habitat for Humanity, Carter addressed this question when he said, "I get a lot more recognition for building homes in partnership with poor people in need than I ever got for the Camp David Accords or for SALT II or for all our [the Carter Center] projects in Africa and Asia or anything I do now since I left the White House." He further explained, "Habitat is not a sacrifice that we [he and Rosalynn] make for others. Habitat is a blessing for those of us who volunteer to help others" (quoted in Fuller and Fuller, 1990, p. 46). President Carter's work with Habitat is clearly not something he has to do; rather, given his background and Christian faith, it is something he wants to do. Helping to provide a decent home often provides hope for an entire family to participate fully in community life.

THE ATLANTA PROJECT

While much of the work of the Carter Center focuses on the international community, the Atlanta Project (TAP) expanded Carter Center programs from the global to the local level of concern. It was Emory University President James T. Laney who first proposed the new domestic focus for programs at the Carter Center, suggesting that the coalition-building approach of President Carter and the Carter Center that had worked so successfully on an international scale could be focused on serious domestic problems ("Atlanta Project targets crime," 1991, p. 4). Carter became convinced of the need for such programs when he and Rosalynn met Baby Pumpkin, a crack-addicted, premature baby hospitalized at an Atlanta hospital they visited in 1991. According to Carter, "We have become more keenly aware of the critical social problems in our own community. The severe challenges faced by Baby Pumpkin and many others who struggle against great odds moved us to create TAP" (quoted in "Your guide to The Atlanta Project," 1994).

While the city of Atlanta in recent years has met with several notable successes, such as being described by *Fortune Magazine* as the best American city in which to do business, and hosting the 1994 Super Bowl and the 1996 Summer Olympic Games, there are still significant problems. These include serious homelessness, 30 percent fewer immunized five-year-olds than in the country of Bangladesh, and being the second-poorest city in the country ("Atlanta Project," 1992, pp. 2–3). For Atlanta to achieve success, according to President Carter, "We need to show it is possible to alleviate hopelessness—both on the part of those in need, and on the part of people who are in a position to help" (quoted in "Atlanta Project targets crime," 1991, p. 5). Developing a partnership between those in need and those who can help became the focus of TAP.

The Carter Center describes TAP, launched in October 1991, as an initiative to channel the talent and goodwill of residents throughout the Atlanta area into one coordinated effort to replace poverty and despair with hope and opportunity. TAP does not attempt to create new social service agencies or organizations; rather, it seeks to more effectively coordinate and link the agencies and organizations that already exist with the people who need their services. In its early stages, TAP coordinator Dan Sweat said that the goal of the project was "to bridge the gap between those in need and government agencies, social and health workers, non-profit organizations, religious institutions, educators and law enforcement" (quoted in "Atlanta Project targets crime," 1991, p. 1). Among the goals of the program are to immunize every child against preventable disease, provide prenatal care, open health clinics in all area schools, develop corporate and religious partnerships with area schools, build and repair housing, assist local police to control violence and drugs in the community, and provide volunteer probation counselors for juvenile delinquents ("Atlanta Project targets crime," 1991, p. 1).

Partnership and volunteerism are the keys or cornerstones for TAP. During its first year, the structure of the program was designed to link those in need in neighborhoods with partners and volunteers through the auspices of the Carter Center. Twenty key neighborhoods or clusters in the three-county Atlanta area were identified. Each cluster had a paid coordinator in an office located at a neighborhood school in order to provide better access to residents. People from targeted neighborhoods worked with the secretariat and advisory board at the Carter Center. The partnership idea came into play as major Atlanta corporations and organizations were asked to sponsor or adopt a cluster and to provide a full-time adviser to coordinate volunteer and economic development efforts in that cluster. Partnerships have been created between the twenty clusters, twenty major corporate sponsors, and eighteen colleges and universities that can offer resources, advice, and assistance.

Among major corporate partners are AT&T, Arthur Andersen, Atlanta Gas and Light, BankSouth, BellSouth, Coca-Cola, Cox Enterprises, Delta Air Lines, Equifax, Equitable Real Estate, Georgia Power, Holland Ware, Home Depot, IBM, Marriott, NationsBank, Sun Trust, Turner Broadcasting, United Parcel Service, and Wachovia ("Corporate volunteers join with clusters," 1992, p. 8). Corporate partners have provided various programs and opportunities for their clusters. For example, partnerships sponsored by BellSouth have worked with literacy programs, Holland Ware has donated one million books, Home Depot has focused on home improvement, Cox Enterprises has addressed communication needs, and paratroopers from Ft. Benning have worked with middle- and high-school students in drug-prevention programs. NationsBank established a three-month pilot program with half a million dollars in short-term financing to assist small businesses in one of the clusters, and the Marriott Corporation hosted a Family Resource Fair for its cluster to make residents more aware of the agencies and programs available to them ("Corporate volunteers join with clusters," 1992, p. 8; Peirce, 1992, p. 2443).

As TAP celebrated its first year of operations, President Carter commented that "cluster coordinators, with the help of their corporate partners and other supporters, have made extraordinary progress in bringing neighbors together to start addressing issues ranging from violence in schools and lack of job skills, to beautifying neighborhoods and participating in the arts" (quoted in

"Neighborhoods embrace the Atlanta Project," 1993, p. 7). Among the initiatives proposed for the second year was for clusters to mount a communitywide offensive against violence called "TAP into Peace." Five thousand volunteers went door-to-door in TAP neighborhoods to begin the program and to gather ideas and suggestions from residents on how to make their communities safer ("Atlanta project begins campaign," 1994, p. 1).

A childhood immunization program was undertaken by TAP in the spring of 1993. The effort was described by the Carter Center as the "most comprehensive immunization program ever mounted in this country" ("Thousands immunized," 1993, p. 1). Addressing the alarmingly low rate of immunization among Atlanta's children, TAP sought to identify, immunize or certify immunization, and begin to track the health-care needs of all children under age six in the targeted three-county Atlanta area.

The program began when 7,000 volunteers went door-to-door in the neighborhoods to identify and gather information on the 54,000 children living in the targeted area. In addition to determining the immunization status of the area's preschool children, a health questionnaire was completed on each child to assist in determining future health-care programs. Information gathered from these health questionnaires was computerized, using equipment provided by IBM, in order to track and provide future information. Following this needs assessment, forty-three immunization sites were set up, and a weeklong free immunization drive was implemented to coincide with the National Pre-School Immunization Week of the U.S. Centers for Disease Control. The program succeeded in immunizing or certifying the immunization records of 17,000 preschoolers during the weeklong program (Scott, 1994, p. C3; "Thousands immunized," 1993, p. 1). In actuality, this immunization program was, in a way, a complement to the Every Child by Two program sponsored by the Carter Center and led by Rosalynn Carter and Betty Bumpers. The families and children participating in the program were rewarded for their participation by a celebration that included an appearance by singer Michael Jackson ("Vaccinations may lead to Jackson concert," 1993, p. 2A). Dr. Julius Richmond, former U.S. surgeon general and professor emeritus at the Harvard Medical School, commended the immunization effort, stating, "By bringing health agencies and others together for this immunization effort, The Atlanta Project is developing a model for the nation" (quoted in "Thousands immunized," 1993, p. 1).

In fact, the intent of TAP was to provide a model for community development that could be used by other cities. To date, a hundred delegations from cities across the country have visited with TAP officials to study the model's duplication. This duplication was part of the intent of the project and would eventually become the America Project, which was established in 1992 as a way to share the experience of TAP with communities around the country.

TAP has experienced several significant accomplishments during its first several years of operation. TAP has raised $14 million in cash support and $14 million in in-kind support toward a five-year operating budget and has inspired schoolchildren to raise an additional $100,000 in spare change. It has enlisted the help of 100,000 volunteers, helped the Atlanta Housing Authority secure a $33.5-million federal grant to rebuild low-income housing, coordinated the efforts of seventy-five public and private housing agencies to avoid fragmentation and overlap, and secured pledges of cooperation and support at the federal level from President Bush and President-elect Clinton ("Corporate volunteers join with clusters," 1992, p. 8). These pledges of support from Bush and Clinton were received by Jimmy Carter during meetings with them during the spring of 1992. Realizing that agencies and services already existed at the federal, state, and local levels, Carter sought better cooperation from federal agencies as TAP proceeded. President Carter met with Bush cabinet members and key Senate and House leaders seeking assistance in waiving some regulations governing federal programs. At the time, TAP Coordinator Dan Sweat stated, "President Bush's Cabinet officers seemed receptive to the idea of making Atlanta a test case. We hope to work with them in a nonpartisan effort to see what might happen if we break down some barriers" (quoted in "Atlanta Project," 1992, p. 6).

President Carter's work to break down barriers and to provide better services to those in need also resulted in an experiment to simplify government paperwork. With the help of President Bush in the form of an executive order, TAP was given unprecedented authority to cut through bureaucratic red tape (Kurylo, 1993a, p. A5). Carter's efforts to streamline and simplify access for those in need continued when he met with Clinton administration officials regarding TAP immunization programs. Carter briefed President Clinton and cabinet officials on TAP, urged better cooperation among federal agencies that deal with programs to aid the urban poor, and found the Clinton administration "very eager" to work with TAP (quoted in Kurylo, 1993b, p. C6). In April 1994, Georgia state and federal officials signed an agreement to test the Georgia Common Access Application, a form that would reduce sixty-four pages of application paperwork to eight pages ("Experiment in easing paperwork," 1994, p. A16; "Jimmy Carter helping simplify government aid," 1994, p. 4A). The six-month test period for the form allowed the poor in urban Atlanta to apply for Aid to Families with Dependent Children, food stamps, Medicaid, Social Security benefits, housing, and the Women, Infants, and Children program by using the simplified form.

Future Force, another TAP program, allowed Atlanta youth to visit Crested Butte, Colorado, to enjoy the resort and helped raise money for TAP. As the youth enjoyed the ski resort, Carter raised $500,000 for TAP by auctioning autographed photographs of former presidents Nixon, Ford, Carter, Reagan, and Bush taken at the dedication of the Reagan Library in 1991 (Scott, 1994, pp. C1, 3; "Jimmy Carter," 1994, p. 4A).

The work of TAP has expanded to include economic development. In 1994, TAP, the Atlanta Chamber of Commerce, and six financial institutions formed Business Community Development Corporation to make available $11.5 million for small-business loans. When the corporation was announced in the spring of

1994, President Carter said, "This is a good example of what can be done when service providers, banks, financial experts, and community groups draw together in a focused effort. We hope this new loan fund will boost small businesses and create new jobs in our city" ("Loan fund," 1994, p. 8).

Taken together, the health, immunization, and tobacco-control programs, the mission of Habitat for Humanity to provide decent and affordable housing, and TAP community development and revitalization efforts all work to improve the daily lives of people in need. In the same way that humanitarian development programs targeted at developing countries improve the health, socioeconomic welfare, and safety of people and remove these factors as potential sources of conflict, these domestic efforts provide similar results. When Americans are healthy and their children are immunized against preventable disease, when they are provided with decent and affordable housing, and when their communities are working to address neighborhood safety and economic concerns, not only are individuals better able to participate fully in society, but the country as a whole is enriched and enhanced. While people in the United States live in relative peace when compared with many developing countries, the conditions under which the poorest of Americans live are, nevertheless, the concern of all Americans. Not only is alleviating disease, substandard housing, and urban decline the right thing to do based on humanitarian principles, but addressing these concerns allows all members of society to participate fully and to contribute, thereby benefiting the nation as a whole.

REFERENCES

All Kids Count goal. (1992, Spring). *Carter Center News*, p. 13.

The Atlanta Project. (1991–1992). Brochure available from the Carter Center, One Copenhill, Atlanta, GA 30307.

Atlanta project begins campaign to stop violence. (1994, Summer). *Carter Center News*, pp. 1, 8–9.

Atlanta project targets crime, poverty, and drug abuse in urban areas. (1991, Fall). *Carter Center News*, pp. 1, 4–5.

The Atlanta Project: Uniting a community. (1992, Spring). *Carter Center News*, pp. 6, 12.

Carter, J. E. (1993, Spring). Proposed tobacco tax would raise money and save lives. *Carter Center News*, p. 2.

Carter, Bumpers immunization goal: Every child by two. (1991, Fall). *Carter Center News*, p. 12.

Carter Center programs, 1994. (1994). Brochure available from the Carter Center, One Copenhill, Atlanta, GA 30307.

Carter, R. (1994). *Helping yourself help others: A book for caregivers*. New York: Times Books.

The challenges of faith and health. (1994, Jan.). A report of the National Conference of the Interfaith Health Program of the Carter Center, supported by the Robert Wood Johnson Foundation. Available from the Carter Center, One Copenhill, Atlanta, GA 30307.

Children and families at risk: Collaborating with our schools. (1995). Report of the Tenth Annual Rosalynn Carter Symposium on Mental Health Policy. Available from the Carter Center, One Copenhill, Atlanta, GA 30307.

Corporate volunteers join with clusters. (1992, Fall). *Carter Center News*, p. 8.

An experiment in easing paperwork: 64 pages reduced to 8. (1994, Apr. 19). *New York Times*, p. A16.

Faith leaders learn how to make their communities healthy. (1994, Summer). *Carter Center News*, pp. 11–12.

Fuller, M., and Fuller, L. (1990). *The excitement is building.* Dallas: Word Publishing.

Health risk appraisal project. (1987, Summer). *Carter Center News*, p. 8.

Healthcare reform must address mental health issues. (1992, Fall). *Carter Center News*, p. 2.

A healthy start for children. (1994, Summer). *Carter Center News*, p. 14.

Helping churches bridge health gap for the poor. (1992, Fall). *Carter Center News*, p. 5.

HFHI ranked among nation's top homebuilders. (1995, Aug./Sept.). *Habitat World*, p. 14.

In perspective. (1994, Summer). *Carter Center News*, p. 2.

Jimmy Carter campaigns to keep guns from kids. (1995, Apr. 30). *Parade Magazine* (*Erie Daily Times*), p. 11.

Jimmy Carter helping simplify government aid. (1994, Apr. 19). *Erie Daily Times* (Associated Press), p. 4A.

Jimmy Carter: Names in the news. (1994, Feb. 23). *Erie Daily Times*, p. 4A.

The Kaiser Family Foundation. (1987, Summer). *Carter Center News*, p. 8.

Kurylo, E. (1993a, Mar. 4). Carter to discuss his war on Atlanta poverty with Clinton aides. *Atlanta Journal–Atlanta Constitution*, p. A5.

———. (1993b, Mar. 5). Carter sees a friend in Clinton: Atlanta in the spotlight. *Atlanta Journal–Atlanta Constitution*, p. C6.

Loan fund will assist small businesses in TAP neighborhoods. (1994, Summer). *Carter Center News*, p. 8.

Mental health: Coverage vital to health care reform. (1993, Spring). *Carter Center News*, p. 10.

Mental health should be part of total healthcare package. (1992, Fall). *Carter Center News*, p. 5.

Mrs. Carter and Mrs. Ford join forces for mental health and substance abuse benefits in national health care reform. (1994, Summer). *Carter Center News*, p. 6.

National organizations urge more coverage for mental health in health care reform. (1993, Fall). *Carter Center News*, p. 5.

Nearly 1,500 organizations join HRA network. (1988, Fall). *Carter Center News*, p. 9.

Neighborhoods embrace the Atlanta Project. (1993, Fall). *Carter Center News*, p. 7.

New affiliates approved by HFHI. (1995, Apr.). *Habitat World*, p. 15.

New books by the Carters. (1995, Winter). *Carter Center News*, p. 10.

Not even one: A report on the crisis of children and firearms. (1994, Feb.). A report produced by the Interfaith Health Program at the Carter Center, and supported by the Carnegie Corporation of New York and the Robert Wood Johnson Foundation. Available from the Carter Center, One Copenhill, Atlanta, GA 30307.

Peirce, N. R. (1992). A former president's finest hour? *National Journal, 24*(43), 2443.

Religious leaders call for reform in U.S. health care. (1989, Fall). *Carter Center News*,
    p. 8.
Scott, P. (1994, Feb. 28). Future Force kids generate hope. *Atlanta Journal–Atlanta
    Constitution*, pp. C1, C3.
Southern tour promotes childhood immunizations. (1992, Fall). *Carter Center News*, p.
    13.
Thousands immunized through Atlanta Project children's health initiative. (1993, Spring).
    Carter Center News, pp. 1, 4–6.
A tribute to Jimmy Carter. (1995, Aug./Sept.). *Habitat World*, p. 16.
Vaccinations may lead to Jackson concert. (1993, Feb. 16). *Erie Daily Times*
    (Associated Press), p. 2A.
Waging peace around the world. (1993). Available from the Carter Center, One
    Copenhill, Atlanta, GA 30307.
Your guide to the Atlanta Project. (1994, Spring). Brochure available from the Carter
    Collaboration Center, P.O. Box 5317, Atlanta, GA 30307-5317.

CHAPTER 10

ASSESSING THE FIRST FIFTEEN YEARS OF THE CARTER POST-PRESIDENCY

Traditionally, the final chapter of a book draws a story to its conclusion, reviews the major episodes to be remembered, and recounts the important lessons to be learned. In the case of Jimmy Carter's post-presidency, there is not yet a conclusion because most, if not all, of the Carter Center programs, projects, and initiatives that have been profiled are ongoing efforts. Further, although President Carter is in his early seventies, he shows no signs of actually retiring, as he continues to champion the causes and issues that have consumed his time over the last fifteen years. Even if he were to retire, the Carter Center would remain as a dynamic and living legacy to his life and his work. By design and planning, through its endowment and formal association with Emory University, the Carter Center will continue the peacemaking work begun by President and Rosalynn Carter long after they are no longer active participants.

Rather than a conclusion, this final chapter should more accurately be thought of as a status report—or perhaps a midterm assessment—of President Carter's most important career, that of peacemaker. As such, President Carter clearly has carved out for himself a unique and valuable role to play since leaving the White House in 1981. Since he has established this role and in doing so has redefined the traditional role of ex-president, three important questions remain to be addressed: What has President Carter accomplished since leaving office? How has he been able to achieve these accomplishments? Why has he pursued the difficult role of peacemaker—what has motivated his pursuit of peace?

REFLECTING ON THE ACCOMPLISHMENTS OF THE FIRST FIFTEEN YEARS

In the last fifteen years, former President Jimmy Carter has not achieved world peace. In many tangible and real ways, however, he has helped to make the world more peaceful. President Carter has not only made the world more peaceful by challenging the parties engaged in armed conflicts to seek jointly the means of resolving or managing their conflict—what have been referred to as the necessary conditions for peace—but he has also cultivated peaceful relations among people by addressing the fundamental human conditions that create the foundations for peace—what have been termed the sufficient conditions for peace. The programs and initiatives of the Carter Center have pursued this dual focus and have achieved a number of significant accomplishments.

The International Negotiation Network (INN) has become the dominant program at the Carter Center for addressing the resolution of armed conflicts. The INN has filled a unique and critical niche or gap in world peacemaking by focusing attention and expertise on those civil conflicts that other organizations have historically been unable to address. In addition to the academic and policy-study activities of the INN in the form of its various consultations, its action orientation has achieved a measure of success in the Ethiopian-Eritrean, Liberian, and Sudanese civil wars over the last several years. Complete success has not been achieved in any of these three cases, but gains have been made in the form of programs to strengthen the emerging democracy created after the Ethiopian-Eritrean civil war, continuing efforts to mediate among the parties in conflict in Liberia, and cease-fires in the Sudan that have facilitated humanitarian aid. These countries have not achieved peace, but they are working toward peace through the assistance of President Carter and the programs at the Carter Center.

Three potential international hot spots were cooled somewhat by diplomatic missions led by President Carter in 1994. Simmering tensions on the Korean Peninsula were prevented from boiling over because President Carter agreed to talk to a North Korean president whom the international community had tried to isolate and sanction into submission. Anyone can speculate as to what might have happened had President Carter not visited North Korea and had the situation been allowed to escalate. The fact of the matter is that when he was invited, he did engage President Kim Il Sung in dialogue, and he initiated diplomatic efforts that would ultimately resolve the immediate crisis and lay the foundation for further talks among the parties in conflict. In Haiti, the very real—if not inevitable—prospect of an armed invasion of a Western Hemisphere neighbor by U.N. and U.S. forces was averted because of President Carter's belief that diplomacy could succeed and his defiant commitment to avoid violence. In this case, it was a virtual certainty that blood would have been shed had the Carter mission not succeeded in convincing the Haitian military to peacefully relinquish power to the democratic will of the Haitian people. While the situation in Bosnia and throughout the former Yugoslavia will likely continue to require the attention of the international community for years to come, President Carter has been a steadfast voice for the use of negotiation over force in resolving these conflicts. In each of these situations, President Carter pursued the path of negotiation and diplomacy against force and confrontation. In each case, he peacefully achieved or pursued the same goals that others threatened to achieve by confrontation or further violence.

As a believer in the principles and promise of democracy, President Carter has championed the cause of democracy for those countries emerging from single-party or repressive military regimes.   Whether in the emerging democracies of the Western Hemisphere or those on the African continent, President Carter, the Council of Freely Elected Heads of Government, and the African Governance Program have worked to ensure that the popular will of the people shapes the leadership and direction of a country. The will of the people and the promise of democracy are furthered as elections are arranged, polling policies are established, and elections are monitored to guarantee free and fair results. Even after elections have taken place, the Carter Center works to assist newly democratic countries in building and strengthening government institutions for future generations. In some cases, this work has meant helping countries with repressive histories reconcile their pasts and build governments that will guarantee basic human rights. Carter Center programs have been committed to providing long-term assistance and counsel in countries where their help is needed and requested. Increasingly, the Carter Center is hopeful that elections can become not only a vehicle for a country to determine its leadership, but also a means for peacefully resolving conflicts at the ballot box rather than on the battlefield.

While the effects of conflict can be measured in terms of civilian and military casualties and the accompanying destruction, the causes of many conflicts may be more difficult to identify and isolate. In many cases, alleviating the conditions of poverty, hunger, disease, and threats to safety begin to address the factors that cause or give rise to armed conflicts. The humanitarian programs operating through the Carter Center, primarily the Global 2000 program, have worked to remove poverty, hunger, and disease as factors contributing to or resulting in armed conflict. By enlisting the brightest minds and newest technologies, by creating new programs when necessary, and by coordinating its efforts with existing programs and organizations when possible, Global 2000 has effectively addressed real problems with practical solutions to achieve significant results. President Carter has served as a catalyst for these efforts by providing the political will to translate the practical solutions into viable programs. The efforts to improve agricultural production and to eradicate Guinea worm disease serve as prime examples of Global 2000's ability to use the best technologies to address serious and devastating problems in developing nations. In collaboration with similar humanitarian aid organizations and agencies and the governments of host countries, these programs result in healthier lives and more prosperous people. Literally hundreds of thousands—if not millions—of people have been spared the devastating effects of famine, preventable childhood diseases, infectious parasites, and blindness as a result of the humanitarian programs operating through the Carter Center. Carter Center programs have always sought to address immediate needs, to promote long-range solutions, and to further the goal of sustainable development in target countries. While there are other humanitarian aid organizations operating throughout the world, none benefits from the ongoing involvement and influence that a former president of the United States can provide.

In the realm of human rights, President Carter has continued his lifelong commitment to protecting and furthering the rights of people everywhere to live in safety from, and without fear of, their own government. This commitment was a hallmark of his presidency and remains a fundamental concern for his post-presidency. The Human Rights Program serves as an advocate for human rights and has worked with several countries to guarantee that past human rights abuses will never be repeated. President Carter has used his stature to intervene personally by contacting heads of state who have reportedly abused the human rights of their citizens. By doing so, he not only directs attention to the abuse, but has been successful in gaining the release of those suffering from such abuse. As with other Carter Center programs, the immediate needs are addressed, while the long-term goals of protecting and promoting human rights are pursued.

Many of the same humanitarian concerns that have shaped the international agenda of President Carter's post-presidency and the programs of the Carter Center are reflected in their domestic agendas. Providing health care and promoting healthy living guide the work of the immunization programs and the Interfaith Health Program operating through the Carter Center. Children in the United States need and deserve the same healthy start in life, through childhood immunization, as children in developing countries. Every child should be immunized, and all children should indeed count. Perhaps because of his own religious beliefs, President Carter has worked to involve all faith communities in achieving the goal of healthful living.

Through the Atlanta Project, President Carter and the Carter Center have turned their considerable development expertise and coalition-building abilities to address the problems of Americans living in poor, inner-city neighborhoods. As with the international programs, this grass-roots effort is attacking real problems and facilitating workable solutions for those in need.

One of President Carter's most visible activities since leaving office, and the image many people most closely associate with him, occurs each summer when he dons his work clothes and picks up his hammer to build homes for Habitat for Humanity. Habitat for Humanity existed before the Jimmy Carter Work Projects began, and its work will continue long after he is no longer able to participate. However, there is perhaps no better testament to President Carter's commitment to his fellow man and to humanity than when this man who once lived in the White House helps to build a decent house for a family in need.

DOING WHAT WORKS:
PRESIDENT CARTER AND PEACEMAKING

There are a number of factors related to President Carter and the design of the Carter Center that begin to explain how he has been able to accomplish the goals he has pursued since leaving office. Perhaps the most important factor is simply that he is a former president of the United States and has chosen to invest the political capital resulting from this unique role or position to produce positive dividends. All presidents, once they have reached office, are able to invest the political capital that brought them to office (that is, the support of the voters who elected them) in pursuit of domestic and foreign policy initiatives and goals. In the case of Jimmy Carter, while the voters in 1980 rejected his leadership and perhaps the direction of his administration, he was, nonetheless, a former leader of the free world. The prestige, experience, connections, and contacts that he made while in office could be tapped while out of office, even though there was no formal position or power associated with the status of "former president." All former presidents, to greater or lesser degrees, have had this political capital. They can and have invested it in the hopes of finding a new political career, cultivating business possibilities, courting celebrity status, or, in the case of Jimmy Carter, furthering the pursuit of peace.

President Carter has used the political capital of the status of former president, his connections, contacts, and experience while in office, and the prestige that surrounds the office to further the broad agenda of peacemaking that has already been outlined. Because he is a former peer to many of the leaders he has dealt with since leaving office, he is generally able to make contact when he calls. Quite simply, when he calls, leaders tend to respond. Further, because of the prestige of his former office, President Carter can attract media attention to situations where he has been unable to make contact. This is particularly true with regard to President Carter's personal intervention on behalf of human rights issues. The Council of Freely Elected Heads of Government, which has been active in democratization efforts, builds on the principle that current and former heads of state can assist countries that are seeking democracy to ensure free and fair elections. President Carter has also been able to use his connections and contacts to act as a catalyst between countries in need and international aid organizations, agencies that provide such aid, and the private sector that can provide needed financial support. He has forged relationships between those in need and the private sector to develop water filters for Guinea worm eradication, to dispense drugs and immunizations, and to obtain the financial resources necessary to revitalize inner-city neighborhoods in Atlanta. The efforts of Global 2000 to improve agricultural development and health care have depended on President Carter's ability to enlist the support of the heads of state in host countries. Rosalynn Carter has also used her position as a former first lady of both Georgia and the United States to build coalitions and cooperation among political spouses to immunize the nation's children.

President Carter's experiences while in office have clearly informed his work while out of office. This is certainly the case with respect to his negotiation and mediation experience. President Carter successfully negotiated nuclear arms agreements, the Panama Canal Treaty, the Camp David Accords, and the release of the U.S. hostages held by the Iranian government. Carter's familiarity with Latin American and Caribbean issues has allowed him to become involved with a number of successful initiatives in that region.   The same patience, determination, and keen negotiation savvy that resulted in the breakthrough Camp David Accords were again in evidence when President Carter gathered the Ethiopians and Eritreans at the Carter Center in 1989. Anyone familiar with the intricate details involved in the ultimate release of the hostages held by Iran can only conclude that President Carter is a seasoned and experienced negotiator and mediator.

In addition to his own experience, President Carter has gathered an excellent staff to operate Carter Center programs. All of the various directors of programs are leading experts and noted scholars in their respective fields. For example, Dr. William Foege has developed and directed several of the center's health-care initiatives following a long and successful career with the U.S. Centers for Disease Control. Dr. Robert Pastor was an advisor to President Carter during his administration, is a well-published scholar in his own right, and directs the Latin American and Caribbean Program. Dr. Donald Hopkins whose 1983 book on smallpox, *Princes and Peasants*, was nominated for a Pulitzer Prize, has brought his expertise in disease eradication to the Carter Center, where he is working to eradicate Guinea worm disease. Last, but not least, the Conflict Resolution Program has benefited from the expertise of scholars at the Harvard Negotiation Project. The Carter Center has gathered some of the world's finest minds to address some of the world's most difficult problems.

While a former president has no formal power or position, there is considerable prestige associated with being a former president of the United States. This prestige can be a formidable source of influence. When President Carter associates himself with a cause or issue, he invests some of this prestige in support of that cause or issue. President Carter's association with Habitat for Humanity International is a prime example of a case where his name recognition and involvement have contributed to the media coverage and overall success of this organization.

By design, the Carter Center is intended to be an action-oriented organization rather than simply another think tank generating policy and position papers or advocating issues and causes. Three principles have guided the work of the center: using a nonpartisan approach to issues and causes, avoiding the duplication of efforts and programs of other organizations and agencies, and being action oriented. The Carter Center's nonpartisan approach to conflict situations and world problems means that President Carter and representatives of the Carter Center are able to talk with and contact parties that those who are politically affiliated or restricted cannot. For President Carter, this means that he can talk to rebel groups and leaders that official government representatives are prohibited from contacting because of partisan political or diplomatic considerations. For example, President Carter could negotiate with the Eritreans, a rebel group that U.N. officials were prevented by charter from contacting. President Carter could meet with Bosnian leaders whom the international community had branded as outlaws and war criminals. In these and other cases,

President Carter and Carter Center representatives can act as private parties seeking to resolve situations rather than as official representatives who must constrain their activities to conform to partisan politics and administrations. This is not to suggest that President Carter acts as a free-lance diplomat without regard for the policies of the United States and the world community. In fact, in most cases, he has been careful to coordinate his efforts with, if not to seek formal endorsement from, the administration in power or other international organizations. President Carter has truly been a diplomat without portfolio. On the other hand, leaders of parties in conflict situations have frequently contacted and sought out President Carter or worked through the Carter Center to help resolve their differences when other more traditional means have failed. The nonpartisan approach makes these contacts possible.

In many ways, President Carter and the programs of the Carter Center have tackled problems ignored or neglected by other organizations. The International Negotiation Network is a good example of how the Carter Center has sought to fill a mediation gap by addressing civil conflicts outside the jurisdiction of international organizations like the United Nations. Since the United Nations could not become involved in these conflicts, this Carter Center program was initiated. In the case of many of the humanitarian assistance programs of Global 2000, the Carter Center programs try not to replicate what other agencies are doing, but rather coordinate their efforts with established programs in an effort to maximize resources. The eradication of Guinea worm disease will occur as a result of the coordinated efforts of several different organizations working collaboratively toward the same goal under the leadership of Global 2000.

Like other policy institutes and organizations, the Carter Center regularly engages in research and academic study related to its programs. Unlike other organizations, the Carter Center is clearly action oriented. As President Carter explained at the opening of a conference on human rights in 1992, "Unless we feel that a direct action will be forthcoming from a conference or session, we do not undertake it" (quoted in "Investigating abuses," 1992, p. 9). The programs and initiatives launched by the Carter Center since its founding have all been based on solid policy research and analysis, but with a clear bias toward practical actions, workable solutions, and tangible results. Much of the policy research and analysis is conducted by experts and fellows working at the Carter Center or scholars associated with Emory University. This mutually beneficial partnership has furthered the missions of both institutions.

The translation of policy research and analysis into practical action is most clearly evident in the programs of the Carter Center. Global 2000 health programs, for example, have been guided by the policy research begun under the Carter administration on closing the gap between our knowledge of health problems and the ability of people to live healthy lives. The agricultural programs of Global 2000 have replicated the success that Nobel laureate Dr. Norman Borlaug had in India in the countries in Africa. The eradication of Guinea worm disease will occur because the research and development efforts of

Du Pont and Precision Fabrics and the resulting technologies were made available to those in need. Democracies in Latin America and Africa will be strengthened as a result of the analyses that have been made of countries that have been successful in establishing democracy, and then translating these lessons into programs and long-term initiatives for emerging democracies. Not only has the Human Rights Program studied human rights abuses, it has worked with countries to create constitutional guarantees to prevent future abuse and to reconcile past histories of abuse. The International Negotiation Network not only conducts and commissions analyses of conflict situations, it formulates action plans designed to resolve these conflicts. Working from a grass-roots approach, the Atlanta Project has identified the problems those living in urban poverty experience and has worked with them to design programs to solve these problems.

The Carter Center's nonpartisan approach to problems, desire to maximize resources through coordinating efforts and minimizing duplication, and translation of research into action combine to create a truly viable organization uniquely suited to addressing a variety of problems. President Carter and the Carter Center have done what is practical and workable in the pursuit of peace. He has acted as an emissary for peace by agreeing to talk with leaders like General Raoul Cedras, President Kim Il Sung, and Radovan Karadzic whom the rest of the world had shunned and demonized. He has done so not because he agrees with their politics or policies, but rather because talking and negotiating are preferable to escalating or continuing the violence. He has acted as an impartial mediator by helping parties arrive at solutions to their problems rather than having solutions imposed on them by force of arms. He has employed his international reputation for fairness and impartiality in order to monitor elections for those countries seeking the promise of democracy. He has successfully negotiated deals that helped to transfer power peacefully to the elected government in Nicaragua and that averted a military invasion in Haiti. In numerous cases, he has sought to establish trust in situations long characterized by suspicion and misunderstanding. Columnist Colman McCarthy aptly characterized President Carter's use of peacemaking techniques that work when he said, "In a world of armies, body bags and wars in more than 30 countries, Carter's ideals appear surreal. Except when put next to the question, what has violence accomplished—besides more of it, which is the definition of the 20th century" (McCarthy, 1994, p. D18). President Carter's work and that of the Carter Center demonstrate that ideals can become realities if they are pursued by the right person supported by the right programs.

DOING HIS BEST AND MAKING THE MOST
OF THE REST OF HIS LIFE

After leaving office, the easiest course for a former president to follow is to write his memoirs, to build his library, to make speeches and comment on current issues, and to retire quietly and comfortably to await the judgment of history. Given the demands of the presidency and the toll that it can take on an individual, perhaps that is the most that Americans should expect of a former president. Jimmy Carter left the White House in the prime of his life and clearly had more work to do and additional goals to achieve before he was ready to retire.

Erwin Hargrove, historian and Carter presidential biographer, suggested in a recent interview that President Carter has been motivated by several factors, including his strong sense of mission that brought him to political life and his strong Southern Baptist religious beliefs. According to Hargrove, Carter "approaches life with a sense of purpose and mission and incredible tenacity." Further, in Hargrove's opinion, "His religion, his faith was the key to his character, a certain kind of Southern Baptist in the Anabaptist tradition that with God all things are possible, that anything can be done" (quoted in "Weekend Edition Saturday," 1994, p. 7). President Carter's sense of purpose or mission seems inseparable from his religious beliefs and convictions. Carter once said, "My Christian faith is just like breathing to me or like being a Southerner or an American. It's all part of the same thing—the sharing, the compassion, the understanding, the dealing with the poor and the destitute and the outcasts" (quoted in Cloud, 1989, p. 63). President Carter's Christian faith guides his compassion for his fellow man and directs him to look for the best in all people and to understand those with whom he must deal. In a way, he believes that anyone can be redeemed and that no situation is beyond hope. Hodding Carter, who worked in the Carter State Department, noted that "he [Carter] does believe that redemption is always possible and one thing you have to be about is providing the redemption that you have had" (quoted in Walsh, 1994, p. A1). Dayle Powell, the former director of the Conflict Resolution Program at the Carter Center, once commented, "Carter is able to look at people like Daniel Ortega [of Nicaragua] and Mengistu [of Ethiopia] and appeal to some higher vision of themselves" (quoted in Bird, 1990, p. 563). Carter does not see his role as one of judging those in conflict in order to determine guilt, but rather seeks to find the common ground that can lead to trust, understanding, reconciliation, and, ultimately, the resolution of the conflict. In characterizing Carter's view of the world in general, Hargrove observed that he "did not see the world as inherently evil and sought peace through understanding rather than confrontation" (1988, p. 8). James Wall, editor of *Christian Century* and President Carter's acquaintance for twenty years, said, "He views the world compassionately," a view that "is grounded in his religion" (quoted in Walsh, 1994, p. A1). While critics have charged that Carter's is a naive and unrealistic view of the world, it is one that has clearly motivated Jimmy Carter to make a positive difference for the world. For Carter, not only is the goal of peace possible and necessary, but because of his religious beliefs, it is the mission to which he has committed his life and his work.

Much has been made of the fact that President Carter has, on five occasions, been nominated for, but never received, the Nobel Prize for Peace. Most recently, there was speculation that his 1994 mission to Haiti would result in his securing the prize. In his always-humble style, Carter commented, "There was no doubt in my mind last year that the Nobel should go to the PLO and the Israeli government. I haven't put anything at stake the way they have. What have I risked?" (quoted in Allen, 1995, p. C1). If gathering awards and recognition were the driving forces behind President Carter's work, he could retire with a room full of honors and accolades. Among the awards that would fill a Carter trophy wall would be the Gold Medal from the International Institute on Human Rights International, the American Arbitration Association Martin Luther King, Jr., Nonviolent Peace Prize, the International Human Rights Award, the Harry S. Truman Public Service Award, the Ansel Adams Conservation Award, the Albert Schweitzer Prize for Humanitarianism, the Philadelphia Liberty Medal, and the J. William Fulbright Prize for International Understanding, just to name a few (Kurylo, 1994, p. A8). In true Carter style, upon the receipt of such awards, he has generally used the monetary prizes to further the work of the Carter Center.

In 1975, presidential candidate Jimmy Carter wrote his campaign autobiography *Why Not the Best?*, in which he recounted an interview he had with Admiral Hyman Rickover before entering the nuclear submarine program. Rickover asked Carter if he had done his best work while in school. Wanting to respond honestly, Carter told the Admiral, "No, sir, I didn't always do my best." Rickover's response to Carter was, "Why not?" This question clearly challenged Jimmy Carter, so much so that when he ran for president in 1976, he, in turn, challenged the American people to strive for the best from their government. He may not have done his best in his academic studies, but in his role as peacemaker, he is seeking the highest of ideals and challenging the world to do what is right. One commentator concluded, "His opinions of what is right and necessary for the world have not changed much since he was president, and in that sense he can be said to be using the [Carter] center to pursue the unfinished business of the Carter administration" ("Presidential libraries," 1989, p. 30). President Carter believes that peace is possible; he has dedicated his best efforts toward the pursuit of peace; and he encourages all people to seek the best and highest ideals of peace and to work toward those ends.

When Jimmy and Rosalynn Carter wrote *Everything to Gain: Making the Most of the Rest of Your Life*, they explained the challenges that confronted their lives after leaving the White House and how they addressed those challenges. They had been defeated at the polls, they were feeling rejected, perhaps somewhat bitter, and yet they found a way to turn that defeat into a positive direction that would guide the rest of their lives. As the Carters determined what that direction might be, following the White House years, and as plans for the Carter Center began to take shape, President Carter recalled telling Rosalynn, "Who knows what we can do if we set our objectives high? We may even be able to do more than if we had won the election in 1980!" (Carter and Carter,

1987, p. 32). President Carter did set his objectives high, and when his final legacy is written, it will undoubtedly be noted that this man, his ideals, and his actions have left an indelible imprint on the rest of humanity.

REFERENCES

Allen, H. (1995, Jan. 19). Carter's mode to joy. *Washington Post*, p. C1.

Bird, Kai. (1990, Nov. 12). The very model of an ex-president. *Nation*, pp. 560–564.

Carter, J. (1975). *Why not the best?* Nashville: Broadman Press.

Carter, J., and Carter, R. (1987). *Everything to gain: Making the most of the rest of your life*. New York: Random House.

Cloud, S. W. (1989, Sept. 11). Hail to the ex-chief. *Time*, pp. 60–63.

Hargrove, E. (1988). *Jimmy Carter as president: Leadership and the politics of the public good.* Baton Rouge: Louisiana State University Press.

Investigating abuses and introducing safeguards in the democratization process. (1992). Conference Report Series, vol. 6, no. 1. Available from the Carter Center, One Copenhill, Atlanta, GA 30307.

Kurylo, E. (1994, Sept. 25). Jimmy Carter at 70. *Atlanta Journal and Atlanta Constitution*, p. A8.

McCarthy, C. (1994, Oct. 4). Carter's proven peacemaking techniques. *Washington Post*, p. D18.

Presidential libraries, his second term. (1989, Sept. 2). *Economist*, pp. 29–30.

Walsh, E. (1994, Sept. 24). When it comes to peace, Carter isn't retiring. *Washington Post*, p. A1.

Weekend Edition Saturday. (1994, Sept. 24). Interview with Erwin Hargrove. Transcript available from National Public Radio, 635 Massachusetts Ave. NW, Washington, DC 20001-3753.

SELECTED
BIBLIOGRAPHY

Assessment mission to Haiti, December 11–14, 1994. (1995, Jan. 5). Working paper series, the Council of Freely Elected Heads of Government. Available from the Carter Center, One Copenhill, Atlanta, GA 30307.

Carter, J. (1975). *Why not the best?* Nashville, TN: Broadman Press.

_____. (1977). *A government as good as its people.* New York: Simon and Schuster.

_____. (1982). *Keeping faith: Memoirs of a president.* New York: Bantam Books.

_____. (1984). *Negotiation: The alternative to hostility.* Macon, GA: Mercer University Press.

_____. (1985). *The blood of Abraham.* Boston: Houghton Mifflin.

_____. (1988). *An outdoor journal.* New York: Bantam Books.

_____. (1992). *Turning point: A candidate, a state, and a nation come of age.* New York: Times Books.

_____. (1993). *Talking peace: A vision for the next generation.* New York: Dutton Children's Books.

Carter, J., and Carter, R. (1987). *Everything to gain: Making the most of the rest of your life.* New York: Random House.

Carter, R. (1984). *First lady from Plains.* Boston: Houghton Mifflin.

_____. (1994). *Helping yourself help others: A book for caregivers.* New York: Times Books.

The challenges of faith and health. (1994, Jan.). A report of the National Conference of the Interfaith Health Program of The Carter Center, supported by the Robert Wood Johnson Foundation. Available from the Carter Center, One Copenhill, Atlanta, GA 30307.

Children and families at risk: Collaborating with our schools. (1995). Report of the Tenth Annual Rosalynn Carter Symposium on Mental Health Policy. Available from the Carter Center, One Copenhill, Atlanta, GA 30307.

Clark, J. C. (1985). *Faded glory: Presidents out of power.* New York: Praeger Publishers.

Conference for global development cooperation. (1992). Conference Report Series, vol. 4, no. 2. Available from the Carter Center, One Copenhill, Atlanta, GA 30307.

Cox, G. (1986). *The ways of peace: A philosophy of peace as action.* New York: Paulist Press.

Cunningham, H. F. (1989). *The presidents' last years: George Washington to Lyndon B. Johnson.* Jefferson, NC: McFarland & Co.

Dateline NBC. (1994, Sept. 23). Minute by minute. Transcript by Burrelle's Information Services, Box 7, Livingston, NJ 07039.

Deng, F. M., and Zartman, I. M. (Eds.). (1991). *Conflict resolution in Africa.* Washington, DC: Brookings Institution.

Electoral reforms in Mexico: Final report. (1993, Nov.). Occasional paper series, vol. 4, no. 1. Available from the Carter Center, One Copenhill, Atlanta, GA 30307.

Ford, G. R. (1979). *A time to heal: The autobiography of Gerald R. Ford.* New York: Berkley Books.

Ford, G. R., and Carter, J. E. (1988). *American agenda: Report to the forty-first president of the United States of America.* Camp Hill, PA: Book-of-the-Month Club.

Fuller, M., and Fuller, L. (1990). *The excitement is building.* Dallas: Word Publishing.

Global 2000, Inc., promoting food self-reliance, improving health standards, and preventing environmental degradation around the world. (undated). Published by the Carter Center of Emory University and Global 2000, Inc. Available from the Carter Center, One Copenhill, Atlanta, GA 30307.

Hargrove, E. C. (1988). *Jimmy Carter as president: Leadership and the politics of the public good.* Baton Rouge: Louisiana State University Press.

Hecht, M. B. (1976). *Beyond the presidency: The residues of power.* New York: Macmillan Publishing Co.

The international negotiation network (INN): A new method of approaching some very old problems. (1991). Occasional Paper Series, vol. 2, no. 2. Available from the Carter Center, One Copenhill, Atlanta, GA 30307.

The international observation of the U.S. elections. (1992, Nov.). Occasional Paper Series, vol. 3, no. 1. Available from the Carter Center, One Copenhill, Atlanta, GA 30307.

Investigating abuses and introducing safeguards in the democratization process. (1992). Conference Report Series, vol. 6, no. 1. Available from the Carter Center, One Copenhill, Atlanta, GA 30307.

Not even one: A report on the crisis of children and firearms. (1994, Feb.). A report produced by the Interfaith Health Program at The Carter Center, and supported by the Carnegie Corporation of New York and the Robert Wood Johnson Foundation. Available from the Carter Center, One Copenhill, Atlanta, GA 30307.

Observing Nicaragua's elections, 1989–1990. (1990). Special Report no. 1 of the Council of Freely Elected Heads of Government. Available from the Carter Center, One Copenhill, Atlanta, GA 30307.

Resolving intra-national conflicts: A strengthened role for non-governmental actors. Conference Report Series, vol. 3, no. 2. Available from the Carter Center, One Copenhill, Atlanta, GA 30307.

Smith, R. N., and Walch, T. (Eds.). (1990). *Farewell to the chief: Former presidents in American public life.* Worland, WY: High Plains Publishing Co.

Waging peace around the world. (1993). Available from the Carter Center, One Copenhill, Atlanta, GA 30307.

Young, J. S. (1988). Foreword. In E. Hargrove, *Jimmy Carter as president: Leadership and the politics of the public good* (p. xii). Baton Rouge: Louisiana State University Press.

INDEX

About the Author

ROD TROESTER is Associate Professor at Behrend College, Pennsylvania State University at Erie.

ISBN 0-275-95444-7

90000>

EAN

9 780275 954444

HARDCOVER BAR CODE

DATE DUE